FRANKLIN COUNTY, GEORGIA MARRIAGES
DECEMBER 1805–DECEMBER 1850

COMPILED BY
MARTHA WALTERS ACKER

Southern Historical Press, Inc.
Greenville, South Carolina

This volume was reproduced
from a personal copy located in
the Publishers private library

Please direct all correspondence and book orders to:
SOUTHERN HISTORICAL PRESS, Inc.
1071 Park West Blvd.
Greenville, SC 29611

Copyright 1987 by:
    Martha W. Ackers
Copyright Transferred 2024 to:
    Southern Historical Press, Inc.
ISBN #978-1-63914-225-5
Printed in the United States of America

THIS PUBLICATION HAS BEEN MADE POSSIBLE IN PART BY A GRANT FROM
THE R.J. TAYLOR, JR. FOUNDATION

TABLE OF CONTENTS

INTRODUCTION

Marriage licenses were not required until 1805 in Georgia. They were granted by the Clerk of the Ordinary Court. The marriage and date were to be returned on the license to the clerk who was to record the marriage.

This work is a comparison of all extant loose marriage licenses from 1805-1850 on file at the Georgia Archives to the marriage licenses recorded in books. There are some remarkable differences in the two records in many cases.

When it is available the marriage license is considered the primary source. The secondary source is the book in which the license was recorded. Serious researchers will want to study both if available. When no license is extant then the marriage book becomes th primary source.

References are as follows:

LICENSE

These are in loose alphabetical order and filed in folders which are in boxes. They have not been microfilmed. When ordering a copy of a license from the Archives, please give the following reference: Franklin County Marriage License Files, Record Group 159-2-3 and the location number given in the reference of each license.

VOLUME 1

The first marriage book (1805-1826) has been laminated and rebound. Some of the pages were bound out of order, and there may be some missing pages.

VOLUME 2

This is a transcription of Volume 1. It is apparently the source used for several printed versions of Franklin Co. marriages, probably because of its readablity compared to other volumes. Unfortunately it is full of errors and inaccuracies. Therefore this volume has been cited only when there is no other source. It is recommended that when in doubt never trust volume 2 because the transcriber himself states that he has had trouble reading the original, and that he has corrected errors. In addition to this problem a group of marriage license found in the 1920's was copied into the back of the book. Fortunately all but one of these licenses has survived.

VOLUME 3

This marriage book(1827-1835) has been laminated and rebound.

VOLUME 4

This book of marriages (1834-1850) has also been laminated and several pages appear to be missing.

VOLUME 5

This volume is not housed at the Archives. For the purpose of this work the microfilmed copy was used to locate additional marriages up through 1850. It is assumed that a copy of the original may be ordered from the Court House at Carnesville. Be aware that the first pages are not numbered and are mixed up. They appear in this order: 3,4,1,2,5.

When ordering copies of records from these volumes from the Archives ask for Franklin Co. Marriage Book Record Group 159-2-24, Location 1752-13.

FRANKLIN COUNTY, GEORGIA MARRIAGES

DECEMBER 1805- DECEMBER 1850

SISSOM, JOHN   16 Dec 1805- Frederick Beall, C.C.O.
  and   19 Dec 1805- Sam'l Everett, J.P.
DODD, SARY   source: volume 1, page 1

CARLTON, JACOB   5 Feb 1806- Frederick Beall, C.C.O.
  and   ....- Frederick Beall, J.P.
CHITHAM, SALLY   source: volume 1, page 1

SMITH, WILLIAM   10 Mar 1806- Frederick Beall, C.C.O.
  and   11 Mar 1806- William Jones, J.P.
BEALL, TEMPE   source: volume 1, page 3

WILKINS, JAMES   12 Mar 1806- Frederick Beall, C.C.O.
  and   14 Mar 1806- William Jones, J.P.
SOWELS, ANN   source: volume 1, page 2

HARRIS, STARLING   5 Apr 1806- Frederick Beall, C.C.O.
  and   7 Apr 1806- William Jones, J.P.
GOBER, ELIZABETH   source: volume 1, page 4

RAMSEY, JAMES   29 Apr 1806- Frederick Beall, C.C.O.
  and   1 May 1806- Tho's Newton, V.D.M.
MESSER, JANE   source: volume 1, page 30

ADAMS, ABSALOM   12 May 1806- Frederick Beall, C.C.O.
  and   18 May 1806- G. Knox, J.P.
PRICKET, MARY   source: volume 1, page 2

1

STOWERS, JOHN
and
FORRESTER, MARGARET

19 May 1806- Frederick Beall, C.C.O.
22 May 1806- James Rylee, M.G.
source: volume 1, page 3

JINKINS, THOMAS
and
BARTON, FRANCES

11 June 1806- Frederick Beall, C.C.O.
26 June 1806- John Mullin, J.P.
source: volume 1, page 4

BUCKNER, DAVID
and
HOLBROOKS, NELLY

28 June 1806- Frederick Beall, C.C.O.
29 June 1806- G. Knox, J.P.
source: volume 1, page 5

WARREN, DAVID
and
KENDRIX, DICA

14 July 1806- Frederick Beall, C.C.O.
16 July 1806- Jno. Collins, J.P.
source: volume 1, page 27

SIMS, NATHANIEL
and
BULLOCK, WINNAFRED

28 July 1806- Frederick Beall, C.C.O.
31 July 1806- G. Knox, J.P.
source: volume 1, page 5

LYNER, JAMES
and
MERREL, ELIZABETH

28 July 1806- Frederick Beall, C.C.O.
...........- Joseph Chandler, J.P.
source: volume 1, page 19

DANIEL, JAMES
and
PAIRPOINT, CHARITY

17 Sept 1806- Frederick Beall, C.C.O.
18 Sept 1806- Ja's Rylee, M.G.
source: volume 1, page 30

BOHANNON, JAMES
and
PATTERSON, RACHEL

27 Sept 1806- Frederick Beall, C.C.O.
9 Oct 1806- Samuel H. Everett, J.P.
source: volume 1, page 6

BAKER, JOHN
and
BRAWNER, AMELIA

26 Oct 1806- Frederick Beall
30 Mar .... - ....
source: volume 1, page 30

PARKER, JESSE
and
HEWSE, POLLEY

26 Oct 1806- Frederick Beall, C.C.O.
...........- Joseph Chandler, J.P.
source: volume 1, page 19

ALLEN, JAMES
and
HOLLEY, POLLEY

20 Nov 1806- Frederick Beall, C.C.O.
.... - Frederick Beall, J.P.
source: volume 1, page 25

HARBER, THO'S
and
MC KEE, ELIZABETH

13 Dec 1806- Frederick Beall, C.C.O.
...........- Frederick Beall, J.P.
source: volume 1, page 25

BUSH, WILLIAM
and
KING, JOYCEY(JOYECY?)

22 Dec 1806- Frederick Beall, C.C.O.
25 Dec 1806- Jno. Collins, J.P.
source: volume 1, page 18

STOVALL, GEORGE
and
CHRISTIAN, NANCY

16 Jan 1807- Frederick Beall, C.C.O.
19 Feb 1807- Tho's Newton, V.D.M.
source: volume 1, page 6

BAKER, CHARLES
and
STOWE, POLLEY

9 Feb 1807- Frederick Beall, C.C.O.
..... 1807- David Garrason, M.G.
source: volume 1, page 12

WALLACE, WILLIAM
and
BLACK, JANET

24 Mar 1807- Frederick Beall, C.C.O.
9 Apr 1807- Tho's Newton, V.D.M.
source: volume 1, page 7

MILLICAN, WILLIAM C.
and
COYLE, REBEKAH

3 Apr 1807- W.F. Bagwell for Frederick
        Beall, C.C.O.
9 Apr 1807- John Jinkins, J.P.
source: volume 1, page 7

ROBINS, WILLIAM
and
HOLLINGSWORTH, MARY

27 Apr 1807- W.F. Bagwell for Frederick
        Beall, C.C.O.
28 Apr 1807- Tho's Hollingsworth, J.P.
source: volume 1, page 8

HAMBLETON, MORDECA STRINGER
and
YORK, DEBERY COOPER

4 May 1807- Frederick Beall, C.C.O.
.... "no return certified of the
above marriage"
source: volume 1, page 12

WALDEN, MICHEAL
and
MC NEAL, LUCY

20 June 1807- W.F. Bagwell for Frederick
        Beall, C.C.O.
23 June 1807- Sam'l H. Everett, J.P.
source: volume 1, page 8

ROSS, RICHARD
and
DENMAN, CATHERINE

12 Oct 1807- Frederick Beall, C.C.O.
...........- "no return certified of
the above marriage"
source: volume 1, page 13

SMITH, WILLIAM
and
KEES, DELILA

12 Oct 1807- Frederick Beall, C.C.O.
.... "no return certified of
the above marriage"
source: volume 1, page 13

HOLLINGSWORTH, BENJAMIN
and
JONES, JOICY

19 Oct 1807(sic)- Frederick Beall, C.C.O.
3 Sept 1809(sic)- Nacy Meeks, M.G.
source: volume 1, page 28

SMITH, THOMAS
and
JACKSON, MARTHA

26 Oct 1807- Frederick Beall, C.C.O.
26 Dec 1807- Littleton Meeks, V.D.M.
source: volume 1, page 9

FORCYTH, WILLIAM and MORGAN, RODY	23 Nov 1807- Frederick Beall, C.C.O. 23 Nov 1807- David Garrison, M.G. source: volume 1, page 13
ALEXANDER, ISAAC and THOMAS, SUSANNAH	16 Dec 1807- M.H. Payne for Frederick Beall, C.C.O. 24 Dec 1807- Tho's Hollingsworth, J.P. source: volume 1, page 9
CHANDLER, ALLEN and BRYAN, POLLY	19 Dec 1807- Frederick Beall, C.C.O. ....- Jos. Chandler, J.P. source: volume 1, page 19
SMITH, JAMES and POE, ELIZABETH	25 Dec 1807- Frederick Beall, C.C.O. .. Jan 1808- Ob. Hooper, J.P. source: volume 1, page 14
ROBERSON, RICHARD and KELLY, ELIZABETH	25 Dec 1807- Frederick Beall, C.C.O. 27 Dec 1807- G. Nox, J.P. source: volume 1, page 14
BANKS, LEVY and ALEXANDER, ELIZABETH	28 Dec 1807- Frederick Beall, C.C.O. 31 Dec 1807- Moses Guest, J.P. source: volume 1, page 10
SEWEL, GREENBERRY and BRASDLE, ANN	29 Dec 1807- Frederick Beall, C.C.O. ....- Frederick Beall, J.P. source: volume 1, page 10
ANDERS, ENOCH and CRUMP, MISSA	24 Feb 1808- Frederick Beall, C.C.O. 25 Feb 1808- Tho's Hollingsworth, J.P. source: volume 1, page 11
HARGROVE, JOHN and BROWN, REBEKAH	2 Mar 1808- Frederick Beall, C.C.O. 3 Mar 1808- Tho's Hollingsworth, J.P. source: volume 1, page 15
BROWN, JOHN and CRAWFORD, MARY	15 Mar 1808- Tho's Hollingsworth for Frederick Beall, C.C.O. 17 Mar 1808- Tho's Hollingsworth, J.P. source: volume 1, page 16
SWAIN, WILLIAM and WILLIAMSON, REBEKAH	19 Mar 1808- Asa Allen for Frederick Beall, C.C.O. 20 Mar 1808- Asa Allen, J.P. source: volume 1, page 11
VAUGHN, HENDRICK and BAGLEY, POLLY	15 May 1808- Frederick Beall, C.C.O. 15 May 1808- Tho's Hollingsworth, J.P. source: volume 1, page 16

GARRISON, JAMES
and
BAKER, MARGARET

28 May 1808- Frederick Beall, C.C.O.
...... 1808- David Garrison, M.G.
source: volume 1, page 15

GRADY, WILLIAM
and
COLLINS, ELIZABETH

6 June 1808- Frederick Beall, C.C.O.
23 June 1808- William Denman, M.G.
source: volume 1, page 17

PRICKET, JOEL
and
DOBS, ELIZABETH

16 July 1808- Frederick Beall, C.C.O.
25 July 1808- Frederick Beall, J.P.
source: volume 1, page 17

LOWRY, CHARLES
and
TONEY, ELIZABETH

30 July 1808- Frederick Beall, C.C.O.
16 Aug 1808- David Garrison, M.G.
source: volume 1 , page 18

ADRINE, FLEMEN F.
and
MCDONALD, MARY

23 Aug 1808- Frederick Beall, C.C.O.
25 Aug 1808- Jno. Collins, J.P.
source: volume 1, page 20

CARTER, THOMAS
and
DAVIS, JINCY(or JINEY)

6 Sept 1808- Frederick Beall, C.C.O.
8 Sept 1808- Jno. Mullin, J.P.
source: volume 1, page 20

GARRISON, CALEB
and
BOX, RACHEL

30 Sept 1808- Frederick Beall, C.C.O.
11 Oct. 1808- ....
source: volume 1, page 22

HOLLAND, UVEY(?)
and
BROWN, PRISCILLA

3 Oct 1808- Frederick Beall, C.C.O.
..........- Littleton Meeks, M.G.
source: volume 1, page 31

LOWRY, JAMES
and
DORSEY, CATY

7 Oct 1808- Frederick Beall, C.C.O.
13 Oct 1808- Frederick Beall (?)
source: volume 1, page 21

COOK, BURRELL
and
LOWERY, ANN

10 Oct 1808- M'k'd Payne for Frederick
            Beall, C.C.O.
11 Oct ....- ....
source: volume 1, page 21

SMITH, WILLIAM
and
WADE, DRISILLA

14 Oct 1808- Frederick Beall, C.C.O.
...........- Littleton Meeks, M.G.
source: volume 1, page 31

GLENN, WILLIAM
and
AARON, ROSA

15 Nov 1808- Frederick Beall, C.C.O.
17 Nov 1808- George Knox, J.P.
source: volume 1, page 29

NIX, WILLIAM
and
STONECYPHER, SUSANNAH

23 Nov 1808(sic)- Frederick Beall, C.C.O.
3 Sept 1809(sic)- Nacy Meeks, M.G.
source: volume 1, page 27

SCOTT, WILLIAM
and
COIL, ANN

26 Nov 1808- M'k'd' Payne for Frederick
            Beall, C.C.O.
29 Nov 1808- Tho's Newton, M.V.D.
source: volume 1, page 21

MC ALLA, THO'S
and
RAMSEY, MARGRET

28 Nov 1808- Daniel Beall for
           Frederick Beall, C.C.O.
1 Dec 1808- Tho's Newton, V.D.M.
source: volume 1, page 22

COLLYER, THOMAS
and
COLLINS, MARY

3 Dec 1808- Frederick Beall, C.C.O.
..........- Littleton Meeks, M.G.
source: volume 1, page 31

HARRISON, REUBEN
and
DIXON, BETHANA

3 Dec 1808- Frederick Beall, C.C.O.
8 Dec 1808- ....
source: volume 1, page 22

BROWN, JOHN
and
STOVALL, MARY

24 Dec 1808- Frederick Beall, C.C.O.
25 Dec 1808- Joseph Chandler, J.P.
source: volume 1, page 26

TRIMBLE, MOSES
and
BAKER, PEGGY

27 Dec 1808- Frederick Beall, C.C.O.
.... - Frederick Beall, J.P.
source: volume 1, page 23

DIXON, DANIEL
and
DORSEY, PRISCILLA

27 Dec 1808- Frederick Beall, C.C.O.
29 Dec 1808- ....
source: volume 1, page 23

DEEN, WILLIAM
and
TOLBERT, PEGGY

28 Dec 1808- Frederick Beall, C.C.O.
29 Dec 1808- Geo. Knox, J.P.
source: volume 1, page 29

WHITE, TIMOTHY L.
and
HARRIS, ELIZABETH

28 Dec 1808- Frederick Beall, C.C.O.
.... - Frederick Beall, J.P.
source: volume 1, page 23

DENMAN, WILLIAM
and
HICKS, MARY

30 Dec 1808- M'k'd' H. Payne for
           Frederick Beall, C.C.O.
1 Jan 1809- Gabriel Martin, J.P.
source: volume 1, page 24

SMITH, JAMES
and
ALLEN, PATCY

6 Jan 1809- Frederick Beall, C.C.O.
6 Jan 1809- James H. Little, J.P.
source: volume 1, page 32

COX, ROBERT R.
and
MOULDER, ELIZABETH

7 Jan 1809- Frederick Beall, C.C.O.
.... - Jno. R. Brown, J.I.C.
source: volume 1, page 24

BULLIN(G), WILLIAM
and
BOLING, AMEY

12 Jan 1809- Sam'l Payne for Frederick
           Beall, C.C.O.
13 Jan 1809- Jno. Collins, J.P.
source: volume 1, page 26

MC CARTER, MATTHEW
and
MAC KINTIRE, PEGGY

16 Jan 1809- M'k'd' H. Payne for
           Frederick Beall, C.C.O.
25 Jan 1809- Tho's Newton
source: volume 1, page 25

MILLIGAN, THO'S
and
CLEGHORN, ELIZABETH

16 Jan 1809- Frederick Beall, C.C.O.
19 Jan 1809- Tho's Newton, V.D.M.
source: volume 1, page 24

CORNELIUS, ABSALOM
and
WARD, MARGARET

15 Mar 1809- Frederick Beall, C.C.O.
19 Mar 1809- John R. Brown, J.I.C.
source: volume 1, page 34

STRICKLAND, WILSON
and
CONLEY, POLLY

17 Mar 1809- Frederick Beall, C.C.O.
23 Mar 1809- Tho's Newton
source: volume 1, page 32

HARRIS, THOMAS
and
TALLEY, JOANNAH

18 Mar 1809- M'k'd' H. Payne for
                Frederick Beall, C.C.O.
.... ‾ ....
source: volume 1, page 26

CARPENTER, JOHN
and
CANADY, ESTHER

24 Mar 1809- Frederick Beall, C.C.O.
25 Mar 1809- John Collins, J.P.
source: volume 1, page 33

LOGEN(?), REUBEN
and
HOOPER, SUSANNAH

5 Apr 1809- Frederick Beall, C.C.O.
6 Apr 1809- Francis Callaway, M.G.
source: volume 1, page 28

CLEVELAND, JOSEPH
and
MEEKS, PATCY

21 Apr 1809- Frederick Beall, C.C.O.
2 May 1809- Nacy Meeks
source: volume 1, page 34

MC KINSEY, PETER
and
RAY, CLOA

30 Apr 1809(sic)- Frederick Beall, C.C.O.
31 Mar 1809(sic)- George Knox, J.P.
source: volume 1, page 29

CONNALLY, DRURY
and
MOORE, NANCY

12 May 1809(sic)- M'k'd Payne for
                Frederick Beall, C.C.O.
7 May 1809(sic) - James Rylee, M.G.
source: volume 1, page 28

MC DOWELL, ROBERT
and
COVINGTON, REBECCA

30 May 1809- Frederick Beall, C.C.O.
3 June 1809- John R. Brown, J.I.C.
source: volume 1, page 35

ROWLAND, DRURY
and
JOHNSTON, ANN

19 June 1809- Frederick Beall, C.C.O.
20 June 1809- Littleton Meeks
source: volume 1, page 45

LOWRY, NATHAN
and
POOL, REBECA

14 July 1809- Frederick Beall, C.C.O.
20 July 1809- James Lowery
source: volume 1, page 33

ROSE, THOMAS
and
BRONNER, ANN

7 Aug 1809- Frederick Beall, C.C.O.
10 Aug 1809- James H. Little, J.P.
source: volume 1, page 34

MANGAM/MANGRAM, SAMUEL
and
BRAWNER, ELIZABETH

2 Sept 1809- Frederick Beall, C.C.O.
7 Sept 1809- James H. Little, J.P.
source: license- 1751-02/4-94
see also volume 1, page 35

HARRISON, ROBERT and SMITH, PHERABY	25 Sept 1809- Frederick Beall, C.C.O. 28 Sept 1809- Nacy Meeks source: volume 1, page 33
MILLS, JOHN and FORESTER, ELENDER	10 Oct 1809- Frederick Beall, C.C.O. 12 Oct 1809- Moses Guest, J.P. source: volume 1, page 32
WARREN, RUBEN and DAVES, ELIZABETH	21 Oct 1809- Frederick Beall, C.C.O. 29 Oct 1809- Jno. Collins, J.P. source: volume 1, page 33
BOSWELL, JAMES and MULLIN, SENA	15 Oct 1809- Frederick Beall, C.C.O. ....- James Chandler, J.I.C. source: volume 1, page 36
PAYNE, THO'S and CARLTON, SARAH	22 Oct 1809- Frederick Beall, C.C.O. 22 Oct 1809- Frederick Beall source: volume 1, page 35
NAIL, EZEKIEL and SPARKS, ELIZABETH	21 Dec 1809- Frederick Beall, C.C.O. 23 Dec 1809- Francis Callaway, O.M.G. source: license- 1751-03/5-105 see also volume 1, page 84
DYE, STEPHEN and WOODSON, ELIZABETH	3 Jan 1810- Frederick Beall,, C.C.O. 3 Jan 1810- W.F. Bagwell, J.P. source: volume 1, page 36
HENLEY, EDMOND and DENMAN, HEPSEBETH	12 Jan 1810- Frederick Beall, C.C.O. 14 Jan 1810- J.R. Brown, J.I.C. source: volume 1, page 37
CHRISTIAN, OBED M. and BARNES, ANNE	17 Jan 1810- Frederick Beall, C.C.O. 18 Jan 1810- Osborn Rogers source: volume 1, page 41
HARRIS, CHARLES and THOMPSON, ELIZABETH	28 Jan 1810- Jno. Collins for Frederick Beall, C.C.O. 28 Jan 1810- John Collins source: volume 1, page 38
BOLES(BALES?), GEORGE and BRYAN, EDITH	4 Feb 1810- Frederick Beall, C.C.O. 4 Feb 1810- Eli Bryan source: volume 1, page 37&46
DODD, PETERSON and MULLIN, ABBA(or MELIA?)	...........- Frederick Beall, C.C.O. 6 Feb 1810- John Collins, J.P. source: volume 1, page 36
RYLEY, EDWARD and WESTBROOK, POLLEY	1 Mar 1810- Frederick Beall, C.C.O. 1 Mar 1810- James H. Little, J.P. source: volume 1, page 38
DEALE, WILLIAM and HAILING, NELLY	18 Mar 1810- Frederick Beall, C.C.O. 18 Mar 1810- Tho's Hollingsworth, J.P. source: volume 1, page 40

HEWEL, JOHN
and
BAKER, ELENER

21 Mar 1810, Frederick Beall, C.C.O.
21 Mar 1810- W.F. Bagwell, J.P.
source: volume 1, page 38

BAKER, WILLIAM
and
BROWN, CATHARINE

5 Apr 1810- Frederick Beall, C.C.O.
5 Apr 1810- Edmond Henley, J.I.C.
source: volume 1, page 42

BLACKWELL, JESSE
and
WILKINS, SARAH

25 Apr 1810- Frederick Beall, C.C.O.
26 Apr 1810- Asa Allen, J.I.C.
source: volume 1, page 43

BLACK, JOHN
and
CAMMON, POLLY

12 May 1810- Frederick Beall, C.C.O.
12 May 1810- W.F. Bagwell, J.P.
source: volume 1, page 40

TOWNS, JOHN
and
SPEARS, ELIZABETH

5 July 1810- Frederick Beall, C.C.O.
8 July 1810- Asa Allen, J.I.C.
source: volume 1, page 37

LEWIS, THOMAS
and
DAY, RACHEL

30 July 1810- Jno. Collins for Frederick
Beall, C.C.O.
30 July 1810- Jno. Collins, J.P.
source: volume 1, page 40

MC QUEEN, ISAAC A.
and
CARRUTH, CINTHIA(?)

30 Aug 1810- Frederick Beall, C.C.O.
...........- W'm Cleghorn, J.P.
source: volume 1, page 84

BROWN, ISAAC
and
LOVELADY, NANCY

11 Sept 1810- Frederick Beall, C.C.O.
11 Sept 1810- John Collins, J.P.
source: volume 1, page 39

DODD, ...
and
SHEFFIELD, POLLY

25 Sept 1810- John Collins for Frederick
Beall, C.C.O.
25 Sept 1810- ....
source: volume 1, page 39

HOLBROOK, JOHN
and
DORSEY, POLLY

26 Sept 1810- M.H. Payne for Frederick
Beall, C.C.O.
27 Sept 1810- John Taber(?), M.G.
source: volume 1, page 43

JOHNSTON, JAMES
and
MISE, SALLY

22 Oct 1810- Frederick Beall, C.C.O.
25 Oct 1810- James H. Little, J.P.
source: volume 1, page 39

DOBBS, WILLIAM
and
COVINTON, CATHERINE

15 Nov 1810- M.H. Payne for Frederick
Beall, C.C.O.
15 Nov 1810- D. Jones, J.P.
source: volume 1 , page 40

THORNTON, ELIJAH
and
FLEMIN, JANE

8 Dec 1810(sic)- Frederick Beall, C.C.O.
20 Dec 1800 (sic)- Tho's Newton, V.D.M.
source: volume 1, page 41

HEDRICK, GURDRAN(?)
and
WILLIAMS, POLLY

15 Dec 1810- M.H. Payne for Frederick
          Beall, C.C.O.
15 Dec 1810- Benjamin King, J.I.C.
source: volume 1, page 47

KING, GEORGE
and
LAWRENCE, ELIZABETH

19 Dec 1810- Frederick Beall, C.C.O.
19 Dec 1810- W.F. Bagwell, J.P.
source: volume 1, page 42

STOVALL, JOSIAH
and
FARMER, LUCY

3 Jan 1811- Frederick Beall, C.C.O.
3 Jan 1811- James Chandler
source: volume 1, page 42

HALL, WILLIAM
and
BENNET, MARY

22 Jan 1811- Frederick Beall, C.C.O.
22 Jan 1811- W.F. Bagwell, J.P.
source: volume 1, page 41

DENMAN, JOHN
and
HOOPER, PATCY

30 Jan 1811- Frederick Beall, C.C.O.
3 Feb 1811- Edmund Henley, J.P.
source: volume 1, page 44

THOMPSON, WILLIAM
and
DAVIS, ELIZABETH

23 Feb 1811- Frederick Beall, C.C.O.
7 Mar 1811- Littleton Meeks
source: volume 1, page 44

BAKER, JAMES
and
SEWEL, MARY

5 Mar 1811- M.H. Payne for Frederick
          Beall, C.C.O.
7 Mar 1811- Edmond Henley, J.I.C.
source: volume 1, page 44

HALEY, LEWDEAY
and
ARENDALL, WINNEYRED

16 Mar 1811- M.H. Payne for Frederick
          Beall, C.C.O.
20 Mar 1811- James H. Little, J.P.
source: volume 1, page 45

CARREL, JOHN W.
and
REDWINE, ELIZABETH

23 Mar 1811- Frederick Beall, C.C.O.
26 Mar 1811- Ja's Lows, Sr.(?), O.D.(?)
source: volume 1, page 49

SANDIDGE, GARRET
and
SMITH, FRANKY

29 Mar 1811- Frederick Beall, C.C.O.
2 Apr 1811- Jno. Mullin, J.P.
source: license- 1751-03/6-128
see also volume 1, page 46

PAYNE, DAVID
and
CHATHAM, POLLY

8 Apr 1811- Frederick Beall, C.C.O.
8 Apr 1811- Francis C. Callaway, M.G.
source: volume 1, page 43

BALENGER, DAVID
and
STEPHENSON, REBECCA

27 May 1811(sic)- Frederick Beall, C.C.O.
12 May 1811(sic)- John Tabor
source: volume 1, page 79

MEEKS, JOHN
and
HENDERSON, ELIZABETH

14 July 1811- Frederick Beall, C.C.O.
23 July 1811- Nacy Meeks
source: volume 1, page 47

SEWEL, JOHN
and
CHRISTIAN, ELIZABETH

24 July 1811- Frederick Beall, C.C.O.
25 July 1811- Edmond Henly, J.I.C.
source: volume 1, page 46

TATUM, WILLIAM
and
THURMOND, PARTHENIA

9 Aug 1811- Frederick Beall, C.C.O.
13 Aug 1811- Benjamin Wofford, J.P.
source: volume 1, page 49

CANE, JOHN
and
HALL, LIDY

12 Oct 1811- Frederick Beall, C.C.O.
25 (5) Nov 1811-........
source: volume 1, page 48&page 80

STRICKLAND, CADE D.
and
BURTON, JINCY

28 Oct 1811- M.H. Payne for Frederick
Beall, C.C.O.
...........- W'm Clayton, J.P.
source: volume 1, page 80

DODD, DAVID
and
SANDERS, SALLEY

31 Oct 1811- Frederick Beall, C.C.O.
31 Oct 1811- John Collins, J.P.
source: volume 1, page 49

WADKINS, BARNET
and
EPPERSON, HANNAH

9 Nov 1811- Frederick Beall, C.C.O.
12 Nov 1811- W'm Jones, J.P.
source: license- 1751-04/8-155

SHOCKLEY, AQUILLA
and
KING, AMELIA

14 Nov 1811- Frederick Beall, C.C.O.
14 Nov 1811- ....
source: volume 1, page 79

STONECYPHER, BENJAMIN
and
COLLINS, ELIZABETH

24 Nov 1811- Frederick Beall, C.C.O.
18 Dec 1811- N. Meeks
source: volume 1, page 85

W'MSON, JOHN
and
BRASDLE, SARAH

12 Dec 1811- Frederick Beall, C.C.O.
12 Dec 1811- W.F. Bagwell, J.P.
source: volume 1, page 47

BROWN, THOMAS
and
WILLIAMS, BARSHEBA

13 Dec 1811- Frederick Beall, C.C.O.
19 Dec 1811- W.F. Bagwell, J.P.
source: license- 1751-01/1-17
see also volume 1, page 47

MORRIS, JOSEPH
and
MOOR(MORE), ANN

24 Dec 1811- Frederick Beall, C.C.O.
24 Dec 1811- Ja's H. Little, J.P.
source: volume 1, page 48

TAILOR, GEORGE
and
MULLIN, LATHY

26 Dec 1811- Frederick Beall, C.C.O.
29 Dec 1811- Ja's Chandler, J.P.
source: volume 1, page 48

SANDERS, JOHN
and
ROBBINS, ALEY

28 Dec 1811- Frederick Beall, C.C.O.
....
source: volume 1, page 45

DENMAN, ABSALEM
and
WILCOX, CLARISSA

28 (sic) Dec 1811- Frederick Beall, C.C.O.
27 (sic) Dec 1811- Edmond Henley, J.I.C.
source: volume 1, page 48

11

HARDEN, SANDLIN
and
STEPHENSON, POLLY

1 Jan 1812- Frederick Beall, C.C.O.
2 Jan 1812- John Taber
source: volume 1, page 90

BRASDLE, JAMES
and
COVINGTON, ELEANOR

4 Jan 1812- Frederick Beall, C.C.O.
5 Jan 1812- W.F. Bagwell, J.P.
source: license- 1751-01/1-10

PRICKET, JESSE
and
ELLIOTT, ELIZABETH

11 Jan 1812- Frederick Beall, C.C.O.
14 Jan 1812- John Tabor
source: volume 1, page 88

GATEWOOD, ROLAND
and
LANE, SENA

17 Jan 1812- W'm Terrell for Frederick
              Beall, C.C.O.
19 Jan 1812- .....
source: license- 1751-02/3--54
see also volume 1, page 91

BROOKS, JOB
and
WOOD, PRISILLA

27 Jan 1812- Frederick Beall, C.C.O.
27 Feb 1812- Boley Conner, J.P.
source: volume 1, page 50

SIMS, HULL
and
ALLEN, POLLY

21 Feb 1812- Frederick Beall, C.C.O.
25 Feb 1812- John Tabor
source: volume 1, page 88

HOLBROOKS, SAMUEL
and
WILSON, HANNAH

5 Mar 1812- Frederick Beall, J.P.
5 Mar 1812- Edmund Henley, J.I.C.
source: license- 1751-02/3-71
see also volume 1, page 79

ARON, WILLIAM
and
BRASHER, DEANNER(?)

30 Mar 1812- Frederick Beall, C.C.O.
31 Mar 1812- Francis Callaway, D.D.(?)
source: volume 1, page 85

GAZAWAY, THOMAS
and
WHEELER, LUCY

22 Apr 1812- Benj. Hollingsworth for
              Frederick Beall, C.C.O.
.... - ....
source: license- 1751-02/3-55
see also volume 1, page 90

SMITH, HEZEKIAH
and
THOMAS, POLLY

11 July 1812- Frederick Beall, C.C.O.
16 July 1812- Francis Callaway, O.M.
source: volume 1, page 50

HODGE, JOHN
and
GOBER, DOLLY

5 Aug 1812- Frederick Beall, C.C.O.
6 Aug 1812- James H. Little, J.P.
source: license- 1751-02/3-71
see also volume 1, page 50

CONNER, JOHN
and
CHAPPLEAR, POLLEY

7 Aug 1812- Frederick Beall, C.C.O.
7 Aug 1812- Joseph Chandler, J.P.
source: license- 1751-01/2-34

MC CARTER, JAMES
and
BROWN, JENSA

1 Sept 1812- Frederick Beall, C.C.O.
1 Sept 1812- James H. Little, J.P.
source: license- 1751-02/4-89

CARTER, ABSALOM
and
WILKESON, NANCY

3 Sept 1812- Frederick Beall, C.C.O.
3 Sept 1812- Joseph Chandler, J.P.
source: volume 1, page 81

PAIN, THOMAS
and
DOBS, ELIZABETH

6 Sept 1812- Frederick Beall, C.C.O.
7 Sept 1812- Bolly Conner, J.P.
source: volume 1, page 80

ELISON, DAVID
and
MAYS, CHARLOTTIE

7 Sept 1812- Frederick Beall, C.C.O.
10 Sept 1812- Nacy Meeks
source: volume 1, page 80

DAVIS, WILLIAM
and
MAYHOE, NANCY

17 Sept 1812- Frederick Beall, C.C.O.
7 Oct 1812- ....
source: volume 1, page 81

CRUMP, RICHARD
and
WHEELER, ELIZABETH

5 Oct 1812- Frederick Beall, C.C.O.
8 Oct 1812- John Tabor
source: volume 1, page 92

PHILIPS, MARK
and
CANN, MARY

26 Oct 1812- Frederick Beall, C.C.O.
26 Oct 1812- James H. Little, J.P.
source: license 1751-03/6-114
see also volume 1, page 91

EPPERSON, PETER
and
WADKINS, RHODY

29 Oct 1812- Frederick Beall, C.C.O.
29 Oct 1812- W'm Jones, J.P.
source: license- 1751-02/3-47

GLOVER, WILLIAM
and
PULLUM, ELIZABETH

27 Nov 1812- Frederick Beall, C.C.O.
28 Nov 1812- Benj. King, J.P.
source: license- 1751-02/3-57

AYERS, ASA
and
VESSELS, OLIVE

19 Dec 1812- Frederick Beall, C.C.O.
19 Dec 1812- John R. Brown, J.P.
source: volume 1, page 69

HANCOCK, ISIAH
and
GOODWIN, NANCY

24 Dec 1812- Jno. Mullin for Frederick
            Beall, C.C.O.
21 Jan 1813- Nacy Meeks
source: volume 1, page 81

LOUGHRIDGE, WILLIAM
and
PULLAM, JERUSHA

7 Jan 1813- Frederick Beall, C.C.O.
10 Feb 1813- Nacy Meeks
source: volume 1, page 82

GOWDY, FRED'K
and
......., ADARINE

21 Jan 1813- Frederick Beall, C.C.O.
29 Jan 1813- James Little, J.P.
source: volume 1, page 83

HALL, WILLIAM H.
and
MERIDA, LUCY

15 Feb 1813- Frederick Beall, C.C.O.
18 Feb 1813- John Cleveland
source: volume 1, page 82

BAGLEY, JAMES
and
ALLEN, ELIZABETH

2 Mar (sic) 1813- Frederick Beall, C.C.O.
4 Feb (sic) 1813- W.F. Bagwell, J.P.
source: volume 1, page 83

KING, BERRY and BRASDLE, REBECCA	16 Mar 1813- Frederick Beall, C.C.O. 25 Mar 1813- Adam Cloud source: volume 1, page 82
ASH, JOHN and NEWTON, MARGARET	17 Mar 1813- Frederick Beall, C.C.O. 18 Mar 1813- Adam Cloud source: volume 1, page 81
BOHANNON, WILLIAM and WHITE, POLLY	2 Apr 1813- Frederick Beall, C.C.O. 8 Apr 1813- W.F. Bagwell source: volume 1, page 83
MAYS, WILLIAM and THOMAS, ELIZABETH	3 Apr 1813- Frederick Beall, C.C.O. 6 Apr 1813- Tho's Newton, V.D.M. source: license- 1751-03/5-97 see also volume 1, page 92
HOLLINGSWORTH, JAMES and JONES, MARY	16 May 1813- Frederick Beall, C.C.O. .... ⁻ .... source: volume 1, page 57
BELL, THOMAS and CLEGHORNE, ELIZABETH	9 June 1813- Frederick Beall, C.C.O. 9 June 1813- Asa Allen, J.I.C. source: license- 1751-01/1-10 see also volume 1, page 90
LANGSTON, JAMES and DAVIS, ELIZABETH	21 June 1813- Darby Henley for Frederick Beall, R. Probate 22 June 1813- Littleton Meeks, M.G. source: license- 1751-02/4-84
GILBERT, WILLIAM and GILBERT, PRISSILLA	7 July 1813(sic)- Frederick Beall, C.C.O. 8 June 1813(sic)- Gabriel Martin, J.P. source: license- 1751-02/3-55 see also volume 1, page 89
MURPHY, ALEXANDER and COLEMAN, SUSANNAH	27 July 1813- Frederick Beall, C.C.O. 27 July 1813- Austin Harden, J.P. source: volume 1, page 89
CHATHAM, CHAFIN and PAYNE, POLLY	28 July 1813- Frederick Beall, C.C.O. 29 July 1813- Francis Callaway source: volume 1, page 86
PENN, WILLIAM and WILSON, ABIGAL	2 Aug 1813- Frederick Beall, C.C.O. 5 Aug 1813- James Lowry, M.G. source: volume 1, page 93
NUNN, THOMAS and WOODALE, FANNY	17 Aug 1813- Frederick Beall, C.C.O. 19 Aug 1813- James Allan, J.I.C. source: license- 1751-03/5-106
DENMAN, MORGAN and GRAY, ELIZABETH	26 Aug 1813- Frederick Beall, C.C.O. 26 Aug 1813- Edmund Henley, J.P. source: volume 1, page 88

PHILLIPS, JAMES
and
MC INTIRE, SARAH

2 Sept 1813- Frederick Beall, C.C.O.
9 Sept 1813- James H. Little, J.P.
source: license- 1751-03/6-114
see also volume 1, page 86

LOWERY, GEORGE
and
COX, ELIZABETH

29 Sept 1813- Frederick Beall, C.C.O.
30 Sept 1813- Littleton Meeks
source: volume 1, page 86

ELSTON, ALLEN
and
TERRELL, MRS. ANNA

4 Oct 1813- Frederick Beall, C.C.O.
21 Nov 1813- Nacey Meeks
source: license- 1751-02/3-47
see also volume 1, page 87

HOMES, JAMES J.
and
NEWTON, ELIZABETH B.

19 Oct 1813- Frederick Beall, C.C.O.
22 Oct 1813- Rev'd Adam Cloud
source: license- 1751-02/3-72
see also volume 1, page 85

WHITTICAR, BENJAMIN
and
BRASDLE, WINNEFRED

25 Oct 1813- Frederick Beall, C.C.O.
29 Oct 1813- Adam Cloud
source: license- 1751-04/8-164
see also volume 1, page 87

CALLAWAY, FRANCIS
and
RUSSEL, SALLY

1 Nov 1813- Frederick Beall, C.C.O.
2 Nov 1813- Nacey Meeks
source: license- 1751-01/2-21
see also volume 1, page 84

NICHELS, DAVID
and
GIBS, MIMA

14 Nov 1813- Frederick Beall, C.C.O.
19 Nov 1813- Francis Callaway, O.M.
source: license- 1751-03/5-106
see also volume 1, page 87

JONES, JOSEPH
and
BOWEN, HEPSEY

2 Dec 1813- Tho's Hollingsworth for
          Frederick Beall, C.C.O.
2 Dec 1813- Tho's Hollingsworth, J.P.
source: license- 1751-02/4-78
see also volume 1, page 88

HODGE, JAMES
and
BOND, JINNEY

30 Dec 1813- Frederick Beall, C.C.O.
6 Jan 1814- Asa Allen, J.I.C.
source: license- 1751-02/3-71

SMITH, RALPH
and
ARTHUR, SALLY

2 Jan 1814- Frederick Beall, C.C.O.
2 Jan 1814- Austin Kendrick, J.P.
source: volume 1, page 89

MANLY, MOSES
and
ATTAWAY, LENA

3 Mar 1814- Frederick Beall, C.C.O.
3 Mar 1814- Adam Cloud
source: license- 1751-02/4-94
see also volume 1, page 90

SMITH, WILLIAM
and
NAIL, SABRY

19 May 1814- Frederick Beall, C.C.O.
27 May 1814- John Cleveland, V.D.M.
source: volume 2, page 104

```
CARPENTER, GEORGE            27 Mar 1814- Frederick Beall, C.C.O.
    and                      27 Mar 1814- James Little, J.P.
HENDRICK, NANCY              source: license- 1751-01/2-23
                             see also volume 1, page 93


HIGGENS, BURWELL            29 Mar 1814- Frederick Beall, C.C.O.
    and                     30 Mar 1814- Francis Callaway, O.M.
HIGGENS, CHARITY            source: license- 1751-02/3-69


PAYN, MIDLETON             23 June 1814- Frederick Beall, C.C.O.
    and                    23 June 1814- W.F. Bagwell, J.P.
HOUS(?HANES?HARRIS?), PATIENCE source: license- 1715-03/5-112
                             see also volume 1, page 93


BEALL, MAT. W.             26 June 1814- Frederick Beall, C.C.O.
    and                    27 June 1814- Francis Stubbs, J.P.-
STEPHENS, REBECCA                       Putnam Co.
                           source: volume 1, page 93,94


WITT, ADAM                 22 July 1814- Frederick Beall, C.C.O.
    and                    23 July 1814- James Mitchell, J.P.
JOHNSON, RACHEL            source: license- 1751-04/8-169
                           see also volume 1, page 89


CALLAWAY, FRANCIS          18 Aug 1814- Frederick Beall, C.C.O.
    and                    11 Sept 1814- Francis Callaway, O.M.
TAYLER, ELIZABETH          source: license- 1751-01/2-21


SMITH, MATHIAS             1 Sept 1814- Frederick Beall, C.C.O.
    and                    1 Sept 1814- John Duncan, J.P.
GARRISON, SUSANNA          source: license- 1751-04/7-138
                           see also volume 1, page 94


HOGWOOD, ASA               9 Sept 1814- Frederick Beall, C.C.O.
    and                    11 Dec 1814- Nace Meeks, J.P.
HIGGINS, ELIZABETH         source: volume 1, page 98


SMITH, THOMAS              15 Sept 1814- Frederick Beall, C.C.O.
    and                    15 Sept 1814- W'm Jones, J.P.
BELL, RUTH                 source: license- 1751-04/7-139


BURTON, ROBERT            23 Sept 1814- Frederick Beall, C.C.O.
    and                   29 Sept 1814- James H. Little, J.P.
CONNALLY, SARAH           source: volume 1, page 98


RACKLEY, SOLOMON          29 Sept 1814- Frederick Beall, C.C.O.
    and                   29 Sept 1814- Austin Kendrick, J.P.
BRIGHT, CHARLOT LOTTEY    source: license- 1715-03/6-122
                          see also volume 1, page 94,95


ASH, JAMES                24 Oct 1814- Frederick Beall, C.C.O.
    and                   27 Oct 1814- James Allan, J.I.C.
MARTIN, NANCY             source: license- 1751-01/1-6
                          see also volume 1, page 94
```

CHANDLER, WYETT   7 Nov 1814- Frederick Beall, C.C.O.
    and   10 Nov 1814- James Allan, J.I.C.
LINER, POLLY (the name Denman was written in first with Liner written in
              over it)   source: license- 1751-01/2-27
                                         see also volume 1, page 95

RICE, WILLIAM   21 Nov 1814- Frederick Beall, C.C.O.
    and   ....   - ....
SIMS, POLLY   source: volume 1, page 97

DOBBS, MOREMAN   17 Dec 1814- Frederick Beall, C.C.O.
    and   25 Dec 1814- Austin Kendrick, J.P.
CAPE, SARAH   source: license- 1751-01/2-44
                                         see also volume 1, page 95

HOLEBROOKS, FRANKY   .... - ....
    and   20 Dec 1814- James Mitchell, J.P.
MULLICAN, ..VRY   source: license- 1751-02/3-72(part missing)
                                         see also volume 1, page 95,96: bride
                                         listed as Iris Milligan, license issued
                                         on 20 Dec 1814 by Frederick Beall, C.C.O.

IRONS, WILLIAM   20 Dec 1814- Frederick Beall, C.C.O.
    and   22 Dec 1814- Edmond Henley, J.I.C.
BEASONS, ELIZABETH   source: license- 1751-02/4-75
                                         see also volume 1, page 96

GOBER, DANIEL   22 Dec 1814- Frederick Beall, C.C.O.
    and   22 Dec 1814- Ja's H. Little, J.P.
ARENDAL, ELIZABETH   source: license- 1751-02/3-57

CHATHAM, WILLIAM   23 Dec 1814- Frederick Beall, C.C.O.
    and   25 Dec 1814- Francis Callaway
PAYNE, RUTH   source: license- 1751-01/2-29

MC INA(?), THOMAS H.   4 Jan 1815- Frederick Beall, C.C.O.
    and   4 Jan 1815- W.F. Bagwell, J.P.
BLACKWELL, ANN   source: volume 1, page 96

HULSEY, PLEASANT   24 Jan 1815- Frederick Beall, C.C.O.
    and   24 Jan 1815- W'm Hulsey, J.P.
BYRD, ELIZABETH   source: license- 1751-02/3-74

ASHWORTH, JAMES   26 Jan 1815- Frederick Beall, C.C.O.
    and   26 Jan 1815- W'm Hulsey, J.P.
BRAISHER, JAMIMAY   source: license- 1751-01/1-6

COUCH, JAMES   30 Jan 1815- Frederick Beall, C.C.O.
    and   30 Jan 1815- Rich'd Shockley, J.P.
WILSON,(?), ABAGAL   source: license- 1751-01/2-35

ROBERTSON, JAMES   19 Feb 1815- Frederick Beall, C.C.O.
    and   20 Feb 1815- Jos. Reed, J.P.
LOWERY, MARGARET   source: license- 1751-03/6-126

GIBSON, JOHN   19 Feb 1815- Frederick Beall, C.C.O.
    and   19 Feb 1815- Clemond Quillian, J.P.
GIBSON, RUHAMA   source: volume 1, page 96

HOLLAND, ALLEN W.
and
COB(?), PATSY B.

17 Mar 1815- Frederick Beall, C.C.O.
17 Mar 1815- George Stovall, J.P.
source: license- 1751-02/3-72

RUSSEL, MARTIN
and
HANES, POLLY

1 Mar 1815- Frederick Beall, C.C.O.
2 Mar 1815- Francis Callaway, O.M.
source: license- 1751-03/6-127
(note: there is a second license in the
file with these names, issued 18 Mar
1815, but with no return data)

PAYNE, ASA
and
GESS, ANNY

26 Mar 1815- Frederick Beall, C.C.O.
26 Mar 1815- Clemond Quillian, J.P.
source: license- 1751-03/5-111
see also volume 1, page 97

ISOM, JAMES
and
EVRETT, ELIZABETH

30 Mar 1815- Frederick Beall, C.C.O.
30 Mar 1815- W'm Hulsey, J.P.
source: license- 1751-02/4-75

DANIEL, RUSSEL
and
GILBERT, ELIZABETH

3 Apr 1815- ....
6 Apr 1815- Gabriel Martin, J.P.
source: volume 2, page 168 (note: this
is not a recorded marriage, and the
license from which the data was copied
is now missing. See Introduction)

GILLEY, WILLIS
and
....., ELIZABETH (HOLCOM?)

10 Apr 1815- Frederick Beall, C.C.O.
18 Apr 1815- John Warmack, J.P.
source: license 1751-02/3-60 (torn)

MAYS, THOMAS
and
BRINLEE, LUVICE

25 Apr 1815- Frederick Beall, C.C.O.
27 Apr 1815- Thomas Newton
source: license- 1751-03/5-97

LOWERY, BENJAMIN
and
BONDS, CHARITY

28 Apr 1815- Frederick Beall, C.C.O.
2 May 1815- Asa Allen, J.I.C.
source: license- 1751-02/4-88

GAZZAWAY, THOMAS, SR.
and
WALLEN, PATSY

1 May 1815- Frederick Beall, C.C.O.
4 May 1815- Moses Guest, J.P.
source: license- 1751-02/3-55

QUILLEN, JAMES
and
PRICHETT, SARAH

16 May 1815- Frederick Beall, C.C.O.
18 May 1815- Clemonds Quillian, J.P.
source: license- 1751-03/6-121

CARPENTER, JONETHEN
and
CASH(or CAGLE?), PEGGY

1 June 1815- Frederick Beall, C.C.O.
.... -..........
source: license- 1751-01/2-23

HARRISON, ROBERT
and
MILLER, SARY

15 June 1815- Frederick Beall, C.C.O.
15 June 1815- W. Hulsey, J.P.
source: license- 1751-02/3-64

REBURN, CORNELIOUS
and
BAXTER, BECCA

17 June 1815- Frederick Beall, C.C.O.
22 June 1815- James H, Little, J.P.
source: license- 1751-03/6-122

BROWN, JAMES
and
FIGGENS, PEGGY

12 July 1815- Frederick Beall, C.C.O.
14 July 1815- Abs. Holcomb, J.P.
source: license- 1751-01/1-17

DOBS, JAMES
and
ARMSTRONG, ANN

12 July 1815- Frederick Beall, C.C.O.
12 July 1815- Clemonds Quillian, J.P.
source: license- 1751-01/2-44

WADKINS, GRIFFIN
and
TOLBERT, MATILDA

13 July 1815- Frederick Beall, C.C.O.
14 July 1815- Francis Callaway, O.M.
source: license- 1751-04/8-155

BREWER, RANDLE
and
COX, LEANNA

26 July 1815- Frederick Beall, C.C.O.
30 July 1815- John M. Gray, M.G.
source: license- 1751-01/1-16

GIDEON, FRANCIS
and
KENDRICK, SUSAN

27 July 1815- Frederick Beall, C.C.O.
28 July 1815- ... Holcomb, J.P.
source: volume 1, page 51

CADEL(?), ISOM
and
CADEL, ELIZABETH

8 Aug 1815- Frederick Beall, C.C.O.
13 Aug 1815- Absalom Holcomb, J.P.
source: license- 1751-03/5-108

FLEMING, JAMES L.
and
ASH, JANE

9 Aug 1815- Frederick Beall, C.C.O.
10 Aug 1815- Thomas Newton
source: volume 1, page 51

WADE, HENRY
and
JORDEN, TEMPY

15 Aug 1815- Frederick Beall, C.C.O.
17 Aug 1815- Abs. Holcomb, J.P.
source: license- 1751-04/8-155

WILLIAMS, WILLIAM
and
HOLBROOKS, JINSEY

21 Aug 1815- Frederick Beall, C.C.O.
24 Aug 1815- Richard Shockley, J.P.
source: license- 1751-C4/8-167

TONEY, HARRIS
and
ROBERSON, REBECCA

21 Aug 1815- Frederick Beall, C.C.O.
24 Aug 1815- Henry David, M.G.
source: license- 1751-04/7-149

GRUVER, JOHN
and
WILLSON, ELIZABETH

6 Sept 1815- Frederick Beall, C.C.O.
7 Sept 1815- W'm Brown, J.P.
source: license- 1751-02/3-60

WADKINS, VINCENT
and
HENDERSON, ELIZABETH

7 Sept 1815- Frederick Beall, C.C.O.
7 Sept 1815- W'm Hulsey, J.P.
source: license- 1751-04/8-155

WALTERS, THOMAS
and
BROWN, ANN

12 Sept 1815- Frederick Beall, C.C.O.
17 Sept 1815- John M. Seay, M.G.
source: license- 1751-04/8-156

BAUZEWELL, MILES
and
HOLD BROOKS, ELEANOR

14 Sept 1815- Frederick Beall, C.C.O.
14 Sept 1815- W'm Hulsey, J.P.
source: license- 1751-01/1-9

GORHAM, THOMAS   10 Oct 1815- W'm Terrell for Frederick
and   Beall, C.C.O.
AVERY, MARY M.   12 Oct 1815- Edmund Henley, J.P.
                                      source: license- 1751-02/3-58

CHANDLER, JEDEDIAH   18 Oct 1815- Frederick Beall, C.C.O.
and   19 Oct 1815- Ja's H. Little, J.P.
MACKY, SARAH   source: license- 1751-01/2-27

BELLAMY, NICHOLAS   27 Oct 1815- Frederick Beall, C.C.O.
and   9 Nov 1815- James H. Little, J.P.
JONES, RODY   source: license- 1751-01/1-10

REDDIN(? RALSTON?), ...   13 Nov 1815- Frederick Beall, C.C.O.
and   16 Nov 1815- Nacey Meeks
INGLAND, RACHEL   source: volume 1, page 52

BAKER, BENJAMIN   10 Dec 1815- Frederick Beall, C.C.O.
and   10 Dec 1815- W.F. Bagwell, J.P.
WILLIAMSON, POLLY   source: license- 1751-01/1-8

NIX, JOHN   3 Feb 1816- Frederick Beall, C.C.O.
and   6 Feb 1816- Nacy Meeks
HOLMES, ELIZABETH   source: volume 1, page 101

HEYRS, DAVID   5 Feb 1816- Frederick Beall, C.C.O.
and   5 Feb 1816- Joseph Walters, J.P.
RAGIN, DICY   source: volume 1, page 52

WATSON, ANDREW   7 Feb 1816- Frederick Beall, C.C.O.
and   10 Feb 1816- Nacy Meeks, J.P.
ISAAC, ELIZABETH   source: volume 1, page 99

WILLIAMSON, JOHN   18 Mar 1816- Frederick Beall, C.C.O.
and   21 Mar 1816- W'm Hulsey, J.P.
THOMPSON, ELIZABETH   source: volume 1, page 100

DAVIS, MATTHEW   20 Mar 1816- Frederick Beall, C.C.O.
and   20 Mar 1816- W'm Hulsey, J.P.
HOLBROOK, DARKES   source: volume 1, page 100

NIX, JAMES   25 Mar 1816- Frederick Beall, C.C.O.
and   27 Mar 1816- Nacy Meeks
HOLMES, LUCY   source: volume 1, page 101

MILLER, JOHN   26 Mar 1816- Frederick Beall, C.C.O.
and   26 Mar 1816- John Duncan, J.P.
HULSEY, ANNY   source: volume 1, page 102

BUSH, JONATHAN   14 Apr 1816- Frederick Beall, C.C.O.
and   14 Apr 1816- Moses Guest, J.P.
CRUMP, DINSELONDY   source: volume 1, page 105

TURK, WILLIAM   17 Apr 1816- Frederick Beall, C.C.O.
and   18 Apr 1816- Tho's Newton
MAYS, JANE   source: volume 1, page 102

THOMPSON, SEBORN
and
LOUGHRIDGE, FANNY

18 Apr 1816- Frederick Beall, C.C.O.
18 Apr 1816- William Hulsey, J.P.
source: volume 1, page 105

GOBER, RICHARD
and
AYRES, POLLY

28 Apr 1816- Frederick Beall, C.C.O.
29 Apr 1816- John Mays, J.P.
source: volume 1, page 107(see also 58)

SHANNON, MOSES
and
CLEVELAND, JEMMIMA

24 Apr 1816- Frederick Beall, C.C.O.
28 Apr 1816- Tryon Patterson, J.P.
source: volume 1, page 100

BOLLS, EBER M.
and
TAYLOR, ELIZABETH B.

21 May 1816- Frederick Beall, C.C.O.
23 May 1816- George Sandivear, M.
source: volume 1, page 107

DOWDY, ARMSTED
and
CROSS, ELIZABETH

28 May 1816- Frederick Beall, C.C.O.
30 May 1816- John Mays
source: volume 1, page 51

ARON, JESSE
and
FLOOD, PATSY

20 June 1816- Frederick Beall, C.C.O.
20 June 1816- James Mitchell, J.P.
source: volume 1, page 105

GARRISON, WILLIAM
and
CRAFT, ELIZABETH

3 July 1816- Frederick Beall, C.C.O.
3 July 1816- William Hulsey, J.P.
source: volume 1, page 106

KNOX, JOHN
and
DENMAN, ELIZABETH

10 July 1816- Frederick Beall, C.C.O.
.... - ....
source: volume 1, page 117

ROSE, JESSE
and
FLEMING, PERMELIA

15 July 1816- Frederick Beall, C.C.O.
18 July 1816- John May, J.P.
source: volume 1, page 102

STOE, WARREN
and
MEDLOCK, ELIZABETH

18 July 1816- Frederick Beall, C.C.O.
18 July 1816- W'm Hulsey, J.P.
source: volume 1, page 99

ELLISON, MOSES
and
ELISON(?), NANCY

24 July 1816- Frederick Beall, C.C.O.
24 July 1816- Littleton Meeks, M.G.
source: volume 1, page 102

RICE, MOSES
and
HOLCOMB, SINTHA

25 July 1816- Frederick Beall, C.C.O.
25 July 1816- Moses Guest, J.P.
source: volume 1, page 105

CRAWFORD, ELIJAH
and
BEASLEY, CLARASY

25 July 1816- Frederick Beall, C.C.O.
1 Aug 1816- Abs. Holcomb, J.P.
source: license- 1751-01/2-36
see also volume 1, page 116

WOOD, ALLEN
and
RAMSEY, ANN

1 Aug 1816- Frederick Beall, C.C.O.
1 Aug 1816- James Mitchell, J.P.
source: volume 1, page 106

THRASHER, WILLI...(torn)
and
SMITH, ELIZABETH

1 Aug 1816- Frederick Beall, C.C.O.
1 Aug 1816- James H. Little, J.P.
source: volume 1, page 136

ALLRED, JOHN
and
WARREN, NANCY

5 Aug 1816- Frederick Beall, C.C.O.
6 Aug 1816- Littleton Meeks, M.G.
source: volume 1, page 103

HARDY, FREEMAN
and
LINNEAR, KEZZIAH

12 Aug 1816- Frederick Beall, C.C.O.
15 Aug 1816- Francis Callaway, O.M.
source: volume 1, page 100

TERRELL, JONATHAN
and
RAMSEY, ELIZABETH

28 Sept 1816(sic)- Frederick Beall, C.C.O.
28 Apr 1816(sic)- ----------
source: volume 1, page 103

MAYS, JAMES
and
BRINDLEY, LUCINDA

30 Sept 1816- Frederick Beall, C.C.O.
30 Sept 1816- Asa Allen, J.I.C.
source: volume 1, page 99

WESTBROOK, THOMAS
and
ALLEN, ELIZABETH

30 Sept 1816- Frederick Beall, C.C.O.
3 Oct 1816- James H. Little, J.P.
source: volume 1, page 103

THOMAS, JAMES L.
and
EVRETT, REBECCA

15 Oct 1816- Frederick Beall, C.C.O.
15 Oct 1816- William Hulsey, J.P.
source: license- 1751-04/7-147
see also volume 1, page 115

HARRIS, NATHANIEL
and
WELBORN, ARGENT

17 Oct 1816- Frederick Beall, C.C.O.
20 Oct 1816- Nacey Meeks
source: volume 1, page 101

HIGGINS, ENOCH
and
HEGGINS, POLLY

18 Oct 1816- Frederick Beall, C.C.O.
.... ‾ ....
source: volume 1, page 117

HENDERSON, JOSEPH
and
REED, NANCY

24 Oct 1816- Frederick Beall, C.C.O.
24 Oct 1816- John Duncan, J.P.
source: license- 1751-02/3-67
see also volume 1, page 108

CLARKSON, JOSEPH
and
GOBER, NANCY

30 Oct 1816- Frederick Beall, C.C.O.
30 Oct 1816- Sam. Lane, O.M.
source: volume 1, page 106

THRASHER, THOMAS
and
ELLIOTT, MIHELIA

6 Nov 1816- Frederick Beall, C.C.O.
6 Nov 1816- Clemond Quillian, J.P.
source: volume 1, page 101

HOLLINGSWORTH, JOHN
and
WHITE, MATILDA

23 Nov 1816- Frederick Beall, C.C.O.
24 Nov 1816- Nace Meeks, O.M.
source: volume 1, page 107

BRANTLY, JOSEPH A.
and
MEEKS, MARTHA

23 Nov 1816- Frederick Beall, C.C.O.
23 Nov 1816- Trion Patterson
source: volume 1, page 53

LOWRY, DAVID
and
COOK, SARAH

5 Dec 1806(sic)- Frederick Beall, C.C.O.
9 Dec 1816(sic)- W'm Jones, J.P.
source: license- 1751-02/4-88
see also volume 1, page 118

SMITH, JOHN T.
and
SHOTWELL, ELIZABETH

6 Dec 1816- Frederick Beall, C.C.O.
10 Dec 1816- Darby Henley, J.P.
source: volume 1, page 103

SIMS, HOPE
and
VARNER, HANNAH

7 Dec 1816- Frederick Beall, C.C.O.
8 Dec 1816- Clemond Quillian, J.P.
source: volume 1, page 107

PUT(?), WILLIAM
and
SANDERS, NANCY

8 Dec 1816- Frederick Beall, C.C.O.
8 Dec 1816- John Duncan, J.P.
source: license- 1751-03/6-120
see also volume 1, page 115

JORDAN, GRAY
and
CHANDLER, PEGGY

17 Dec 1816- Frederick Beall, C.C.O.
19 Dec 1816- Jos. Chandler, J.P.
source: volume 1, page 116

BRADY, ENOCH
and
DAVIS, NANCY

19 Dec 1816- Frederick Beall, C.C.O.
.... - ....
source: volume 1, page 104

ANDREWS, WILLIAM
and
POE(? ROE?), REBECKAH

22 Dec 1816- Frederick Beall, C.C.O.
.... - ....
source: volume 1, page 104

BOSWELL, WILLIAM
and
WHITWORTH, LAVISA

23 Dec 1816(sic)- Frederick Beall, C.C.O.
20 Dec 1816(sic)- Francis Callaway, Jr.,
                 M.G.
source: volume 1, page 106

WORTHY, ANDERSON
and
ANDREWS, SUSANNAH

23 Dec 1816- Frederick Beall, C.C.O.
.... - ....
source: volume 1, page 104

ISOM, JOHN
and
HENDERSON, SINAH

24 Dec 1816- Frederick Beall, C.C.O.
....   - John Duncan, J.P.
source: license- 1751-02/4-75
see also volume 1, page 115

RICKELS, JOSIAH
and
TUCKER, POLLY

25 Dec 1816- Frederick Beall, C.C.O.
26 Dec 1816- Richard C. Bond, J.P.
source: volume 1, page 104

ANTHONY, DAVID
and
CHANDLER, MRS. ELIZABETH

27 Dec 1826(sic)- Frederick Beall, C.C.O.
29 Dec 1816(sic)- Henry David, M.G.
source: volume 1 , page 58 and 108

MELLEN(?), MICHAEL
and
JONES, SARAH

30 Dec 1816- Frederick Beall, C.C.O.
2 Jan 1817- Nacy Meeks
source: volume 1, page 121

SHOTWELL, JOHN
and
HENLEY, SALLY

6 Jan 1817- Frederick Beall, C.C.O.
.... - ....
source: volume 1, page 117

MAYS, THOMAS
and
CHANDLER, MARTHA

22 Jan 1817- Frederick Beall, C.C.O.
.... - ....
source: volume 1, page 99

HULSEY, JOHN
and
GARRISON, ELLENDER

23 Jan 1817- Frederick Beall, C.C.O.
23 Jan 1817- W'm Hulsey, J.P.
source: license- 1751-02/3-74
see also volume 1, page 110

INGRAM, MARTIN
and
PEEK, NANCY

25 Jan 1817- Frederick Beall, C.C.O.
25 Jan 1817- W'm Hulsey, J.P.
source: volume 1, page 122

LOWRY, JOHN W.
and
TRIMBLE, ELIZABETH

27 Jan 1817- Frederick Beall, C.C.O.
28 July 1817- R. Weems, J.P.
source: license- 1751-02/4-88

IVIE, JOHN
and
GLASS, NANCY

28 Jan 1817- Frederick Beall, C.C.O.
29 Jan 1817- Littleton Meeks
source: volume 1, page 58 and 118

REDWINE, JESSE
and
HUNT, ELIZABETH

30 Jan 1817- Frederick Beall, C.C.O.
2 Feb 1817- James Hutto, M.G.
source: volume 1, page 122

WILSON, WILLIAM
and
SISSON, ELIZABETH

30 Jan 1817- Frederick Beall, C.C.O.
30 Jan 1817- W'm Hulsey, J.P.
source: license- 1751-04/8-168

SANDERS, ARON
and
THOMASON, MORNING

4 Feb 1817- Frederick Beall, C.C.O.
4 Feb 1817- John Duncan, J.P.
source: license- 1751-03/6-128
see also volume 1, page 113

MILLER, ROBERT
and
WALLRAVEN, ELIZABETH

19 Feb 1817- Frederick Beall, C.C.O.
20 Feb 1817- W'm Hulsey, J.P.
source: license- 1751-03/5-99
see also volume 1, page 113

AYRES, JOHN
and
PAYNE, EDY

12 Feb 1817- Frederick Beall, C.C.O.
13 Feb 1817- Francis Callaway
source: volume 1, page 122

LOWREY, JAMES
and
TONEY, NANCY

18 Feb 1817- Frederick Beall, C.C.O.
18 Feb 1817- John Mays, J.P.
source: volume 1, page 109

BLACKWELL, JEDIAH
and
HENDERSON, NANCY

20 Feb 1817- Frederick Beall, C.C.O.
20 Feb 1817- John Duncan, J.P.
source: license- 1751-01/1.12
see also volume 1, page 110

MILLER, ASARIEL
and
HALEY, DICE

5 Mar 1817- Frederick Beall, C.C.O.
6 Mar 1817- Asa Allen, J.I.C.
source: license- 1751-03/5-99
see also volume 1, page 111

RUSSEL, JA'S
and
ACOLS, ANN

30 Mar 1817- Frederick Beall, C.C.O.
3 Apr 1817- Francis Callaway, O.M.
source: volume 1, page 123

ARTHUR, W'M
and
MILLER, MARY

8 Apr 1817- Frederick Beall, C.C.O.
8 Apr 1817- ....
source: volume 1, page 123

THOMPSON, JESSE
and
SMITH, CHARITY

13 Apr 1817- Frederick Beall, C.C.O.
13 Apr 1817- W'm Hulsey, J.P.
source: license- 1751-04/7-148
see also volume 1, page 113

MILLS, DYAL
and
GIBSON, JUDAH

15 Apr 1817- Frederick Beall, C.C.O.
17 Apr 1817- Clemonds Quillian, J.P.
source: license- 1751-03/5-99
see also volume 1, page 108

MC KENTIRE, JOSEPH
and
LITTLE, NANCY

10 May 1817- Frederick Beall, C.C.O.
15 May 1817- Asa Allen, J.I.C.
source: license- 1751-02/4-92
see also volume 1, page 110

MARTIN, WILLIAM
and
RUCKER, NANCY

28 May 1817- Frederick Beall, C.C.O.
27 May 1817- Littleton Meeks, O.M.G.
source: volume 1, page 118

DUNEHOO, JAMES
and
WILSON, ELIZABETH

29 May 1817- Frederick Beall, C.C.O.
29 May 1817- E.V.J.(?), J.I.C.
source: volume 1, page 118

CARTER, JOHN TILMAN
and
STARNS, CATY

1 June 1817- Frederick Beall, C.C.O.
1 June 1817- L. Meeks
source: volume 1, page 119

BROWN, W'M
and
RESE (or ROSE?), NANCY

12 June 1817- Frederick Beall, C.C.O.
12 June 1817- James H. Little, J.P.
source: volume 1, page 123

HATEN (or HEETON?), SAMUEL
and
NORWOOD, MARY

15 June 1817- Frederick Bell, C.C.O.
............- John Duncan, J.P.
source: license- 1751-02/3-65
see also volume 1, page 110

LOWRY, JOHN
and
AYRES, ELIZABETH

30 June 1817- Frederick Beall, C.C.O.
3 July 1817- Caleb Garrison, J.P.
source: license- 1751-02/4-88
see also volume 1, page 114

BALLARD, LEWIS
and
DOBBS, MEEKY

15 July 1817- Frederick Beall, C.C.O.
15 July 1817- Clemonds Quillian, J.P.
source: license- 1715-01/1-9
see also volume 1, page 111

MOLDER, JACOB
and
WESTBROOK, MARTHA

23 July 1817- Frederick Beall, C.C.O.
24 July 1817- James Mitchell, J.P.
source: license- 1751-03/2-101
see also volume 1, page 109

BROCK, WILLIAM
and
HOLLINGSWORTH, HANNAH

29 July 1817- Frederick Beall, C.C.O.
29 July 1817- Tho's Hollingsworth, J.P.
source: license- 1751-01/1-16
see also volume 1, page 112

WEST, THOMAS
and
HEWEY (?HERVEY?), ELEENER

30 July 1817- Frederick Beall, C.C.O.
31 July 1817- John Mayes, J.P.
source: license- 1751-04/8-159
see also volume 1, page 114

CHANDLER, GREEN
and
HOWINGTON, POLLY

18 Aug 1817- Frederick Beall, C.C.O.
21 Aug 1817- Henry David, M.G.
source: license- 1751-01/2-27
see also volume 1, page 111

MCDONALD, HUGH
and
LOGGINS, ANN

19 Aug 1817- Frederick Beall, C.C.O.
21 Aug 1817, Littleton Meeks
source: volume 1, page 58 & 119

THRASHER, GEORGE
and
WHITE, ALENDER

24 Aug 1817- Frederick Beall, C.C.O.
26 Aug 1817- James Mitchell, J.P.
source: license- 1751-04/7-149
see also volume 1, page 109

ANTHONY, MARTIN
and
CHANDLER, ELIZABETH

27 Aug 1817- Frederick Beall, C.C.O.
31 Aug 1817- Henry David, M.G.
source: volume 1, page 114

PAYNE, JOHN
and
YORK, RUTH

28 Aug 1817- Frederick Beall- C.C.O.
28 Aug 1817- Th. Hollingsworth, J.P.
source: license- 1751-03/5-111
see also volume 1, page 111

POOL, JAMES
and
BURTON, MARTHA

22 Sept 1817- Frederick Beall, C.C.O.
23 Sept 1817- Caleb Garrison, J.P.
source: volume 1, page 120

CHITWOOD, DAN'L
and
MC CRACKEN, POLLY

1 Oct 1817- Frederick Beall, C.C.O.
3 Oct 1817- Hutson Moss, J.P.
source: volume 1, page 123

FANNEN, JNO.
and
MC INGTIRE, ZALENDA

15 Oct 1817- Frederick Beall, C.C.O.
18 Oct 1817- Gabriel Martin, J.P.
source: volume 1, page 123

SHALLEN, JA'S
and
YEARLOW, ELIZABETH

30 Oct 1817- Frederick Beall, C.C.O.
30 Oct 1817- Jno. Duncan, J.P.
source: volume 1, page 124

VAUGHN, DAVID
and
SEWELL, SARAH

5 Nov 1817- Frederick Beall, C.C.O.
.... - Edmund Henley, J.I.C.
source: volume 1, page 58

PRICKET, JOSIAH
and
BAKER, POLLY

9 Nov 1817- Frederick Beall, C.C.O.
14 Nov 1817- James Hutton, M.G.
source: license- 1751-03/6-119
see also volume 1, page 135

CARNES(?), PETER
and
COLLEM, ELIZABETH

13 Nov 1817- Frederick Beall, C.C.O.
13 Nov 1817- W'm Hulsey, J.P.
source: volume 1, page 124

RAMSEY, JOHN
and
TATE, ELIZABETH

13 Nov 1817- Frederick Beall, C.C.O.
13 Nov 1817- James Mitchell, J.P.
source: volume 1, page 121

HENSLEE, DAVID S.
and
PAYNE, RHODA

13 Nov 1817- Frederick Beall, C.C.O.
13 Nov 1817- Lit. Meeks
source: volume 1, page 119

BALLENGER, JOHN
and
STEPHENSON, ELIZABETH

15 Nov 1817- Frederick Beall, C.C.O.
18 Nov 1817- W'm Redwine, J.P.
source: volume 1, page 124

LAIN, ROBERT
and
CLEAVLAND, ANNE

17 Nov 1817- Frederick Beall, C.C.O.
20 Nov 1817- W'm Legg, J.P.
source: volume 1, page 124

CAWDELL, DAVID
and
SIMS, REBECCA

25 Nov 1817- Frederick Beall, C.C.O.
25 Nov 1817- Caleb Garrison, J.P.
source: volume 1, page 120

WALTERS, ELIJA
and
BOLIN, NANCY

27 Nov 1817- Frederick Beall, C.C.O.
...........- Adam Loony, J.P.
source: volume 1, page 120

CAROL(? or CASEE?), JNO.
and
BOLEN, PRISILEY

4 Dec 1817- Frederick Beall, C.C.O.
5 Dec 1817- Hutson Moss, J.P.
source: volume 1, page 125

......., ... (blank)
and
MICHOLDS, ANN

6 Dec 1817- Frederick Beall, C.C.O.
7 Dec 1817- W'm Legg, J.P.
source: volume 1, page 125

THOMPSON, JOHN (or JOBE)
and
HALL, JUDAH

7 Dec 1817- Frederick Beall, C.C.O.
7 Dec 1817- John Perkin, J.P.
source: volume 1, page 59

THOMPSON, JAMES A.
and
LINCH, MARTHA

27 Dec 1817- Frederick Beall, C.C.O.
27 Dec 1817- Liddleton Meeks
source: volume 1, page 52

OSBOURN, DANIEL
and
STOUT (? or STOVAL?), DICY

10 Jan 1818- Frederick Beall, C.C.O.
11 Jan 1818- Caleb Garrison, J.P.
source: license- 1751-03/5-107
see also volume 1, page 136

BOND, LEONARD
and
CASH, SALLY

12 Jan 1818- Frederick Beall, C.C.O.
12 Jan 1818- Francis Callaway, Jr.
source: volume 1, page 122

GRIFFIN, ASA
and
LITTLE, NANCY

15 Jan 1818- Frederick Beall, C.C.O.
15 Jan 1818- Littleton Meeks
source: volume 1, page 136

ROBERTSON, DAVID
and
THOMAS, SALLIE

23 Jan 1818- Frederick Beall, C.C.O.
25 Jan 1818- Francis Callaway, Jr.
source: volume 1, page 121

BOND, WRITE
and
WILKESON, POLLEY

19 Feb 1818- Frederick Beall, C.C.O.
19 Feb 1818- F. Callaway, Jr.
source: volume 1, page 125

JONES, MARTIN
and
GARRISON, MRS. JUDAY E.

16 Feb 1818- Frederick Beall, C.C.O.
19 Feb 1818- C. Garrison, J.P.
source: volume 1, page 133

MANLY, DANIEL B.
and
HOPPER, WINNEY

17 Feb 1818- Frederick Beall, C.C.O.
17 Feb 1818- Royal Bryan, J.P.
source: volume 1, page 59

CARTER, ABCOL
and
CHANDLER, MALEDA(or MATILDA?)

26 Feb 1818- Frederick Beall, C.C.O.
26 Feb 1818- John Sandridge, M.G.
source: volume 1, page 125

WESTBROOK, JOHN
and
JENES(?), NANCY

2 Mar 1818- Frederick Beall, C.C.O.
3 Mar 1818- Ja's H. Little, J.P.
source: license- 1751-04/8-160
see also volume 1, page 126

PEDAN, JAMES
and
BAKER, POLLY

3 Mar 1818- Frederick Beall, C.C.O.
3 Mar 1818- R. Wims, J.P.
source: volume 1, page 129

HALL, SEBORN
and
SMITH, NANCY

15 Mar 1818- Frederick Beall, C.C.O.
15 Mar 1818- R.C. Quillian, J.P.
source: volume 1, page 59

MC MILLEN, JOHN
and
CLARK, DICY

17 Mar 1818- Frederick Beall, C.C.O.
19 Mar 1818- Francis Callaway, SR., O.M.
source: volume 1, page 126

ARON, THO'S
and
SMITH, SUSANNAH

22 Mar 1818- Frederick Beall, C.C.O.
22 Mar 1818- Clemond Henley, J.I.C.
source: volume 1, page 53

JONES, DREWRY
and
BARTON, DOLLY

28 Mar 1818- Frederick Beall, C.C.O.
29 Mar 1818- Absalom Holcom, J.P.
source: volume 1, page 126

JONES, WILLIAM
and
HOWEL, ANNY

5 Apr 1818- Frederick Beall, C.C.O.
5 Apr 1818- Gabriel Smith, J.P.
source: license- 1751-02/4-78
see also volume 1, page 133

DENMAN, JAMES and LICAT(?), ...	8 Apr 1818- Frederick Beall, C.C.O. 16 Apr 1818- Tryon Patterson, J.P. source: volume 1, page 127 (page torn) see also volume 2, page 147 which lists the bride as <u>Sarah Licat</u>
INGLAND, DAVID and FIELD, SUSANNER	23 Apr 1818- Caleb Griffith for Frederick Beall, C.C.O. 11 May 1818- Nacy Meeks source: volume 1, page 127
WILSON, NATHANIEL and BURT, ...	26 Apr 1818- Frederick Beall, C.C.O. 26 Apr 1818- W'm Legg, J.P. source: volume 1, page 135 (page torn) see also volume 2, page 159 which shows the bride as <u>Susannah Burt</u>
KEITH, MEMBRUM and MC COY, NANCY	28 Apr 1818- Frederick Beall, C.C.O. 30 Apr 1818- Andrew Dorsey, J.P. source: volume 1, page 127
DOOLEY, JOHN and GARTNEY, REBECCA	15 May 1818- Frederick Beall, C.C.O. 17 May 1818- F. Callaway, O.M.G. source: volume 1, page 127
CAWTHON, CLABURN and PULLIAM, JARUSHA	23 May 1818- Frederick Beall, C.C.O. 27 May 1818- Adam Looney source: volume 1, page 127
ALLEN, COL. ASA and WOOD, MRS. ANN	16 June 1818- Frederick Beall, C.C.O. 18 June 1818- James H. Little, J.P. source: volume 1, page 130
DEEN, WILLIAM and PEARE, ELIZABETH	20 June 1818- Frederick Beall, C.C.O. 25 June 1818- Rich'd Bond, J.P. source: volume 1, page 130
HIGGINS, THO'S and SMITH, ELIZABETH	29 June 1818- Frederick Beall, C.C.O. 2 July 1818- Andrew Dorsey, J.P. source: volume 1, page 130
DUDLEY, JOHN and JONES, ANN	13 July 1818- Frederick Beall, C.C.O. 16 July 1818- Clemond Quillian, J.P. source: volume 1, page 131
MOSS, JOHN and BOATWRIGHT, NANCY	16 July 1818- Frederick Beall, C.C.O. 16 July 1818- Francis Callaway, O.M.G. source: volume 1, page 131
BEALL, RUSSEL G. and DENT, CLOE S.	29 July 1818- Frederick Beall, C.C.O. 13 Aug 1818- W'm E. Adams, J.P.- Putnam Co. source: volume 1, page 131
POE, JOHN and DAVIS, WINNEY(?)	30 July 1818- Frederick Beall, C.C.O. 30 July 1818- Enock Brady, J.P. source: volume 1, page 129

```
WOODSON, WILLIAM              14 Aug 1818- Frederick Beall, C.C.O.
   and                       20 Aug 1818- Hardy Brown, J.P.
SWAN, CATY                   source: volume 1, page 59


......., THO'S              2 Sept 1818- Frederick Beall, C.C.O.
   and                      27 Sept 1818- Clemond Quillian, J.P.
ROSE, RODA                  source: volume 1, page 129


CRAWFORD, JOHN              14 Sept 1818- Frederick Beall, C.C.O.
   and                      14 Sept 1818- Andrew Dorsey, J.P.
VESSELS, POLLY              source: volume 1, page 129


BRUMBLET, STEPHEN           22 Sept 1818- Frederick Beall, C.C.O.
   and                      22 Sept 1818- Clemond Quillian, J.P.
ANDREWS, MARTHA             source: volume 1, page 129


HERRIN, W'M                 30 Sept 1818- Frederick Beall, C.C.O.
   and                      1 Oct 1818- James Mitchell, J.P.
MOLDER, SALLIE              source : volume 1, page 126


PATRICK, JOHN H.            3 Oct 1818- Frederick Beall, C.C.O.
   and                      29 Oct 1818- Edmund Henley, J.I.C.
MITCHELL, NACY(?)           source: volume 1, page 128


PULLUM, THO'S              5 Oct 1818- Frederick Beall, C.C.O.
   and                      8 Oct 1818- Edmond Henley, J.I.C.
BURRIS, MATILDA             source: volume 1, page 128


BRENDLEE, ASA               8 Oct 1818- Frederick Beall, C.C.O.
   and                      8 Oct 1818- Reuben Thornton, M.G.
BOWEN, POLLY                source: volume 1, page 128


AKINS, WILLIAM              20(?) Oct 1818- Frederick Beall, C.C.O.
   and                      19 Oct 1818(sic)- Francis Callaway, Sr.
CHATHAM, RODA               source: volume 1, page 135


JONES, MICAJAH             29 Oct 1818- Frederick Beall, C.C.O.
   and                      29 Oct 1818- C. Quillian, J.P.
ASHWORTH, ELIZABETH         source: volume 1, page 128


LINNER(or SIMMS?), ELISHA   19 Nov 1818- Frederick Beall, C.C.O.
   and                      22 Nov 1818- Clemond Quillian, J.P.
TRENTHAM, ANN               source: volume 1, page 126


SEWEL, SAMUEL               2 Dec 1818- Frederick Beall, C.C.O.
   and                      3 Dec 1818- James H. Little, J.P.
TRIMBLE, LUCY               source: volume 1, page 130


SIMMONS, HOLEMAN F.         22 Dec 1818- Frederick Beall, C.C.O.
   and                      24 Dec 1818- James Allen, J.P.
BURNES, SARAH E.H.          source: volume 1, page 59


STONE, HILLERY             17 Jan 1819- Frederick Beall, C.C.O.
   and                      17 Jan 1819- Edmund Henley, J.I.C.
BAGWELL, MATILD(sic)        source: license- 1751-04/7-142
                            see also volume 1, page 53
```

HILL, WILLIAM
and
NANCE, HARRIET

31 Jan 1819- Frederick Beall, C.C.O.
31 Jan 1819- John Brewster, J.I.C.
source: license- 1751-02/3-69
see also volume 1, page 135

RAY, ROBBERT
and
BRAMLETT, MARY

1 Feb 1819- Frederick Beall, C.C.O.
1 Feb 1819- Andrew Dorsey, J.P.
source: volume 2, page 161- found and
recorded 1 May 1878 by L.N. Tribble,
Ordinary.

SMITH, HENRY
and
HENING, MARGARET

9 Feb 1819- Frederick Beall, C.C.O.
14(?) Feb 1819- Adam Looney, J.P.
source: volume 1, page 136

DAVIS, HENRY H.
and
WALTERS, MRS. POLLY, WIDOW OF
JOHN WALTERS, deceased

21 Feb 1819-Adam Looney for Frederick
Beall, C.C.O.
21 Feb 1819- Adam Looney, J.P.
source: license- 1751-01/2-41
see also volume 1, page 53

MARAL, ISHAM
and
WALTERS, PHEBY

11 Mar 1819- Adam Looney for Frederick
Beall, C.C.O.
11 Mar 1819- George Vandiver
source: volume 1, page 54

GRAVES, JEREMIAH
and
BARNETT, JANE

1(?) Mar 1819- Frederick Beall, C.C.O.
14 Mar 1819- F. Callaway, Jr., O.M.
source: license- 1751-02/3-59
see also volume 1, page 131

ATHER, BARNY
and
JONES, SOPHIA

1 May 1819- Frederick Beall, C.C.O.
2 May 1819- Hamilton Wynne, J.P.
source: volume 1, page 60

MC MULLEN, WILLIAM
and
BEALL, AMELIA

13 May 1819- Frederick Beall, C.C.O.
.... - ....
source: license- 1751-02/4-92
see also volume 1, page 54

TURNER, AS. A.
and
JONES, MARTHA

6 July 1819- Frederick Beall, C.C.O.
6 July 1819- Francis Callaway, O.M.G.
source: volume 1, page 134

MAREDITH, TIGNAL
and
STOVALL, MARY ANN

19 July 1819- A. Looney for Frederick
Beall, C.C.O.
.... - ....
source: volume 1, page 54

HARRIS, WILLIAM
and
MILLER, DISA

17 Aug 1819- Frederick Beall, C.C.O.
19 Aug 1819- J. Hammond, J.I.C.
source: volume 1, page 55

BROWN, JOHN M.
and
CHEEK, ELIZABETH

20 Sept 1819- Frederick Beall, C.C.O.
23 Sept 1819- Richard Bond, J.P.
source: volume 1, page 56

31

DEAR(?), WILLIAM
and
H...., LUIS..

23 Aug 1819- Frederick Beall, C.C.O.
24 Aug 1819- Andrew Dorsey, J.P.
source: volume 1, page 131 (page torn)
see also volume 2, page 153 which shows
the bride as Louisa Hobbs

BACKSTER, W'M
and
CONALLY, THURSY

16 Sept 1819- Frederick Beall, C.C.O.
23 Sept 1819- John Mays, J.P.
source: volume 1, page 132

DENMAN, FELIX G.
and
HUCHERSON, ANN

22 Sept 1819- Frederick Beall, C.C.O.
30 Sept 1819- Francis Callaway, Jr.,
           O.M.G.
source: license- 1751-01/2-43
see also volume 1, page 133

TABER, ISAAC
and
WHEELER, ABBA

3 Oct 1819- Frederick Beall, C.C.O.
3 Oct 1819- Andrew Dorsey, J.P.
source: license- 1751-04/7-145
see also volume 1, page 55

ADISON, BRAZEL
and
CRUMP, JANE

3 Oct 1819- Frederick Beall, C.C.O.
3 Oct 1819- Clemond Quillian, J.P.
source: volume 1, page 134

TAYLOR, HIRAM
and
BLAIR, SALLY

8 Oct 1819- Frederick Beall, C.C.O.
10 Oct 1819- Francis Callaway, M.G.
source: volume 1, page 60

SHOEMATE, BERRYMAN D.
and
FARROW, SURSEY(?)

29 Oct 1819- Frederick Beall, C.C.O.
29 Oct 1819- James H. Little, J.P.
source: license- 1751-04/7-134
see also volume 1, page 134

MC LURE, JOHN
and
FENOT, CHARATY

1 Nov 1819- Frederick Beall, C.C.O.
.... - ....
source: volume 1, page 54

SPEARS, ROLAND
and
SEWELL, COMFORT

8 Nov 1819- Frederick Beall, C.C.O.
9 Nov 1819- J. Hammond, J.I.C.
source: license- 1751-04/7-141
see also volume 1, page 136

SMITH, JAMES
and
BURTT, SARAH

18 Nov 1819- Frederick Beall, C.C.O.
18 Nov 1819- Clemond Quillian, J.P.
source: license- 1751-04/7-137
see also volume 1, page 56

OSBERN, NELSON
and
WATSON, LUCY

17 Dec 1819- Frederick Beall, C.C.O.
21 Dec 1819- John M. Smith, J.P.
source: license- 1751-03/5-107
see also volume 1, page 133

DAVIS, JAMES H.
and
MC FARLIN, SALLIE

26 Dec ...- Frederick Beall, C.C.O.
4 Jan 1820- F. Callaway, Jr., O.M.G.
source: volume 1, page 131

32

MARTIN, WESTLEY
and
ROGERS, BETSY

28 Dec 1819- Frederick Beall, C.C.O.
28 Dec 1819- Gabriel Martin, J.P.
source: volume 1, page 134

BIRTT, JOHN
and
SMITH, POLLY

12 Jan 1820- Frederick Beall, C.C.O.
13 Jan 1820- Clemon Quillian, J.P.
source: volume 1, page 54

BURNS, WILLIAM
and
CHEEK, JANE

17 Jan 1820- Frederick Beall, C.C.O.
3 Feb 1820- Richard C. Bond, J.P.
source: volume 1, page 56

BRAMLET, NATHANIEL
and
GOBER, JINNY

11 Feb 1820- Frederick Beall, C.C.O.
17 Feb 1820- Ja's H. Little, J.P.
source: license- 1751-01/1-15
see also volume 1, page 132

PIERCE, WILLIAM
and
HOLBROOK, BETSEY

13 Feb 1820- Frederick Beall, C.C.O.
13 Feb 1820- Clemonds Quillian, J.P.
source: license- 1751-03/6-115
see also volume 1, page 57

DUNAGIN, JOSEPH
and
BEALL, LUCY

14 Feb 1820- Frederick Beall, C.C.O.
15 Feb 1820- Francis Callaway, Sr., O.M.
source: volume 1, page 55

RAMSEY, ELI
and
STRANGE, ELIZABETH

28 Feb 1820- Frederick Beall, C.C.O.
29 Feb 1820- J. Hammons, J.I.C.
source: volume 1, page 57

HOPGOOD, HEZEKIAH
and
EDWARDS, PATSEY

19 Feb 1820- Frederick Beall, C.C.O.
24 Feb 1820- James H. Little, J.P.
source: volume 1, page 57

...NEAL, JOHN C.
and
BEARD, POLLY

6 Mar 1820- Frederick Beall, C.C.O.
9 Mar 1820- F. Callaway, Jr.
source: volume 1, page 132(part torn off)
see also volume 2, page 154 which shows
the groom's name as John C. McNeal

VAUGHN, PETER
and
SEWELL, DEBORA

6 Mar 1820- Frederick Beall, C.C.O.
9 Mar 1820- F. Callaway, Jr.
source: license- 1751-04/8-152
see also volume 1, page 132

BARBER, SAMPSON
and
FOWLER, PATCY(or Polly?)

23 Mar 1820- Frederick Beall, C.C.O.
26 Mar 1820- James H. Little, J.P.
source: volume 1, page 60

SMITH, MARK
and
SMITH, ALLY

10 Apr 1820- Frederick Beall, C.C.O.
10 Apr 1820- Clemond Quillian, J.P.
source: volume 1, page 60

CARNES, JOHN P.
and
CASH, LIDIA H.

18 Apr 1820- Frederick Beall, C.C.O.
18 Apr 1820- Francis Callaway, Jr., O.M.G.
source: license- 1751-01/2-23
see also volume 5, page 91

ATTAWAY, WILLIAM
and
DUNLOT, LUCY

22 May 1820- Frederick Beall, C.C.O.
31 May 1820- John Sandridge
source: volume 1, page 60

FREEMAN, HENRY
and
HUCHERSON, ABISHA

21 July 1820- Frederick Beall, C.C.O.
23 July 1820- Henry David, M.G.
source: volume 1, page 61

CRAWFORD, HUGH
and
EDINS, ELIZABETH

1 Mar 1821(?)- Frederick Beall, C.C.O.
4 Mar 1821- F. Callaway, O.M.G.
source: license- 1751-01/2-36
see also volume 5, page 91

HOUSE, DARLING B.
and
BRYANT, JINNY

15 Mar 1821- Frederick Beall, C.C.O.
20 Mar 1821- Stephen Chatham, J.P.
source: volume 1, page 61

STOE, JAMES
and
BRYAN, ELIZABETH

26 Mar 1821- Frederick Beall, C.C.O.
26 Mar 1821- Stephen Chatham, J.P.
source: license- 1751-04/7-141
see also volume 4, page 127

ECHOLS, ABRAM
and
HAYS, MARY

23 Aug 1821- Frederick Beall, C.C.O.
...........- Littleton Meeks, M.G.
source: license- 1751-02/3-46

HOLLY, PLEASANT
and
ALLEN, MATILDA

28 Aug 1821- Frederick Beall, C.C.O.
30 Aug 1821- James H. Little, J.P.
source: volume 1, page 62

LUADING, JOHN
and
JACKSON, AMELIA

13 Oct 1821- Frederick Beall, C.C.O.
15 Oct 1821- Joseph Dunlap, J.P.
source: volume 1, page 61

HOLLY, WILLIAM
and
RAMSEY, ELIZABETH

13 Dec 1821- Frederick Beall, C.C.O.
13 Dec 1821- J. Hammond, J.P.
source: volume 1, page 61

SARTIN, JOHN
and
BOND, VILY(?)

18 Dec 1821- Frederick Beall, C.C.O.
20 Dec 1821- John B. McMillon, J.P.
source: volume 1, page 62

ALLEN, HUDSON H.
and
CUNELIUSON, A.

22 Jan 1822- Frederick Beall, C.C.O.
24 Jan 1822- James H. Little, J.P.
source: volume 1, page 64

SPARKS, WILLIAM J.
and
PUCKETT (PRICKETT?), NAOMA

12 Feb 1822- Frederick Beall, C.C.O.
14 Feb 1822- James Hargrove, O.M.
source: volume 1, page 64

BROWN, JAMES
and
SMITH, SARAH

15 Feb 1822- Frederick Beall, C.C.O.
16 Feb 1822- John H. Patrick
source: volume 1, page 69

SWIFT, TYRE
and
CHANDLER, RHODA

11 July 1822- Frederick Beall, C.C.O.
11 July 1822- F. Callaway, O.M.G.
source: volume 1, page 62

BROWN, WILLIAM
and
SMITH, MORNING

21 Aug 1822- Frederick Beall, C.C.O.
21 Aug 1822- Richard Smith, J.P.
source: volume 1, page 63

PAYNE, JOHN W.
and
HALL, JULY

10 Oct 1822- Frederick Beall, C.C.O.
10 Oct 1822- James Martin, J.P.
source: volume 1, page 64

BEALL, JOSIAH
and
DENT, ANN

15 Oct 1822- Frederick Beall, C.C.O.
17 Oct 1822- W'm Garrett, J.P.
source: volume 1, page 62

TUCKER, LEWIS
and
GOBER, MARIAH(? MARIAN?)

29 Oct 1822- Frederick Beall, C.C.O.
31 Oct 1822- James H. Little, J.P.
source: volume 1, page 63

PIERCE, JAMES
and
STOVALL, NANCY

9 Nov 1822- Frederick Beall, C.C.O.
.... - ....
source: license- 1751-03/6-115
see also volume 5, page 91

HICKUMBOTTAM, FRANCIS
and
JONES, MARTHA

18 Nov 1822(sic)- Frederick Beall, C.C.O.
18 Nov 1823(sic)- John Patrick
source: volume 1, page 65

LOWRY, AMOS
and
ALBRITTON, ELIZA

2 Dec 1822- Frederick Beall, C.C.O.
3 Dec 1822- Samuel S. Gerrald, M.O.G.
source: volume 1, page 63

KENNON(?), DAVID
and
HUNT, MARY

7 Dec 1822- Frederick Beall, C.C.O.
12 Dec 1822- Tho's Payne
source: volume 1, page 63

HOLCUM, RUSSELL
and
MEEKS, SUSAN(or LURAN?)

21 Dec 1822(sic)- Frederick Beall, C.C.O.
26 Jan 1822(sic)- Donald McDonald
source: volume 1, page 63

DONAHOO, CERNELIUS R.
and
PARKS, NANCY

28 Dec 1822- Frederick Beall, C.C.O.
29 Dec 1822- John Sandrige, M.G.
source: volume 1, page 64

WESTBROOK, JOSHUA
and
BELLAMY, LEAVYCY

1 Jan 1823- Frederick Beall, C.C.O.
2 Jan 1823- John Mays, J.P.
source: volume 1, page 66

WELLBORN, WILLIAM R.
and
BUSH, MALISSA

2 Jan 1823- Frederick Beall, C.C.O.
2 Jan 1823- Henry David, M.G.
source: volume 1, page 68

HAMBY, LEVY
and
CLARK, ELIZABETH

13 Jan 1823- Frederick Beall, C.C.O.
14 Jan 1823- John H. Patrick, J.P.
source: volume 1, page 66

WALLS, ZACHERIAH
and
MOSLEY (or MARBRY), SALLIE

15 Jan 1823(sic)- F. Beall, C.C.O.
25 Jan 1824(sic)- John Mays, J.P.
source: volume 1, page 69

SHELTON(? SPITTON?), WILKY   6 Feb 1823- Frederick Beall, C.C.O.
and   6 Feb 1823- Z. Chandler
HULSE(? or KESLER?), SARAH   source: volume 1, page 68

AUSTIN, THOMAS   12 Mar 1823(sic)- Frederick Beall, C.C.O.
and   11 Mar 1823(sic)- John C. Adderhold,
WOOLBRIGHT, MARY   J.I.C.
                                source: volume 1, page 66

WILSON, PETER   13 Mar 1823- Frederick Beall, C.C.O.
and   16 Mar 1823- John B. McMillian, J.P.
BAKER, JINNY   source: volume 1, page 65

SUTLEY, MICHAEL   19 Mar 1823- Frederick Beall, C.C.O.
and   20 Mar 1823- Samuel S. Gerrald, M.O.G.
WILSON, POLLY   source: volume 1, page 65

WILLIAMS, WRIGHT   12 Apr 1823(sic)- Frederick Beall, C.C.O.
and   24 Apr 1824(sic)- John Mays, J.P.
ROBERTSON, RODY(?)   source: volume 1, page 68

SHELTON, RICHMOND   24 Apr 1823- Frederick Beall, C.C.O.
and   24 Apr 1823- James H. Little, J.P.
GARRISON, NANCY   source: volume 1, page 66

TATE, SOLOMON   15 July 1823- Frederick Beall, C.C.O.
and   17 July 1823- W'm Herring, J.P.
CHANDLER, MARY   source: volume 1, page 67

TAPP, WILLIS   27 Aug 1823- Frederick Beall, C.C.O.
and   28 Aug 1823- W'm Turk
WADE, NANCY   source: volume 1, page 68

HALL, GEORGE   30 Aug 1823- Frederick Beall, C.C.O.
and   31 Aug 1823- William Johnson
THOMISON, LUCY   source: volume 1, page 67

WILLIAMSON, JOHN   16 Oct 1823- Frederick Beall, C.C.O.
and   16 Oct 1823- Tho's King, J.P.
CARLTON, ELIZA   source: volume 1, page 64

GIBSON, DANIEL   27 Oct 1823- Frederick Beall, C.C.O.
and   30 Oct 1823- William Johnson, J.P.
COUCH, MARY   source: volume 1, page 67

STRANGE, JOHN   26 Nov 1823- Frederick Beall, C.C.O.
and   26 Nov 1823- W'm Johnson, J.P.
JOHNSON, ANN   source: volume 1, page 68

DUNNAHO, JAMES   18 Nov 1823- Frederick Beall, C.C.O.
and   20 Nov 1823- Asa Allen, J.I.C.
JORDEN, JANE   source: volume 1, page 65

HERREN(?), JOEL   11 Dec 1823- Frederick Beall, C.C.O.
and   11 Dec 1823- Thomas King, J.P.
CHATHAM, ESTER(?)   source: volume 1, page 67

PAYNE, MARTIN
and
PAYNE, KEZIAH

15 Dec 1823- Frederick Beall, C.C.O.
19 Dec 1823- Rev'd Henry Harden
source: volume 1, page 67

KING, BERRY
and
COOK, LUCY

20 Dec 1823- Frederick Beall, C.C.O.
21 Dec 1823- Tho's King, J.P.
source: volume 1, page 66

CONLY, CHARLES M.
and
CONLEY, DISA

16 Jan 1824- Frederick Beall, C.C.O.
.........- ....
source: volume 1, page 70

WILLIS, JOHN A.
and
DAVIS, ELIZABETH

29 Mar 1824- Frederick Beall, C.C.O.
1 Apr 1824- Chesly Cothon
source: volume 1, page 70

HUMPHREYS, GEORGE
and
MC INTIRE, ZILLA

1 Apr 1824- Frederick Beall, C.C.O.
1 Apr 1824- A. Allen, J.I.C.
source: volume 1, page 71

TONEY, JOHN, JR.
and
BRUMLY, ELIZA

17 Apr 1824- Frederick Beall, C.C.O.
17 Apr 1824- A.F. Ash, J.P.
source: volume 1, page 70

HOLBROOKS, CHRISTOPHER
and
CHRISTIAN, SARAH

3 June 1824- Frederick Beall, C.C.O.
3 June 1824- Tho's King
source: volume 1, page 70

GREEN, TANDY H.
and
WHITE, OBEDIENCE

22 July 1824- Frederick Beall, C.C.O.
26 July 1824- R. Williams, J.P.
source: volume 1, page 72

SANDERS, LEWIS
and
MILLNER/MILLER, PRUDENCE

4 Aug 1824- Frederick Beall, C.C.O.
5 Aug 1824- W'm Cawthon, J.P.
source: volume 1, page 71& 72

COUCH, REUBEN
and
SEWEL, JINNY

13 Aug 1824- Frederick Beall, C.C.O.
19 Aug 1824- F. Caliway, M.G.
source: volume 1, page 69

BROWN, JESSE
and
SMITH, SARY

16 Aug 1824- Frederick Beall, C.C.O.
19 Aug 1824- F. Calaway
source: volume 1, page 72

GOBER, HIRAM
and
GOBER, BETSY(?)

26 Aug 1824- Frederick Beall, C.C.O.
26 Aug 1824- Z. Chandler, J.P.
source: volume 1, page 69

COCKRAM, FRED'K
and
BAXTER, DORCAS

31 Aug 1824- Frederick Beall, C.C.O.
31 Aug 1824- W'm Herring, J.P.
source: volume 1, page 71

KITCHEN, GEORGE
and
JOHNSTON, ANNA

2 Sept 1824- Frederick Beall, C.C.O.
2 Sept 1824- A. Williams
source: volume 1, page 69

ASH, ALEXANDER F.
and
MC CRACKEN, ELIZABETH

5 Oct 1824- Frederick Beall, C.C.O.
7 Oct 1824- James H. Little, J.P.
source: volume 1, page 71

CHANLER, STEPHEN
and
ADDERHOLD, ANNA

6 Oct 1824- Frederick Beall, C.C.O.
7 Oct 1824- W'm Cawthon, J.P.
source: volume 1, page 72

BAKER, CHRISTOPHER
and
SPEARS, SINTHA

8 Nov 1824- Frederick Beall, C.C.O.
18 Nov 1824- Zacheriah Chandler
source: volume 1, page 71

STOVALL, JAMES
and
GARNER, NANCY

25 Nov 1824- Frederick Beall, C.C.O.
25 Nov 1824- B.S. Murrell, J.P.
source: volume 1, page 70

SANDERS, CALVIN
and
MILLER, SARAH

22 Dec 1824- Frederick Beall, C.C.O.
23 Dec 1824- W'm   Cawthon, J.P.
source: volume 1, page 72

BOHANON(?), JAMES S.
and
PATTERSON(?), MARY

5 Jan 1825- Frederick Beall, C.C.O.
13 Jan 1825- ... Bramblet
source: volume 1, page 74

JOHNSTON, SAMUEL
and
RUCKER, SINTHA

6 Jan 1825- Frederick Beall, C.C.O.
6 Jan 1825- M.G. Thorton(?)
source: volume 1, page 72

HARDY, ARMSTED
and
NORWOOD, LUCY

8 Jan 1825- Frederick Beall, C.C.O.
13 Jan 1825- Littleton Meeks
source: volume 1, page 73

ADERHOLD, ISAAC
and
STOVEALL, SALLY

14 Jan 1825- Frederick Beall, C.C.O.
16 Jan 1825- F. Callaway, O.M.G.
source: license- 1751-01/1-3

CASH, HENRY C.
and
HENIG, ELIZA

20 Jan 1825- F. Beall, C.C.O.
20 Jan 1825- F. Callaway, O.M.G.
source: license- 1751-01/2-25

CHANDLER, DANIEL
and
YEARGIN, ANNY

11 Feb 1825- Frederick Beall, C.C.O.
12 Feb 1825- Charles L. Linkers(sic)
source: volume 1, page 74

HUMPHREYS, JAMES
and
JORDAN, BEYNA(?)

20 Mar 1825- Frederick Beall, C.C.O.
22 Mar 1825- Royal Bryan, J.P.
source: volume 1, page 73

HALL, ROBERT H.
and
LOVING, LOUIZA

21 Mar 1825- Frederick Beall, C.C.O.
21 Mar 1825- Robert Williams, J.P.
source: volume 1, page 75

FREEMAN, HENRY
and
MAYFIELD, MARTHA

21 Apr 1825- Frederick Beall, C.C.O.
21 Apr 1825- W'm J. Parks, M.G.
source: volume 1, page 74

CONNALY, CHRISTOPHER
and
MC INTIRE, ELIZABETH

16 June 1825- Frederick Beall, C.C.O.
16 June 1825- Z. Chandler, J.P.
source: volume 1, page 74

COOK, FRANCIS T.
and
HOOD, EDA S.

18 June 1825- Frederick Beall, C.C.O.
18 June 1825- W'm Hughes
source: volume 1, page 75

CARTER, AUSTIN
and
FINCH, POLLY

20 June 1825- Frederick Beall, C.C.O.
20 June 1825- Elijah Stephens, J.P.
source: volume 1, page 75

CONALLY, SAMUEL W.
and
CHRISTIAN, PYRIDE(?)

21 June 1825- Frederick Beall, C.C.O.
21 June 1825- Z. Chandler, J.P.
source: volume 1, page 74

STANDLIN(?), YOUNG
and
MC INTIRE, JANE

4 July 1825- Frederick Beall, C.C.O.
5 July 1825- H.H. Allen, J.P.
source: volume 1, page 78

CONALY, WILLIAM
and
CHRISTIAN, CINUS(? EINUS?)

26 July 1825- Frederick Beall, C.C.O.
26 July 1825- Z. Chanler, J.P.
source: volume 1, page 73

F. GARRELL, SAMUEL
and
BLANKENSHIP, NANCY

12 Aug 1825- Frederick Beall, C.C.O.
15 Aug 1825- Thomas King
source: volume 1, page 73

WELLS, THO'S
and
RAMSEY, MARTHA

17 Aug 1825- Frederick Beall, C.C.O.
18 Aug 1825- M.H. Payne, J.I.C.
source: volume 1, page 78

SUTLY, DAVID
and
WHITYCAR, MARTHA

20 Aug 1825- Frederick Beall, C.C.O.
21 Aug 1825- Tho's King, J.P.
source: volume 1, page 73

HONEY, WILLIAM
and
PARR, JIRSEY (JINSEY?)

31 Aug 1825- Frederick Beall, C.C.O.
31 Aug 1825- Z. Chandler, J.P.
source: volume 1, page 73

HARRIS, LITTLE
and
HANBY(? HANLEY?), ANY

6 Sept 1825- Frederick Beall, C.C.O.
6 Sept 1825- W'm Hughing(?)
source: volume 1, page 78

BELL, ADDAM
and
MC FARLAND, ELEANOR

20 Nov 1825- Frederick Beall, C.C.O.
20 Nov 1825- Royal Bryan, J.P.
source: volume 1, page 78

WATERS, JEREMIAH
and
TATE, ELIZA C.

24 Nov 1825- Frederick Beall, C.C.O.
29 Nov 1825- John Bramblet, M.G.
source: volume 1, page 75

CARPENTER, JOSHUA
and
SIMS, AGGY

25 Nov 1825- Frederick Beall, C.C.O.
28 Nov 1825- Thomas King, J.P.
source: volume 1, page 75

HAMPTON, HENRY and THORNTON, ELIZA	26 Nov 1825- F. Beall, C.C.O. 28 Nov 1825- Littleton Meeks, M.G. source: license- 1751-02/3-62
BAIRD, ABSALOM J. and BRYAN, SALLEY	1 Dec 1825- Frederick Beall, C.C.O. 4 Dec 1825- Royal Bryan source: volume 1, page 78
THOMAS, EZEKIAL and MONTGOMERY, SALLY/SARAH	24 Jan 1826- Frederick Beall, C.C.O. 29 Jan 1826- George H. Cosper, M.G. source: license- 1751-04/7-147
CHANDLER, LEWIS and PREWETT, POLLY	24 Jan 1826- Frederick Beall, C.C.O. 31 Jan 1826- Henry David, M.G. source: license- 1751-01/2-27 see also volume 3, page 73
POOL, WILLIAM and CLARKSON, KIZIA	13 Feb 1826- Frederick Beall, C.C.O. 16 Feb 1826- Littleton Meeks source: license- 1751-03/6-116 see also volume 4, page 161
STUBS, BENTON and GOODSON, NANCY	21 Feb 1826- Frederick Beall, C.C.O. 21 Feb 1826- John Bramblet source: license- 1751-04/7-144
CROW, WILLIAM T. and BLACKWELL, ELIZABETH	22 Feb 1826- Frederick Beall, C.C.O. 23 Feb 1826- Z. Chandler, J.P. source: license- 1751-01/2-38
VINES(?), JOHN and AYRES, JINNY	2 Mar 1826- Frederick Beall, C.C.O. 2 Mar 1826- J. Hammond, J.P. source: license- 1751-04/8-154
THORNTON, REV. DOZIER and PULLIAM, JANE	24 May 1826- Frederick Beall, C.C.O. 24 May 1826- John Bramblet, M.G. source: license- 1751-04/7-149 see also volume 3, pagen 32
MILLS, CHESLEY and AYRES, MARTHA	3 June 1826- Frederick Beall, C.C.O. 6 June 1826- Frederick Freeman, J.P. source: license- 1751-03/5-99
PAYNE, FLEMING and AYERS, EVELINE	23 July 1826- F. Beall, C.C.O. 23 July 1826- Robert Williams, J.P. source: license- 1751-03/5-111
SLAYTON, BENJAMIN and VESSELS, CHARLOTTE	7 Aug 1826- Frederick Beall, C.C.O. 8 Aug 1826- Harris Toney, J.P. source: license- 1751-04/7-135
WHITTAKER, JOHN and SUTLEY, SUSAN	7 Aug 1826- Frederick Beall, C.C.O. 10 Aug 1826- Frederick Freeman, J.P. source: license- 1751-04/8-164
MITCHELL, RUBIN and JONES, LUIZA	27 Sept 1826- Frederick Beall, C.C.O. 28 Sept 1826- Henry Freeman, J.I.C. source: license- 1751-03/5-100

CAMP, JOHN
and
CAWTHON, FANNY

9 Nov 1826- Frederick Beall, C.C.O.
9 Nov 1826- J. Bramblet, M.G.
source: license- 1751-01/2-21
see also volume 3, page 21

MEDOWS/MEADOWS, JEDEDIAH
and
GOBER, MARGARETTE

17 Jan 1827- Tho's King. C.C.O.
23 Jan 1827- W.J. Parks, M.G.
source: license- 1751-03/5-98
see also volume 3, page 2

NEEL(?), WILLIAM
and
ECHOLLS, ANN

31 Jan 1827- Thomas King, C.C.O.
1 Feb 1827- Robert Williams, J.P.
source: license- 1751-04/7-142
see also volume 3, page 1 which shows
the groom's name as KEEL

HALEY, JAMES
and
KEESLER, ELIZABETH

3 Feb 1827- Thomas King, C.C.O.
4 Feb 1827- Asa Payne, J.P.
source: license- 1751-02/3-61
see also volume 3, page 1

PINSON, STERLING
and
BURTON, POLLY

10 Feb 1827- Thomas King, C.C.O.
4 Mar 1827- George Vandiver, M.G.
source: license- 1751-03/6-115
see also volume 3, page 2

BUSH, DANIEL
and
NEAL, ELIZABETH

19 Feb 1827- Thomas King, C.C.O.
8 Mar 1827- W.J. Parks
source: license- 1751-01/1-20
see also volume 3, page 3

WHITTIN, ALVIN E.
and
JONES, CATHARINE W.

20 Feb 1827- Thomas King, C.C.O.
22 Feb 1827- Henry Freeman, J.I.C.
source: license- 1751-04/8-164
see also volume 3, page 3

PAIR, INGRAM
and
VAUGHAN, AIRY

6 Mar 1827- Thomas King, C.C.O.
7 Mar 1827- Royal Bryan, J.P.
source: license- 1751-03/5-108
see also volume 3, page 1

SARTAIN, TAPLEY
and
WILLIAMS, RACHAEL

6 Mar 1827- Thomas King, C.C.O.
7 Mar 1827- John Bramblett, M.G.
source: license- 1751-04/6-128
see also volume 3, page 20

MAYBRY, JOSHUA
and
DEFOOR, DRUICILLER

23 Mar 1827- Thomas King, C.C.O.
27(29?) Mar 1827- C's D. Jenkins, J.P.
source: license- 1751-03/5-97
see also volume 3, page 1

WHITE, BURRELL
and
PULLIAM, FRANCES

26 Mar 1827- Thomas King, C.C.O.
29 Mar 1827- Royal Bryan, J.P.
source: license- 1751-04/8-162
see also volume 3, page 4

AVEREY, JAMES
and
PULLIAM, SARAH

4 Apr 1827- Thomas King, C.C.O.
4 Apr 1827- John Bramlet, M.G.
source: license- 1751-01/1-6
see also volume 3, page 32

WHITE, THOMAS T.
and
CONNALLY, MARY

7 Apr 1827- Thomas King, C.C.O.
8 Apr 1827- W'm Gilmore, J.P.
source: license- 1751-04/8-162
see also volume 3, page 2

JONES, WILLIAM
and
HIGGINBOTHAM, RACHEL

12 Apr 1827- Thomas King, C.C.O.
14 Apr 1827- Robert Williams, J.P.
source: license- 1751-02/4-78
see also volume 3, page 3

CAUDELL, DAVID
and
BRIDGES, MRS. ELIZABETH

26 Apr 1827- Thomas King, C.C.O.
26 Apr 1827- Sam'l Jackson, J.P.
source: license- 1751-01/2-26
see also volume 3, page 4

CHANDLER, AMBROSE
and
WHITE, JERUSHA

1 May 1827- Thomas King, C.C.O.
3 May 1827- Charles D. Jenkins, J.P.
source: license- 1751-01/2-27
see also volume 3, page 2

WILSON, ANDREW
and
STEGALL, LENCY(?)

9 June 1827- Thomas King, C.C.O.
9 June 1827- Maxfield H. Payne, J.I.C.
source: license- 1751-04/8-168
see also volume 3, page 5

MC JENKINS, JIMMY(?)
and
VAUGHAN, NARSISA

12 June 1827- Thomas King, C.C.O.
14 June 1827- F. Callaway, M.G.
source: volume 3, page 50

CHRISTIAN, GEORGE M.
and
JONES, SARAH J.

2 July 1827- Thomas King, C.C.O.
5 July 1827- W'm J. Parks, M.G.
source: license- 1751-01/2-31
see also volume 3, page 6

MISE, WARREN
and
CLARKSON, ELIZABETH

3 July 1827- Thomas King, C.C.O.
3 July 1827- W'm Turk, J.I.C.
source: license- 1751-03/5-100
see also volume 3, page 5

HILLHOUSE, ELIJAH
and
MAULDIN, NANCY

16 July 1827- Thomas King, C.C.O.
16 July 1827- Littleton Meeks, M.G.
source: license- 1751-02/3-70
see also volume 3, page 42

MCCARTA, JAMES H.
and
STOE, NANCY

24 July 1827- Thomas King, C.C.O.
26 July 1827- Samuel Mosely, J.P.
source: license- 1751-02/4-89
see also volume 3, page 4

HARRISON, LARKIN
and
HARRISON, FRANCIS

26 July 1827- Thomas King, C.C.O.
29 July 1827- Dozier Thornton, M.G.
source: license- 1751-02/3-64
see also volume 3, page 5

COKER, CHALTON
and
CHANDLER, MATILDA

29 July 1827- Thomas King, C.C.O.
29 July 1827- John B. McMillion, J.P.
source: license- 1751-01/2-33
see also volume 3, page 28

WADE, JOHN
and
PEEK, LUCY

6 Aug 1827- Thomas King, C.C.O.
7 Aug 1827- John B. McMillion, J.P.
source: license- 1751-04/8-155
see also volume 3, page 13

MC KELVY, JOHN
and
ATTAWAY, CHRISTIAN

8 Aug 1827- Thomas King, C.C.O.
9 Aug 1827- John B. McMillian, J.P.
source: license- 1751-02/4-92
see also volume 3, page 12

ROBERTS, MOSES
and
TABOR, MILLY

9 Oct 1827- Thomas King, C.C.O.
11 Oct 1827- John B. McMillion, J.P.
source: license- 1751-03/6-125
see also volume 3, page 12

LOVIL, SAMUEL C.
and
BLALOCK, ELLA

9 Oct 1827- Thomas King, C.C.O.
14 Oct 1827- John Crocker, J.P.
source: license- 1751-02/4-88
see also volume 3, page 8

ATTAWAY, JOHN T.C.
and
AVERY, MARY

11 Oct 1827- Thomas King, C.C.O.
11 Oct 1827- John B. McMillion, J.P.
source: license- 1751-01/1-6
see also volume 3, page 12

BAIRD, WILLIAM W.
and
MC CALL, REBECCA

13 Oct 1827- Thomas King, C.C.O.
16 Oct 1827- Royal Bryan, J.P.
source: license- 1751-01/1-8
see also volume 3, page 6

TOWNSEND, JOEL W.
and
ACKER, MARY T.

22 Oct 1827- Thomas King, C.C.O.
25 Oct 1827- David Garrison, E.M.C.
source: license- 1751-04/7-149
see also volume 3, page 10

MINYARD, RICHARD
and
CHANDLER, REBECCA

24 Oct 1827- Thomas King, C.C.O.
24 Oct 1827- Frederick Freeman, J.P.
source: license- 1751-03/5-100
see also volume 3, page 6

KING, THOMAS M.
and
SUTLEY, MARY

1 Nov 1827- Thomas King, C.C.O.
1 Nov 1827- Frederick Freeman, J.P.
source: license- 1751-02/4-83
see also volume 3, page 7

THOMASON, SOLOMON D.
and
WORD, HARRIETT

3 Nov 1827- Thomas King, C.C.O.
8 Nov 1827- M.H. Payne, J.I.C.
source: license- 1751-04/7-148
see also volume 3, page 7

JONES, LEWIS D.
and
BUSH, MARIAH L.

6 Nov 1827- Thomas King, C.C.O.
15 Nov 1827- W'm J. Parks, M.G.
source: license- 1751-02/4-78
see also volume 3, page 9

DYAR, JOEL H.
and
SANDERS, RACHEL

8 Nov 1827- Thomas King, C.C.O.
8 Nov 1827- John B. McMillion, J.P.
source: license- 1751-01/2-45
see also volume 3, page 13

DENMAN, CHRISTOPHER
and
CAGLE, SARY

8 Nov 1827- Thomas King, C.C.O.
8 Nov 1827- F. Calloway, M.G.
source: license- 1751-01/2-43
see also volume 3, page 9

SMITH, JOHNSON T.
and
ENGLISH, MARGARETT

9 Nov 1827- Thomas King, C.C.O.
11 Nov 1827- Nathan Gunnels, J.P.
source: license- 1751-04/7-138
see also volume 3, page 32

GARRISON, JAMES H.
and
DAVISON, NANCY B.

10 Nov 1827- Thomas King, C.C.O.
15 Nov 1827- D. Garrison, M.G.
source: license- 1751-02/3-54
see also volume 3, page 10

PUCKETT, EDMUND D.
and
PULLIAM, NANCY

12 Nov 1827- Thomas King, C.C.O.
13 Nov 1827- Royal Bryan, J.P.
source: license- 1751-03/6-119
see also volume 3, page 7

BROWN, ROBERT
and
CAUDELL, MRS. HANNAH

13 Nov 1827- Thomas King, C.C.O.
13 Nov 1827- Sam'l Jackson, J.P.
source: license- 1751-01/1-17
see also volume 3, page 8

HOUSTON, JOHN K.
and
WATSON, HARRIETT S.

17 Nov 1827- Thomas King, C.C.O.
2 Dec 1827- John B. McMillion, J.P.
source: license- 1751-02/3-73
see also volume 3, page 11

HOUSE, DARLING B.
and
ROGERS, MARGET

19 Nov 1827- Thomas King, C.C.O.
22 Nov 1827- Robert Williams, J.P.
source: license- 1751-02/3-73
see also volume 3, page 19

SIMS, JOHN
and
ROGERS, RHODY

19 Nov 1827- Thomas King, C.C.O.
19 Nov 1827- Rob't Williams, J.P.
source: license- 1751-04/7-135
see also volume 3, page 18

LAUGHRIDGE, JOHN C.
and
MURDOCK, ELIZABETH S.

21 Nov 1827- Thomas King, C.C.O.
22 Nov 1827- Elijah Stephens, J.P.
source: license- 1751-02/4-84
see also volume 3, page 18

HEMPHILL, ROBERT
and
BRANNUM, MARY

11 Dec 1827- Thomas King, C.C.O.
13 Dec 1827- William J. Parks, M.G.
source: license- 1751-02/3-67
see also volume 3, page 9

MANLEY, ISAAC D.
and
ATTAWAY, TELITHA

13 Dec 1827- Thomas King, C.C.O.
13 Dec 1827- J. Hammond, J.P.
source: license- 1751-02/4-94
see also volume 3, page 8

CROW, RANDOLPH
and
SEWELL, ELIZABETH

18 Dec 1827- Thomas King, C.C.O.
20 Dec 1827- Frederick Freeman, J.P.
source: license- 1751-01/2-38
see also volume 3, page 9

TURMAN, SIMEON
and
AVERY, NANCY

18 Dec 1827- Thomas King, C.C.O.
19 Dec 1827- John Bramblet, M.G.
source: license- 1751-04/7-150
see also volume 3, page 20

DOBBS, LODOWICK
and
DOBBS, DELILA

18 Dec 1827- Thomas King, C.C.O.
20 Dec 1827- Asa Payne, J.P.
source: license- 1751-01/2-44
see also volume 3, page 11

CHATHAM, JAMES
and
YARBROUGH, NANCY

24 Dec 1827= Thomas King, C.C.O.
25 Dec 1827- Frederick Freeman, J.P.
source: license- 1751-01/2-29
see also volume 3, page 10

NEAL, STEPHEN H.
and
MALONE, LAURA W.

26 Dec 1827- Thomas King, C.C.O.
3 Jan 1828- Littleton Meeks
source: license- 1751-03/5-105
see also volume 4, page 135

BRYAN, WILLIAM
and
BRYAN, ALIS

31 Dec 1827- Thomas King, C.C.O.
1 Jan 1828- John Sandidge, M.G.
source: license- 1751-01/1-18
see also volume 3, page 10

DEVERALL, JOHN
and
HUDSON, ELIZABETH

31 Dec 1827- Thomas King, C.C.O.
3 Jan 1828- W'm J. Parks, M.G.
source: license- 1751-01/2-43
see also volume 3, page 15

HEATON, WILLIAM
and
ADERHOLD, MRS. MARY M.

..........- T. King, C.C.O.
1 Jan 1828- John Crocker, J.P.
source: license- 1751-02/3-67
see also volume 3, page 11

GRAY, GARRET
and
JENKINS, JINCEY

1 Jan 1828- Thomas King, C.C.O.
1 Jan 1828- Chesley Cawthon, J.P.
source: license- 1751-02/3-59
see also volume 3, page 132

ALMAN, WILLIAM
and
FOWLER, NANCY

7 Jan 1828- Thomas King, C.C.O.
8 Jan 1828- Zack Chandler, J.P.
source: license- 1751-01/1-4
see also volume 3, page 14

PAYNE, SAMUEL T.
and
MC CRACKEN, MARGARETT

7 Jan 1828- Thomas King, C.C.O.
10 Jan 1828- Howel Mangum, J.P.
source: license- 1751-03/5-112
see also volume 3, page 16

ANGLING, WILLIAM
and
SEWELL, ELIZABETH

15 Jan 1828- Thomas King, C.C.O.
17 Jan 1828- W'm J. Parks, M.G.
source: license- 1751-01/1-5
see also volume 3, page 14

WILLIAMS, ELISHA
and
TONEY, SINTHA

16 Jan 1828- Thomas King, C.C.O.
16 Jan 1828- Howel Mangum, J.P.
source: license- 1751-04/8-166
see also volume 3, page 15

ATTAWAY, JAMES
and
AVERY, MATILDA

16 Jan 1828- Thomas King, C.C.O.
17 Jan 1828- John B. McMillion
source: license- 1751-01/1-6
see also volume 3, page 13

MOTES, DREWRY V.
and
BRANNAM, FRANCES

16 Jan 1828- Thomas King, C.C.O.
17 Jan 1828- W'm J. Parks, M.G.
source: license- 1751-03/5-103
see also volume 3, page 14

WESTBROOK, STEPHEN B.
and
HUNT, ELIZABETH

19 Jan 1828- Thomas King, C.C.O.
24 Jan 1828- W'm J. Parks, M.G.
source: license- 1751-04/8-160
see also volume 3, page 15

MIZE, THOMAS
and
CAPE, LEVINA

20 Jan 1828- Thomas King, C.C.O.
20 Jan 1828- Tho's Garrison, J.P.
source: license- 1751-03/5-101
see also volume 3, page 17

SANDERS, SAMUEL
and
SKELTON, ANN

24 Jan 1828- Thomas King, C.C.O.
24 Jan 1828- John B. McMillion, J.P.
source: license- 1751-03/6-128
see also volume 3, page 28

WALTERS, JACKSON M.
and
CAWTHON, POLLY

7 Feb 1828- Thomas King, C.C.O.
12 Feb 1828- Dozier Thornton, M.G.
source: license- 1751-04/8-156
see also volume 3, page 17

CLARK, ZACHERIAH
and
DAVIS, POLLYANN

7 Feb 1828- Thomas King, C.C.O.
21 Feb 1828- Samuel Jackson, J.P.
source: license- 1751-01/2-32
see also volume 3, page 16

GRAHAM, JONATHAN
and
PAYNE, IRENE

27 Feb 1828- Thomas King, C.C.O.
28 Feb 1828- W'm Beall, J.P.
source: license- 1751-02/3-59
see also volume 3, page 16

ELAXANDER, JOHN P.
and
TATE, ELIZABETH

28 Feb 1828- Thomas King, C.C.O.
28 Feb 1828- Charles D. Jenkins, J.P.
source: license- 1751-01/1-4
see also volume 3, page 17

BOWEN, ANDREW
and
GROVER, MILLEY

3 Mar 1828- Thomas King, C.C.O.
6 Mar 1828- Zach. Chandler, J.P.
source: license- 1751-01/1-14
see also volume 3, page 18

JEFFERS, JOHN
and
NICKSON, FRANCES

23 Mar 1828- Thomas King, C.C.O.
23 Mar 1828- Rob't Williams, J.P.
source: license- 1751-02/4-77
see also volume 3, page 19

COCKBURN, JEREMIAH
and
HENSON, JOANNAH

26 Mar 1828- Thomas King, C.C.O.
27 Mar 1828- Robert Williams, J.P.
source: license- 1751-01/2-33
see also volume 3, page 19

THOMAS, EZEKIEL
and
COCKRUM, SALLY

14 Apr 1828- Thomas King, C.C.O.
17 Apr 1828- Francis Callaway, M.G.
source: volume 3, page 50

WOODS, EALY
and
ABET, MARY

17 Apr 1828- Thomas King, C.C.O.
17 Apr 1828- Howel Mangum, J.P.
source: license- 1751-04/8-169
see also volume 3, page 20

THORNTON, REUBEN
and
WARTERS, ELIZABETH

8 May 1828- Thomas King, C.C.O.
8 May 1828- John Bramblet, M.G.
source: license- 1751-04/7-149
see also volume 3, page 34

CLARK, WILEY
and
WHITEHEAD, FRANCES

9 May 1828- Thomas King, C.C.O.
9 May 1828- John Bramblet, M.G.
source: license- 1751-01/2-32
see also volume 3, page 33

PHILLIPS, JOSEPH E.
and
PASCHAL, HARRIETT

10 May 1828- Thomas King, C.C.O.
15 May 1828- W'm J. Parks, M.G.
source: license- 1751-03/6-114
see also volume 3, page 22

BRYANT, WILLIAM
and
HIDE, SALLY

10 May 1828- Thomas King, C.C.O.
11 May 1828- W'm Gilmore, J.P.
source: license- 1751-01/1-18
see also volume 3, page 21

CARVER, HENRY
and
WHISENANT, BARBARA

13 May 1828- Thomas King, C.C.O.
13 May 1828- Samuel Mosely, J.P.
source: license- 1751-01/2-25
see also volume 3, page 24

FAGENS, MOSES
and
SMITH, MRS. PHEBE

1 June 1828- Thomas King, C.C.O.
1 June 1828- Sam'l Jackson, J.P.
source: license- 1751-02/3-48
see also volume 3, page 21

CAWTHON, WILKINSON T.
and
CAMP, SARAR

15 June 1828- Thomas King, C.C.O.
15 June 1828- Royal Bryan, J.P.
source: license- 1751-01/2-26
see also volume 3, page 22

MEADERS, CHRISTOPHER
and
GARRISON, CANDAS

9 July 1828- Thomas King, C.C.O.
10 July 1828- W'm J. Parks, M.G.
source: license- 1751-03/5-98
see also volume 3, page 22

HENDRIX, JOHN J.
and
GROSE, MRS. SUSY(? or SARY?)

3 Aug 1828- Thomas King, C.C.O.
3 Aug 1828- Sam'l Jackson, J.P.
source: license- 1751-02/3-67
see also volume 3, page 23

CLARK, JOHN
and
BAIRD, ANN C.

7 Aug 1828- Thomas King, C.C.O.
12 Aug 1828- Royal Bryan, J.P.
source: license- 1751-01/2-32
see also volume 3, page 23

GLENN, FRANKLIN
and
CARSON, SUSAN T.

7 Aug 1828- Thomas King, C.C.O.
7 Aug 1828- Nathan Gunnels, J.P.
source: license- 1751-02/3-57
see also volume 3, page 33

HAMMETT, JAMES
and
TATE, SARAH

16 Aug 1828- Thomas King, C.C.O.
17 Aug 1828- William Beall, J.P.
source: license- 1751-02/3-62
see also volume 3, page 30

TEASLEY, JAMES S.
and
REED, SUSAN W.

9 Sept 1828- Thomas King, C.C.O.
9 Sept 1828- Joel W. Townsend, E.M.C.
source: license- 1751-04/7-146
see also volume 3, page 23

NOLES, SAMUEL
and
ROBERTSON, SARAH

5 Sept 1828- Thomas King, C.C.O.
7 Sept 1828- Elijah Stephens, J.P.
source: license- 1721-03/5-106
see also volume 3, page 24

DODD, LEMUEL(?)
and
SMITH, DIANAH F.

7 Sept 1828- Thomas King, C.C.O.
7 Sept 1828- Nathan Gunnels, J.P.
source: license- 1751-01/2-44
see also volume 3, page 44

ATTAWAY, PARNAL
and
COX, ANNAH

4 Oct 1828- Thomas King, C.C.O.
4 Oct 1828- John Bramblett, M.G.
source: volume 3, page 52

WILSON, JOHN F.
and
STUBBS, POLLY P.

6 Oct 1828- Thomas King, C.C.O.
9 Oct 1828- Joel W. Townsend, P.G.
source: license- 1751-04/8-168
see also volume 3, page 24

MITCHELL, WILLIAM
and
BAIRD, REBECCA

6 Oct 1828- Thomas King, C.C.O.
9 Oct 1828- Chesley Cawthon, J.P.
source: license- 1751-03/5-100
see also volume 3, page 25

ROBERTS, BARNET
and
CAUDELL, MRS. PHEBE

12 Oct 1828- Thomas King, C.C.O.
12 Oct 1828- Sam'l Jackson, J.P.
source: license- 1751-03/6-125
see also volume 3, page 25

STOVALL, FERDINAND
and
REED, CINTHA

16 Oct 1828- Thomas King, C.C.O.
23 Oct 1828, B.S. Merrell, J.P.
source: license- 1751-04/7-143
see also volume 3, page 26

FREEMAN, JAMES
and
CHANDLER, MARTHA

17 Oct 1828- Thomas King, C.C.O.
23 Oct 1828- Job Hammond, J.P.
source: license- 1751-02/3-51
see also volume 3, page 25

ANDREWS, ADAM
and
SANFORD, ADALINE

22 Oct 1828- Thomas King, C.C.O.
23 Oct 1828- Abner Mize, J.P.
source: license- 1751-01/1-5
see also volume 3, page 36

SHANNON, THOMAS M.
and
GUNNELLS, AVIS

25 Oct 1828- Thomas King, C.C.O.
30 Oct 1828- Job Hammond, J.P.
source: license- 1751-04/7-133
see also volume 3, page 26

BLAIR, LEVI
and
SMITH, NANCY

4 Nov 1828- Thomas King, C.C.O.
6 Nov 1828- Sam. Mosley, J.P.
source: license- 1751-01/1-13
see also volume 3, page 27

FORD, WILLIAM
and
SMITH, CERREN

4 Nov 1828- Thomas King, C.C.O.
4 Nov 1828- Zach. Chandler, J.P.
source: license- 1751-02/3-49
see also volume 3, page 27

THOMAS JOHN
and
MITCHELL, ELIZABETH

4 Nov 1828- Thomas King, C.C.O.
6 Nov 1828- Chesley Cawthon, J.P.
source: license- 1751-04/7-147
see also volume 3, page 133

SEWEL, JOSHUA
and
JOHNSON, NANCEY

9 Nov 1828- Thomas King, C.C.O.
9 Nov 1828- John Bramblet, M.G.
source: license- 1751-03/6-131
see also volume 3, page 33

CHANDLER, DANIEL
and
HARBOUR, KATHARINE

15 Nov 1828- Thomas King, C.C.O.
20 Nov 1828- Job Hammond, J.P.
source: license- 1751-01/2-27
see also volume 3, page 26

HOOPER, JOHNSON M.
and
CHATHAM, BERNICY

18 Nov 1828- Thomas King, C.C.O.
18 Nov 1828- W'm Beall, J.P.
source: license- 1751-02/3-72
see also volume 3, page 27

DAILY, WILLIAM
and
NEEL, LUCY

24 Nov 1828- Thomas King, C.C.O.
25 Dec 1828- W'm J. Parks, M.G.
source: license- 1751-01/2-40
see also volume 3, page 41

WESTBROOK, REUBEN W.
and
HALL, TABITHA

4 Dec 1828- Thomas King, C.C.O.
4 Dec 1828- David Carson, J.P.
source: license- 1751-04/8-160
see also volume 3, page 29

GILLISPIE, JAMES
and
YARBROUGH, ELIZABETH

23 Dec 1828- Thomas King, C.C.O.
25 Dec 1828- Howel Mangum, J.P.
source: license- 1751-02/3-56
see also volume 3, page 29

MURREY, JOSIAH
and
CATLETT, SARY

23 Dec 1828- Thomas King, C.C.O.
23 Dec 1828- Howel Mangum, J.P.
source: license- 1751-03/5-104
see also volume 3, page 28

ROSE, HARDY
and
FREEMAN, POLLEY

24 Dec 1828- Thomas King, C.C.O.
24 Dec 1828- Henry David, M.G.
source: license 1751-03/6-126
see also volume 3, page 29

```
RUMSEY, RICHARD                    28 Dec 1828- Thomas King, C.C.O.
    and                            28 Dec 1828- Richard Smith, J.P.
JENTRY, ELIZABETH                  source: license -1751-03/6-127
                                   see also volume 3, page 30


NANCE, ELI L.                      30 Dec 1828- Thomas King, C.C.O.
    and                            30 Dec 1828- Richard Smith, J.P.
LUALLING, TABITHA                  source: license- 1751-03/5-105
                                   see also volume 3, page 30


JOHNSON, JESSE                     1 Jan 1829- Thomas King, C.C.O.
    and                            1 Jan 1829- William Beall, J.P.
HINSON, ALSEY                      source: license- 1751-02/4-77
                                   see also volume 3, page 31


ALLEN, MATTHEW                     5 Jan 1829- Thomas King, C.C.O.
    and                            13 Jan 1829- Asa Payne, J.P.
VAUGHTERS, LUCINDA                 source: license- 1751-01/1-4
                                   see also volume 3, page 35


PHILLIPS, JAMES                    8 Jan 1829- Thomas King, C.C.O.
    and                            8 Jan 1829- Job Hammond, J.P.
DEARING, ELIZABETH                 source: license- 1751-03/6-114
                                   see also volume 3, page 31


JONES, CHARLES                     9 Jan 1829- Thomas King, C.C.O.
    and                            15 Jan 1829- N. Gunnels, J.P.
CHRISTIAN, SARAH                   source: license- 1751-02/4-78
                                   see also volume 3, page 34


PRUITT, ROBERT W.                  13 Jan 1829- Thomas King, C.C.O.
    and                            13 Jan 1829- Littleton Meeks, M.G.
LITTLE, IZEBELLA                   source: license- 1751-03/6-119
                                   see also volume 3, page 42


JONES, MICAJAH                     13 Jan 1829- Thomas King, C.C.O.
    and                            14 Jan 1829- Maxfield H. Payne, J.I.C.
ASHWORTH, MARY                     source: license- 1751-02/4-78
                                   see also volume 3, page 34


TATE, COOPER B.                    14 Jan 1829- Thomas King, C.C.O.
    and                            15 Jan 1829- Job Hammond, J.P.
WHITE, NANCY                       source: license- 1751-04/7-145
                                   see also volume 3, page 35


RAMSEY, MADISON                    17 Jan 1829- Thomas King, C.C.O.
    and                            22 Jan 1829- Asa Payne, J.P.
CRUMP, RAHTHA                      source: license- 1751-03/6-122
                                   see also volume 3, page 35


KNOX, SAMUEL                       22 Jan 1829- Thomas King, C.C.O.
    and                            10 Feb 1829- B.S. Merrell, J.P.
REED, MARY M.                      source: license- 1751-02/4-83
                                   see also volume 3, page 47


HATHCOCK, WILLIAM                  23 Jan 1829- Thomas King, C.C.O.
    and                            25 Jan 1829- Nathan Gunnels, J.P.
TRIMBLE, ARMINDA                   source: license- 1751-02/3-65
                                   see also volume 3, page 31
```

JOHNSTON, JON
and
GOBER, MRS. MARY

24 Jan 1829- Thomas King, C.C.O.
29 Jan 1829- Sam'l Jackson, J.P.
source: license- 1751-02/4-77
see also volume 3, page 37

PAYNE, CHESLEY
and
BURGESS, MATILDA

26 Jan 1829- Thomas King, C.C.O.
27 Jan 1829- B.S. Merrell, J.P.
source: license- 1751-03/5-111
see also volume 3, page 36

TILLMAN, BERRY G.
and
MARTIN, SARY ARMANDA

27 Jan 1829- Thomas King, C.C.O.
29 Jan 1829- W'm J. Parks, M.G.
source: license- 1751-04/7-149
see also volume 3, page 36

LANGSTON, JOHN
and
SHANNON, SOPHIA

31 Jan 1829- Thomas King, C.C.O.
4 Feb 1829- W'm J. Parks, M.G.
source: license- 1751-02/4-84
see also volume 3, page 43

LANGSTON, ALEXANDER
and
SHANNON, ELIZABETH

31 Jan 1829- Thomas King, C.C.O.
4 Feb 1829- W'm J. Parks, M.G.
source: license- 1751-02/4-84
see also volume 3, page 43

MORROW, WILLIAM
and
MITCHELL, MARY

7 Feb 1829- Thomas King, C.C.O.
10 Feb 1829- John Maples, J.P.
source: license- 1751-03/5-103
see also volume 3, page 38

BROWN, HUGH
and
CAUDELL, MRS. MARY

19 Feb 1829- Thomas King, C.C.O.
19 Feb 1829- Sam'l Jackson, J.P.
source: license- 1751-01/1-17
see also volume 3, page 37

STAPLES, WILLIM N.
and
THORNTON, MARTHA G.

6 Mar 1829- Thomas King, C.C.O.
12 Mar 1829- Henry David, M.G.
source: license- 1751-04/7-141
see also volume 3, page 37

WILLIAS, FIELAND T.
and
OLOVER, CATY

10 Mar 1829- Thomas King, C.C.O.
10 Mar 1829- B.S. Merrell, J.P.
source: license- 1751-04/8-168
see also volume 3, page 48

BARRY, BARTLEY
and
BRUCE, MARY

18 Mar 1829- Thomas King, C.C.O.
24 Mar 1829- Francis Callaway, M.G.
source: license- 1751-01/1-9
see also volume 3, page 38

COBB, ISAAC E.
and
CHANDLER, FRANCES C.

22 Mar 1829- Thomas King, C.C.O.
22 Mar 1829- James R. Smith, M.G.
source: license- 1751-01/2-33
see also volume 3, page 39

NEAL, WILLIAM
and
GOBER, ELIZABETH

23 Mar 1829- Thomas King, C.C.O.
24 Mar 1829- Nathan Gunnels, J.P.
source: license- 1751-03/5-105
see also volume 3, page 40

THOMAS, JESSE
and
JACKSON, RHODA

25 Mar 1829- Thomas King, C.C.O.
26 Mar 1829- Chesley Cawthon, J.P.
source: license- 1751-04/7-147
see also volume 3, page 40

HARDY, HENRY W.
and
ISBEL, SARAH

27 Mar 1829- Thomas King, C.C.O.
29 Mar 1829- James R. Smith, M.G.
source: license- 1751-02/3-63
see also volume 3, page 38

BELLAMY, JOHN
and
JONES, REBECCAH

30 Mar 1829(sic)- Thomas King, C.C.O.
3 Mar 1829(sic)- Howell Mangum, J.P.
source: license- 1751-01/1-10
see also volume 3, page 39

ROBERTS, JESSE
and
BRIANT, MARTHA

6 Apr 1829-Thomas King, C.C.O.
6 Apr 1829- Howell Mangum, J.P.
source: license- 1751-03/6-125
see also volume 3, page 39

WILLSON, WILLIAM
and
WALTERS, ELIZABETH

9 Apr 1829- Thomas King, C.C.O.
9 Apr 1829- Royal Bryan, J.P.
source: license- 1751-04/8-168
see also volume 3, page 40

MARTIN, JAMES
and
WHEELER, KATHARINE

16 Apr 1829- Thomas King, C.C.O.
16 Apr 1829- Dudley Ayers, J.P.
source: license- 1751-03/5-95
see also volume 3, page 41

DOBBS, MARTAN
and
FULBRIGHT, PARTHENY

18 Apr 1829- Thomas King, C.C.O.
19 Apr 1829- Dudley Ayers, J.P.
source: license- 1751-01/2-44
see also volume 3, page 41

SLOAN, WILLIAM
and
HACKETT, ELIZA T.

23 May 1829- Thomas King, C.C.O.
26 May 1829- A.W. Ross
source: license- 1751-04/7-135
see also volume 3, page 42

BOLCH, GEORG A.
and
MC CLAY, LETTY

26 May 1829- Thomas King, C.C.O.
26 May 1829- B.S. Merrell, J.P.
source: license- 1751-01/1-13
see also volume 3, page 49

YORK, WILLIAM
and
MARTIN, TABITHA

26 May 1829- Thomas King, C.C.O.
26 May 1829- Reuben Thornton, M.G.
source: volume 3, page 51

PERKINS, HIRAM B.
and
RAY, SUSAN

9 June 1829- Thomas King, C.C.O.
14 June 1829- Dudley Ayers, J.P.
source: license- 1751-03/5-113
see also volume 3, page 47

LEDBETTER, JAMES V.
and
SISK, MARTHA R.

11 July 1829- Thomas King, C.C.O.
14 July 1829- John B. Chappel, M.G.
source: license- 1751-02/4-85
see also volume 3, page 44

WHITE, BENJAMIN H.
and
SMITH, MARGET

18 July 1829- Thomas King, C.C.O.
18 July 1829- Ch's D. Jenkins, J.I.C.
source: license- 1751-04/8-162
see also volume 3, page 43

DENMAN, WILLIAM S.
and
PARR, DARKIS

23 July 1829- Thomas King, C.C.O.
23 July 1829- B.S. Merrell, J.P.
source: license- 1751-01/2-43
see also volume 3, page 48

GARRISON, JEDIDIAH
and
BRADLEY, ELIZABETH

5 Aug 1829- Thomas King, C.C.O.
7 Aug 1829- Sam'l Jackson, J.P.
source: license- 1751-02/3-54
see also volume 3, page 45

ALEXANDER, JAMES S.
and
HUMPHRIS, ELIZABETH

13 Aug 1829- Thomas King, C.C.O.
13 Aug 1829- Job Hammond, J.P.
source: license- 1751-01/1-4
see also volume 3, page 45

SARTAIN, ELIJAH
and
WILLIAMS, SARAH

26 Aug 1829- Thomas King, C.C.O.
26 Aug 1829- Howell Mangum, J.P.
source: license- 1751-03/6-128
see also volume 3, page 45

CHANDLER, ASA
and
CLARK, JANE

27 Aug 1829- Thomas King, C.C.O.
27 Aug 1829- Francis Callaway, M.G.
source: license- 1751-01/2-27
see also volume 3, page 48

WIDEMAN, HENRY
and
SEWELL, MILLEY

3 Sept 1829- Thomas King, C.C.O.
3 Sept 1829- Joel W. Townsend, M.E.
source: license- 1751-04/8-164
see also volume 3, page 44

YORK, WILLIAM
and
COSBY, NANCY

4 Sept 1829- Thomas King, C.C.O.
6 Sept 1829- Sam'l T. Payne, J.P.
source: volume 3, page 55

RAMSAY, JAMES
and
CHRISTIAN, FANNEY

6 Sept 1829- Thomas King, C.C.O.
7 Sept 1829- G.L. Sandridge, J.I.C.
source: license- 1751-03/6-122
see also volume 3, page 49

CHANDLER, WILLIAM
and
HARBOUR, NANCY

9 Sept 1829- Thomas King, C.C.O.
10 Sept 1829- Zach. Chandler, J.P.
source: license- 1751-01/2-27
see also volume 3, page 46

HARPER, JOHN
and
SANDERS, MARY

20 Sept 1829- Thomas King, C.C.O.
20 Sept 1829- Reuben Thornton, M.G.
source: license- 1751-02/3-63
see also volume 3, page 46

WEATHERLEY, AARON
and
ROBISON, MARY

22 Sept 1829- Thomas King, C.C.O.
22 Sept 1829- C.D. Jenkins, J.I.C.
source: license- 1751-04/8-158
see also volume 3, page 47

CROW, WILLIAM S.
and
WEST, MALINDA

24 Sept 1829- Thomas King, C.C.O.
24 Sept 1829- Job Hammond, J.P.
source: license- 1751-01/2-38
see also volume 3, page 46

SEWELL, ASA
and
MITCHELL, NANCY M.

7 Oct 1829- Thomas King, C.C.O.
8 Oct 1829- John Bramblett, M.G.
source: volume 3, page 53

ACKER, WILLIAM S.
and
WHITE, ELIZABETH

23 Oct 1829- Thomas King, C.C.O.
27 Oct 1829- R. Tharriton(?), M.G.
source: license- 1751-01/1-1
see also volume 3, page 49

SEWELL, GREEN B.
and
VAUGHAN, SUSANNAH

24(26?) Oct 1829- Thomas King, C.C.O.
26 Oct 1829- John Bramblett, M.G.
source: volume 3, page 52

WILMOTT, ELY T.
and
WYLEY, JANE

2 Nov 1829- Thomas King, C.C.O.
2 Nov 1829- Howell Mangrum, J.P.
source: volume 3, page 51

AARON, WILLIAM
and
RUDD, REBECCA

3 Nov 1829- Thomas King, C.C.O.
3 Nov 1829- Job Hammond, J.P.
source: license- 1751-01/1-1
see also volume 3, page 50

PAYNE, THOMAS
and
AYERS, OLIVE

8 Nov 1829- Thomas King, C.C.O.
8 Nov 1829- Sam'l T. Payne, J.P.
source: volume 3, page 56

GARRISON, SAULBURY
and
BRAWNER, SARAH

10 Nov 1829- Thomas King, C.C.O.
10 Nov 1829- David Garrison, M.G.
source: volume 3, page 56

PERRY, WILLIAM A.
and
WILLIAMS, SARAH

18 Nov 1829- Thomas King, C.C.O.
18 Nov 1829- Henry David, M.G.
source: volume 3, page 51

CHANDLER, THOMAS
and
JACKSON, MARY

24 Nov 1829- Thomas King, C.C.O.
26 Nob 1829- Asa Chandler, M.G.
source: license- 1751-01/2-27
see also volume 3, page 72

WHITE, OBADIAH
and
SPARKS, JEMIMA

6 Dec 1829- Thomas King, C.C.O.
6 Dec 1829- C.D. Jenkins, J.I.C.
source: volume 3, page 58

LOONEY, JOSEPH C.
and
WRIGHT, PERMELY

10 Dec 1829- Thomas King, C.C.O.
10 Dec 1829- John Burton, J.P.
source: license- 1751-02/4-87
see also volume 3, page 111

HILL, CALEB
and
RUSSEL, MARGARETT

19 Dec 1829- Thomas King, C.C.O.
22 Dec 1829- John Catlett, J.P.
source: volume 3, page 53

TILLER, PEYTON
and
BAKER, SALLY

19 Dec 1829- Thomas King, C.C.O.
19 Dec 1829- Nathan Gunnels, J.P.
source: volume 3, page 56

VAUGHAN, JAMES
and
SEWELL, NANCY

24 Dec 1829- Thomas King, C.C.O.
24 Dec 1829- John Bramblett, M.G.
source: volume 3, page 52

WATKINS, WILEY
and
REED, PERMELA N.

2 Jan 1830- Thomas King, C.C.O.
2 Jan 1830- B.S. Merrell, J.P.
source: license- 1751-04/8-158
see also volume 3, page 72

BARBER, WILLIAM A.
and
HUDGINS, NANCY

16 Jan 1830- Thomas King, C.C.O.
17 Jan 1830- John Maples, J.P.
source: volume 3, page 55

FREEMAN, BENAJAH
and
MC CARTER, SUSAN

2 Feb 1830- Thomas King, C.C.O.
2 Feb 1830- Nathan Gunnels, J.P.
source: volume 3, page 57

CAWTHON, ORVILLE
and
HARRISON, ELIZABETH

3 Feb 1830- Thomas King, C.C.O.
11 Feb 1830- S. Hymer, M.G.
source: volume 3, page 65

ROBERTSON, WILLIAM
and
MAYS, MATILDA

4 Feb 1830- Thomas King, C.C.O.
4 Feb 1830- Henry David, M.G.
source: volume 3, page 61

YORK, JOHN G.
and
THOMASON, ANNY B.

3 Feb 1830- Thomas King, C.C.O.
9 Feb 1830- Dudley Ayers, J.P.
source: volume 3, page 55

THOMASON, JOHN W.
and
DICKERT, LIBBY

10 Feb 1830- Thomas King, C.C.O.
14 Feb 1830- Dudley Ayers, J.P.
source: volume 3, page 54

TONEY, HEDRICK
and
ROSE, ANNY

15 Feb 1830- Thomas King, C.C.O.
16 Feb 1830- Howell Mangrum, J.P.
source: volume 3, page 54

MASON, SQUIRE
and
MILLS, LOUISA

15 Feb 1830- Thomas King, C.C.O.
16 Feb 1830- Dudley Ayers, J.P.
source: volume 3, page 54

COSBY, AUSTIN W.
and
REED, MARGARET A.

20 Feb 1830- Thomas King, C.C.O.
23 Feb 1830- Rob't Pulliam, J.I.C.
source: volume 3, page 53

SCOTT, AGRIPPA
and
GRAY, JANE

24 Feb 1830- Thomas King, C.C.O.
24 Feb 1830- Benjamin Laughridge, J.P.
source: volume 3, page 66

SMITH, ALFORD
and
NEAL, CAROLINE

3 Mar 1830- Thomas King, C.C.O.
3 Mar 1830- Henry David, M.G.
source: volume 3, page 59

WADE, JAMES
and
RYLEY, ELIZABETH

.... - Thomas King, C.C.O.
4 Mar 1830- Henry David, M.G.
source: volume 3, Page 60

KING, JOHN C.
and
BORUM, MARY

9 Mar 1830- Thomas King, C.C.O.
11 Mar 1830- John Catlett, J.P.
source: volume 3, page 60

AYERS, LARKIN C.
and
AYERS, ELIZABETH

13 Mar 1830- Thomas King, C.C.O.
18 Mar 1830- Asa Payne, J.P.
source: volume 3, page 64

SEWELL, NICHOLAS
and
TOWNS, ELIZABETH

22 Mar 1830- Thomas King, C.C.O.
25 Mar 1830- Nathan Gunnels, J.P.
source: volume 3, page 57

SHELTON, ABSALOM H.
and
PATTERSON, MILLY

23 Mar 1830- Thomas King, C.C.O.
23 Mar 1830- Benj. Laughridge, J.P.
source: volume 3, page 62

PRITCHARD, SION B.
and
HEADEN, ELIZABETH

24 Mar 1830- Thomas King, C.C.O.
24 Mar 1830- G.L. Sandidge, J.I.C.
source: volume 3, page 61

DOBBS, SOLOMON
and
CARSON, FANNY

25 Mar 1830- Thomas King, C.C.O.
25 Mar 1830- Lewis Ballard, M.G.
source: volume 3, page 60

WATSON, SAMUEL
and
JONES, HARRIETT

29 Mar 1830- Thomas King, C.C.O.
1 Apr 1830- Henry David, M.G.
source: volume 3, page 59

STOVALL, DAVID
and
MC COLLAY(?), MARGARET

29 Mar 1830- Thomas King, C.C.O.
31 Mar 1830- Henry David, M.G.
source: volume 3, page 59

GILLISPIE, PICKENS
and
MORROW(?), NANCY

3 Apr 1830- Thomas King, C.C.O.
4 (6?) Apr 1830- John Catlett, J.P.
source: volume 3, page 61

SLACK, JOSEPH
and
TATOM, MARY J.

20 Apr 1830- Thomas King, C.C.O.
22 Apr 1830- Hiram Russell, J.P.
source: volume 3, page 58

BERRY, JOHN
and
ELLIS, MARTHA

22 Apr 1830- Thomas King, J.P.
22 Apr 1830- Richard Smith, J.P.
source: license- 1751-01/1-11
see also volume 3, page 90

WHITE, DAVID
and
JONES, MARY H.

25 Apr 1830- Thomas King, C.C.O.
25 Apr 1830- Charles D. Jenkins, J.I.C.
source: volume 3, page 58

DUNSON, WILLIAM
and
COOK, SARAH

11 May 1830- Thomas King, C.C.O.
12 May 1830- Henry David, M.G.
source: volume 3, page 63

CHANDLER, LINSEY
and
SEWELL, MATILDA

20 May 1830- Thomas King, C.C.O.
30 May 1830- Noah Looney, J.P.
source: volume 3, page 57

SMITH, WILLIAM B. and AGE, SARAH	14 June 1830- Thomas King, C.C.O. 14 June 1830- Richard Smith, J.P. source: license- 1751-04/7-139 see also volume 3, page 81
WILLIAMS, BENAJAH and SPARKS, MALINDA	22 June 1830- Thomas King, C.C.O. 22 June 1830- M.W. Vandiver, M.G. source: volume 3, page 63
NUCKOLS, SAMUEL and SANDIDGE, ELIZA C.	24 July 1830- Thomas King, C.C.O. 29 July 1830- Dozier Thornton, M.G. source: volume 3, page 64
GARRISON, CASSEL and BAKER, ELIZABETH	9 Aug 1830- Thomas King, C.C.O. 10 Aug 1830- John Catlett, J.P. source: license- 1751-02/3-54 see also volume 3, page 75
PARKS, HENRY and PULLIAM, SARAH	11 Aug 1830- Thomas King, C.C.O. 11 Aug 1830- Dozier Thornton, M.G. source: volume 3, page 65
BANKS, ROBERT T. and JONES, FRANCES S.	12 Aug 1830- Thomas King, C.C.O. 12 Aug 1830- S. Hymer, M.G. source: volume 3, page 64
CLARK, JACOB and AUSBERN, LUCY	21 Aug 1830- Thomas King, C.C.O. 21 Aug 1830- John Catlett, J.P. source: license- 1751-01/2-32 see also volume 3, page 76
MC CARTER, ALEXANDER and MC DOW, LUCY	22 Aug 1830- Thomas King, C.C.O. 22 Aug 1830- Nathan Gunnels, J.P. source: volume 3, page 67
SHURDON, WILLIAM and GARRISON, TRYPHENA	6 Sept 1830- Thomas King, C.C.O. 7 Sept 1830- John Catlett, J.P. source: license- 1751-04/7-134 see also volume 3, page 73
DEFOOR, MARTIN and TABOR, SUSAN	13 Sept 1830- Thomas King, C.C.O. 14 Sept 1830- Oliver C. Miller, preacher source: volume 3, page 63
EDWARDS, THOMAS G. and WILKINSON, SOPHIA	20 Sept 1830- Thomas King, C.C.O. 23 Sept 1830- Chesley Cawthon, J.P. source: volume 3, page 66
GOBER, JOHN, SR. and JONES, SARAH	21 Sept 1830- Thomas King, C.C.O. 23 Sept 1830- G.L. Sandridge, J.I.C. source: volume 3, page 67
MC FARRON, JOHN H. and MAULDEN, ELIZABETH	23 Sept 1830- Thomas King, C.C.O. 23 Sept 1830- Asa W. Allen, J.P. source: volume 3, page 65

DAVIS, JAMES
and
ANTHONY, MARY

25 Sept 1830- Thomas King, C.C.O.
25 Sept 1830- B.S. Merrell, J.P.
source: license- 1751-01/2-41
see also volume 3, page 71

SMITH, JACOB
and
WILLIAMS, ELIZAAN

29 Sept 1830- Thomas King, C.C.O.
29 Sept 1830- Sam'l McCollum, J.P.
source: volume 3, page 67

RODGERS, ROBERT
and
RUDD(or READ?), NANCY

2 Oct 1830- Thomas King, C.C.O.
3 Oct 1830- Henry David, M.G.
source: volume 3, page 66

STOKES, WILLIAM
and
ILEY, BARBARA

8 Oct 1830- Thomas King, C.C.O.
10 Oct 1830- Royal Bryan, J.P.
source: volume 3, page 62

NOGGLE, JACOB
and
BING, MARTHA

10 Oct 1830- Thomas King, C.C.O.
10 Oct 1830- Benjamin Loughridge, J.P.
source: license- 1751-03/5-106
see also volume 3, page 78

PARKS, WILBORN(?)
and
HAINS, NANCY

14 Oct 1830- Thomas King, C.C.O.
14 Oct 1830- S. Hymer, Minister
source: license- 1751-03/5-109
see also volume 3, page 108

SAYER, ICHABOD
and
THOMASON, MARY

16(14?) Oct 1830- Thomas King, C.C.O.
16(14?) Oct 1830- Sam'l T. Payne, J.P.
source: volume 3, page 68

HARRISON, HUGH
and
HANNAN(?), CARLINE W.

17 Oct 1830- Thomas King, C.C.O.
17 Oct 1830- Benjamin Laughridge, J.P.
source: license- 1751-02/3-64
see also volume 3, page 77

GARNER, OSBURN
and
BALDWIN, MARY

20 Oct 1830- Thomas King, C.C.O.
20 Oct 1830- Benjamin Laughridge, J.P.
source: license- 1751-02/3-53
see also volume 3, page 78

ANDERSON, WILLIAM
and
MORGAN, ELIZABETH

28 Oct 1830- Thomas King, C.C.O.
4 Nov 1830- John Catlett, J.P.
source: license- 1751-01/1-5
see also volume 3, page 74

PARKS, MARSHALL
and
MEWBOURN, MARY

3 Nov 1830- Thomas King, C.C.O.
3 Nov 1830- S. Hymer, Minister
source: license- 1751-03/5-109
see also volume 3, page 109

SCOTT, ASA
and
MC FARLAN, LUCINDA

4 Nov 1830- Thomas King, C.C.O.
4 Nov 1830- Benjamin Laughridge, J.P.
source: license- 1751-03/6-130
see also volume 3, page 77

HAYNES, STEPHEN
and
PARKS, MARY

4 Nov 1830- Thomas King, C.C.O.
4 Nov 1830- S. Hymer, Minister
source: license- 1751-02/3-66
see also volume 3, page 108

ANDERSON, JAMES
and
ARROWWOOD, MARTHA

7 Nov 1830- Thomas King, C.C.O.
7 Nov 1830- G.L. Sandidge, J.I.C.
source: license- 1751-01/1-5
see also volume 3, page 68

MITCHELL, RILEY
and
COMBS, HARRIETT M.

10 Nov 1830- Thomas King, C.C.O.
11 Nov 1830- Z. Chandler, J.P.
source: license- 1751-03/5-100
see also volume 3, page 69

SOSEBEE, ABNER
and
PAYNE, MALINDIA

11 Nov 1830- Thomas King, C.C.O.
12 Nov 1830- Robert Williams, J.P.
source: license- 1751-04/7-140
see also volume 3, page 84

CROW, LEVI
and
CARSON, MARY

15 Nov 1830- Thomas King, C.C.O.
18 Nov 1830- Lewis Ballard, M.G.
source: license- 1751-01/2-38
see also volume 3, page 69

FRY, DRURY
and
FREEMAN, MARGARET

16 Nov 1830- Thomas King, C.C.O.
... Nov 1830- Nathaniel R. Hood, J.P.
source: license- 1751-02/3-52
see also volume 3, page 84

SIMMONS, WILLIAM
and
MITCHELL, ARCADA

24 Nov 1830- Thomas King, C.C.O.
30 Nov 1830- Henry David, M.G.
source: license- 1751-04/7-135
see also volume 3, page 72

ALLBRITTON, PHILLIP L.
and
MERRELL, MARY F.

28 Nov 1830- Thomas King, C.C.O.
28 Nov 1830- Royal Bryan, J.P.
source: license- 1751-01/1-4
see also volume 3, page 69

GREEN, JOHN
and
HUGHES, ELIZABETH

8 Dec 1830- Thomas King, C.C.O.
9 Dec 1830- John Maples, J.P.
source: license- 1751-02/3-59
see also volume 3, page 70

CROW, THOMAS J.
and
SEWELL, JANE

14 Dec 1830- Thomas King, C.C.O. •
16 Dec 1830- Woodson Blackenship, J.P.
source: license- 1751-01/2-38
see also volume 3, page 70

LEADBETTER, JOHN
and
WILLIAMS, SUSAN

20 Dec 1830- Thomas King, C.C.O.
30 Dec 1830- John B. Chappel, M.G.
source: license- 1751-02/4-85
see also volume 3, page 70

NEAL, WILLIAM F.
and
KEY, MARY D.

20 Dec 1830- Thomas King, C.C.O.
20 Dec 1830- N. Gunnels, J.P.
source: license- 1751-03/5-105
see also volume 3, page 76

STOVALL, JAMES
and
EDWARDS, SARAH

23 Dec 1830- Thomas King, C.C.O.
23 Dec 1830- Job Hammond, J.P.
source: license- 1751-04/7-143
see also volume 3, page 71

WILEY, JOHN B.
and
JONES, NANCY

23 Dec 1830- Thomas King, C.C.O.
23 Dec 1830- Job Hammond, J.P.
source: license- 1751-04/8-165
see also volume 3, page 71

GRAY, JOHNSON
and
JENKINS, LILEY(?)

27 Dec 1830- Thomas King, C.C.O.
27 Dec 1830- Benjamin Laughridge, J.P.
source: volume 3, page 62

BARTON, CLOUD
and
BIRD, MARTHA H.

8 Jan 1831- Thomas King, C.C.O.
13 Jan 1831- Noah Looney, J.P.
source: license- 1751-01/1-9
see also volume 3, page 68

SEWELL, GREEN B.
and
SEEGAR, WINNY

10 Jan 1831- Thomas King, C.C.O.
13 Jan 1831- Nathan Gunnels, J.P.
source: license- 1751-03/6-132
see also volume 3, page 75

HOLCOMBE, SPENCER
and
LAWRENCE, PEGGY

13 Jan 1831- Thomas King, C.C.O.
13 Jan 1831- John Catlett, J.P.
source: license- 1751-02/3-71
see also volume 3, page 73

CHANDLER, DUDLEY J.
and
JOLLY, NANCY

19 Jan 1831- Thomas King, C.C.O.
20 Jan 1831- Nath'l R. Reed, J.P.
source: license- 1751-01/2-27
see also volume 3, page 75

OSBURN, AMOS
and
DAVISEN, RACHAEL

3 Feb 1831- Thomas King, C.C.O.
3 Feb 1831- L. Meeks, M.G.
source: license- 1751-03/5-107
see also volume 3, page 88

STARRITT, BENJAMIN
and
ILEY, CYNTHA

12 Feb 1831- Thomas King, C.C.O.
15 Feb 1831- Nelson Osborn, M.G.
source: license- 1751-04/7-142
see also volume 3, page 78

MORRIS, HENRY J.
and
ALLEN, ASENITH

14 Feb 1831- Thomas King, C.C.O.
24 Feb 1831- W'm Alexander, J.P.
source: license- 1751-03/5-102
see also volume 3, page 76

HOWINGTON, WILLIAM R.
and
SEEGAR, SUSANNAH

28 Feb 1831- Thomas King, C.C.O.
3 Mar 1831- Jacob Strickland, J.P.
source: license- 1751-02/3-74
see also volume 3, page 79

DOBBS, GREENBERRY
and
GOODSON, PATSY

4 Mar 1831- Thomas King, C.C.O.
10 Mar 1831- Absalom Holcomb, J.I.C.
source: license- 1751-01/2-44
see also volume 3, page 79

GLAZIER, CHARLES R.
and
MC CARTER, SARAH

8 Mar 1831- Thomas King, C.C.O.
8 Mar 1831- Nathan Gunnels, J.P.
source: license- 1751-02/3-57
see also volume 3, page 74

STOKES, WADDY
and
STARRITT, MALINDA

14 Mar 1831- Thomas King, C.C.O.
15 Mar 1831- Nelson Osborn, M.G.
source: license- 1751-04/7-142
see also volume 3, page 74

JAOURDEN, ARCHABEL
and
TATE, LOUCINDAY

17 Mar 1831- Thomas King, C.C.O.
17 Mar 1831- W'm Tabor, J.P.
source: license- 1751-02/4-79
see also volume 3, page 91

FIELD, SAMUEL
and
BAGWELL, MARTHA W.

21 Mar 1831- Thomas King, C.C.O.
22 Mar 1831- C.D. Jinkins, J.I.C.
source: license- 1751-02/3-48
see also volume 3, page 77

HARRIS, WILLIAM
and
WOODS, MANDY MELVIRY

25 Apr 1831- Thomas King, C.C.O.
25 Apr 1831- Richard Smith, J.P.
source: license- 1751-02/3-63
see also volume 3, page 83

COKERHAM, MATTHEW B.H.
and
HOOPER, MARTHA

9 May 1831- Thomas King, C.C.O.
24 May 1831- Lewis Ballard, M.G.
source: license- 1751-01/2-34
see also volume 3, page 84

MC CAUL, FRANCIS
and
MC NEAL, NANCY

14 May 1831- Thomas King, C.C.O.
19 May 1831- Noah Looney, J.P.
source: license- 1751-02/4-89
see also volume 3, page 83

REED, NATHAN L.
and
DOWNS, SARAH ANN

22 May 1831- Thomas King, C.C.O.
22 May 1831- W'm Burroughs, J.P.
source: license- 1751-03/6-123
see also volume 3, page 82

BUSH, HEZEKIAH
and
AYERS, RUTHA

23 May 1831- Thomas King, C.C.O.
27 May 1831- Rob't Williams, Esq'r
source: license- 1751-01/1-20
see also volume 3, page 81

BEALL, HORATIO
and
STARRITT, POLLEY

28 May 1831- Thomas King, C.C.O.
31 May 1831- Royal Bryan, J.P.
source: license- 1751-01/1-10
see also volume 3, page 82

MC ENTIRE, THOMAS C.
and
ALLEN, LOUISA H.

22 June 1831- Thomas King, C.C.O.
30 June 1831- W'm J. Parks, M.G.
source: license- 1751-02/4-91
see also volume 3, page 83

PAYNE, AMBROSE
and
BRIANT, LOVADA L.

26 June 1831- Thomas King, C.C.O.
26 June 1831- S. Hymer, Minister
source: license- 1751-03/5-111
see also volume 3, page 107

CHATHAM CHAFIN
and
LACEY, SYLVANA

28 June 1831- Thomas King, C.C.O.
28 June 1831- Job Hammond, J.P.
source: license- 1751-01/2-29
see also volume 3, page 82

ROUS, MARTIN
and
JACKSON, DISEY

2 July 1831- Thomas King, C.C.O.
3 July 1831- Bartlett Jones, J.P.
source: license- 1751-03/6-126
see also volume 3, page 85

GARVIN, MICAJER
and
KELLY, ANNY

14 July 1831- Thomas King, C.C.O.
14 July 1831- S. Hymer, Minister
source: license- 1751-02/3-54
see also volume 3, page 108

VAUGHN, OTAWAY W.
and
DODSON, ELIZABETH

4 Aug 1831- Thomas King, C.C.O.
4 Aug 1831- Bartlet Jones, J.P.
source: license- 1751-04/8-152
see also volume 3, page 85

MEEKS, NACEY
and
CHALMERS, ELIZAR

4 Aug 1831-Thomas King, C.C.O.
4 Aug 1831- Samuel Morgan, J.P.
source: license- 1751-01/2-27
see also volume 3, page 89

LOWRY, ISOM
and
BASKIN, MARY

8 Aug 1831- Thomas King, C.C.O.
11 Aug 1831- John Bramblet, M.G.
source: license 1751-02/4-88
see also volume 3, page 103

BEALL, FREDERICK
and
MC MILLION, MARGERY

9 Aug 1831- Thomas King, C.C.O.
9 Aug 1831- W'm J. Parks, M.G.
source: license- 1751-01/1-10
see also volume 3, page 81

BUSH, EDMUND T.
and
BORDERS, ADALINE

20 Aug 1831- Thomas King, C.C.O.
25 Aug 1831- Reuben Thornton
source: license- 1751-01/1-20
see also volume 3, page 85

CHAPPLIER, BENJAMIN
and
MILUM, ELIZABETH

21 Aug 1831- Thomas King, C.C.O.
21 Aug 1831- B.S. Merrell, J.P.
source: license- 1751-01/2-28
see also volume 3, page 80

PAYNE, JOHN H.
and
BELLAMY, ELIZABETH

1 Sept 1831- Thomas King, C.C.O.
6 Sept 1831- Hiram Bennett, J.P.
source: license- 1751-03/5-111
see also volume 3, page 86

STOE, WILLIAM
and
CATLETT, SUSANNAH

22 Sept 1831- Thomas King, C.C.O.
22 Sept 1831- Samuel Jackson, J.P.
source: license- 1751-04/7-142
see also volume 3, page 80

WHITAKER, SEABORN
and
COMPTON, DENCRIA(? DENERIA?)

24 Sept 1831- Thomas King, C.C.O.
25 Sept 1831- Nelson Osbern, M.G.
source: license- 1751-04/8-161
see also volume 3, page 86

MILLS, WILLIAM
and
JONES, RUTHA

25 Sept 1831- Thomas King, C.C.O.
25 Sept 1831- Lewis Ballard, M.G.
source: license- 1751-03/5-99
see also volume 3, page 134

FIN(N), MID(D)LETON
and
SKELTON, SYNTHA

27 Sept 1831- Thomas King, C.C.O.
27 Sept 1831- S. Hymer, Minister
source: license- 1751-02/3-49
see also volume 3, page 109

MANLEY, WILLIAM
and
TUCKER, NANCY

27 Sept 1831- Thomas King, C.C.O.
27 Sept 1831- Job Hammond, J.P.
source: license- 1751-02/4-94
see also volume 3, page 95

TUCKER, BENJAMIN, JR.
and
LEGRAND, SARAH

28 Sept 1831- Thomas King, C.C.O.
29 Sept 1831- Job Hammond, J.P.
source: license- 1751-04/7-149
see also volume 3, page 94

WILSON, JAMES H.
and
STUBBS, SARAH T.

5 Oct 1831- Thomas King, C.C.O.
6 Oct 1831- Woodson Blankinship, J.P.
source: license- 1751-04/8-168
see also volume 3, page 86

TURK, THEODORE
and
LITTLE, ELIZABETH M.

5 Oct 1831- Thomas King, C.C.O.
6 Oct 1831- Asa W. Allen, J.P.
source: license- 1751-04/7-150
see also volume 3, page 87

MEEKS, MARTIN
and
MORRIS, SUSAN

12 Oct 1831- Thomas King, C.C.O.
13 Oct 1831- Littleton Meeks
source: license- 1751-03/5-98
see also volume 3, page 80

WILLIAMS, JOHN
and
NEAL, ELIZABETH

18 Oct 1831- Thomas King, C.C.O.
18 Oct 1831- Nathan Gunnels, J.P.
source: license- 1751-04/8-166
see also volume 3, page 105

CROW, JOHN W.
and
PORTER, AVES

20 Oct 1831- Thomas King, C.C.O.
20 Oct 1831- George W. Humphries, J.P.
source: license- 1751-01/2-38
see also volume 3, page 87

HENDRICK, JEREMIAH
and
CRAWFORD, SARAH

25 Oct 1831- Thomas King, C.C.O.
3 Nov 1831- Nelson Osbern, M.G.
source: license- 1751-02/3-67
see also volume 3, page 94

PAYNE, THOMAS
and
VERNER, SELLENDA

30 Oct 1831(?)- Thomas King, C.C.O.
30 Oct 1831- Rob't Williams, J.P.
source: license- 1751-03/5-112
see also volume 3, page 91

WILLIAMS, MARTIN
and
KESLER, MARY

30 Oct 1831- Thomas King, C.C.O.
30 Oct 1831- Sam'l Jackson, J.P.
source: license- 1751-04/8-167
see also volume 3, page 79

STUBBS, JOHN U.
and
WILSON, MARTHA P.

1 Nov 1831- Thomas King, C.C.O.
3 Nov 1831- W. Blankinship, J.P.
source: license- 1751-04/7-144
see also volume 3, page 88

JACKSON, THOMAS
and
CATLETT, MARY

12 Nov 1831- Thomas King, C.C.O.
13 Nov 1831- Joseph Byers, M.G.
source: license- 1751-04/4-76
see also volume 3, page 99

TAPP, CURTISS
and
CASY, NANCY

16 Nov 1831- Thomas King, C.C.O.
18 Nov 1831- Reuben Thornton, M.G.
source: license- 1751-04/7-145
see also volume 3, page 115

WARMACK, JESSE P.
and
SCOTT, WILLINDA

27 Nov 1831- Thomas King, C.C.O.
27 Nov 1831- Benj. Laughridge, J.P.
source: license- 1751-04/8-157
see also volume 3, page 139

MARTIN, BRISON
and
MEADOWS, SALLY

28 Nov 1831- Thomas King, C.C.O.
5 Dec 1831- Jacob Strickland, J.P.
source: license- 1751-03/5-95
see also volume 3, page 97

BOSWELL, JOHN
and
JOHNSON, LOUISA

6 Dec 1831- Thomas King, C.C.O.
7 Dec 1831- Bartlet Jones, J.P.
source: license- 1751-01/1-14
see also volume 3, page 89

MILLS, JAMES
and
BENNET, EZEBETH

8 Dec 1831- Thomas King, C.C.O.
8 Dec 1831- Robert Williams, J.P.
source: license- 1751-03/5-99
see also volume 3, page 98

CARROLL, JOHN F.
and
KIRK, NANCY

11 Dec 1831- Thomas King, C.C.O.
11 Dec 1831- Carter White, J.P.
source: license- 1751-01/2-23
see also volume 3, page 132

PAYNE, THOMAS, JR.
and
ADCOCK, MARY ANN

14 Dec 1831, Thomas King, C.C.O.
16 Dec 1831- Rob't Williams, J.P.
source: license- 1751-03/5-112
see also volume 3, page 96

ROGERS, JOHNSON
and
JOHNSON, AGGY

15 Dec 1831- Thomas King, C.C.O.
15 Dec 1831- Noah Looney, J.P.
source: license- 1751-03/6-126
see also volume 3, page 94

RAMSEY, HAMPTON
and
HENSON, SARAH

16 Dec 1831- Thomas King, C.C.O.
22 Dec 1831- Hiram Bennett, J.P.
source: license- 1751-03/6-122
see also volume 3, page 89

LANGSTON, ELIHU
and
NEAL, MARTHA H.

19 Dec 1831- Thomas King, C.C.O.
20 Dec 1831- Nathan Gunnels, J.P.
source: license- 1751-02/4-84
see also volume 3, page 101

PULLIAM, BENJAMIN S.
and
TURMON, ELENDER

22 Dec 1831- Thomas King, C.C.O.
23 Dec 1831- Dozier Thornton, M.G.
source: license- 1751-03/6-120
see also volume 3, page 90

BURTON, JOHN
and
HARRISON, NANCY

22 Dec 1831- Thomas King, C.C.O.
23 Dec 1831- S. Hymer, Minisyer
source: license- 1751-01/1-20
see also volume 3, page 114

SEWELL, JAMES A.
and
VAUN, MARY

23 Dec 1831- Thomas King, C.C.O.
23 Dec 1831- John Bramblet, M.G.
source: license- 1751-03/6-132
see also volume 3, page 103

BLACKWELL, JOEL
and
EDWARDS, JUDAH ANN

24 Dec 1831- Thomas King, C.C.O.
27 Dec 1831- Job Hammond, J.P.
source: license- 1751-01/1-12
see also volume 3, page 93

BENNETT, COOPER
and
MILLS, NANCY

31 Dec 1831- Thomas King, C.C.O.
1 Jan 1832- Hiram Bennett, J.P.
source: license- 1751-01/1-11
see also volume 3, page 92

JOLLY, JOHN P.
and
COOK, MARY

1 Jan 1832- Thomas King, C.C.O.
1 Jan 1832- Jacob Strickland, J.P.
source: license- 1751-02/4-78
see also volume 3, page 97

DAVIS, HEZEKIAH
and
BREWER, SARAH

1 Jan 1832- Thomas King, C.C.O.
1 Jan 1832- Benj. Laughridge, J.P.
source: license- 1751-01/2-41
see also volume 3, page 92

SAXON, JAMES
and
HARISSON, NANCY

1 Jan 1832- Thomas King, C.C.O.
1 Jan 1832- Benjamin Laughridge, J.P.
source: license- 1751-03/6-128
see also volume 3, page 93

ANDERS, WILLIAM
and
MC CARTER, MARY

5 Jan 1832- Thomas King, C.C.O.
5 Jan 1832- Nathan Gunnels, J.P.
source: license- 1751-01/1-5
see also volume 3, page 105

CHANDLER, ELZA
and
JOHNSON, ELIZABETH

6 Jan 1832- Thomas King, C.C.O.
8 Jan 1832- Noah Looney, J.P.
source: license- 1751-01/2-27
see also volume 3, page 93

WALTERS, MICAJAH
and
COCKERHAM, MARY

11 Jan 1832- Thomas White, C.C.O.
13 Jan 1832- W'm Burroughs, J.P.
source: license- 1751-04/8-156
see also volume 3, page 99

ALEXANDER, SAMUEL F.
and
NEAL, MAHULDAH

11 Jan 1832- Thomas King, C.C.O.
12 Jan 1832- John S. Wilson, M.G.
source: license- 1751-01/1-4
see also volume 3, page 87

BOBO, BENJAMIN H.
and
FAIN, MARY

12 Jan 1832- Thomas King, C.C.O.
12 Jan 1832- Dozier Thornton, M.G.
source: license- 1751-01/1-13
see also volume 3, page 88

BALLENGER, JOHN
and
WILLIAMS, LENRY(?)

23 Jan 1832- Thomas King, C.C.O.
24 Jan 1832- John Bramblet, M.G.
source: license- 1751-01/1-9
see also volume 3, page 102

HUNT, ESLEY
and
DAILEY, SUSAN

25 Jan 1832- Thomas King, C.C.O.
31 Jan 1832- Nathan Gunnels, J.P.
source: license- 1751-02/3-74
see also volume 3, page 101

HAYS, JACKSON
and
GREEN, NANCY

26 Jan 1832- Thomas King, C.C.O.
26 Jan 1832- Benjamin Stonecypher, J.P.
source: license- 1751-02/3-66
see also volume 3, page 90

KESLAR, GEORGE
and
MILLER, MARY

26 Jan 1832- Thomas King, C.C.O.
26 Jan 1832- Sam'l Jackson, J.P.
source: license- 1751-02/4-82
see also volume 3, page 98

WILEY, GEORGE W.
and
JONES, JANE

28 Jan 1832(sic)- Thomas King, C.C.O.
4 Jan 1832(sic)- Woodson Blankenship, J.P.
source: license- 1751-04/8-165
see also volume 3, page 91

SARTIN, JOHN, SR.
and
COKER, MARYAN

28 Jan 1832- Thomas King, C.C.O.
29 Jan 1832- John Bramblet, M.G.
source: license- 1751-03/6-128
see also volume 3, page 102

PATERSON, CALVIN W.
and
ATAWAY, ELIZABETH

8 Feb 1832- Thomas King, C.C.O.
9 Feb 1832- S. Hymer, Min.
source: license- 1751-03/5-110
see also volume 3, page 109

WEEMS, JOHNSON
and
LEACH, PAMELIA

11 Feb 1832- Thomas King, C.C.O.
12 Feb 1832- Woodson Blankenship, J.P.
source:license- 1751-04/8-159
see also volume 3, page 95

MABURY, JAMES
and
COLLYER, SARAH

12 Feb 1832- Thomas King, C.C.O.
12 Feb 1832- Benjamin Stonecypher, J.P.
source: license- 1751-02/4-89
see also volume 3, page 106

PATTERSON, JOHN
and
HOBGOOD, PAMELIA

15 Feb 1832- Thomas King, C.C.O.
15 Feb 1832- Chesley Cawthon, J.P.
source: license- 1751-03/5-110
see also volume 3, page 128

FULLER, COPER B.
and
STONECIPHER, ANNEY

16 Feb 1832- Thomas King, C.C.O.
16 Feb 1832- C.D. Jenkins, J.I.C.
source: license- 1751-02/3-52
see also volume 3, page 92

VAWTER, HIRAM
and
GLENN, ELIZABETH

21 Feb 1832- Thomas King, C.C.O.
23 Feb 1832- Hiram Bennett, J.P.
source: license- 1751-04/8-153
see also volume 3, page 100

GOODE, DANIEL
and
HORTON, ARTIMISSA

1 Mar 1832- Thomas King, C.C.O.
1 Mar 1832- John Catlett, J.P.
source: license- 1751-02/3-58
see also volume 3, page 96

RILEY, WILLIAM
and
CHANDELAR, LUCINDY

1 Mar 1832- Thomas King, C.C.O.
1 Mar 1832- Henry David, M.G.
source: license- 1751-03/6-125
see also volume 3, page 99

BRAMLET, JOHN
and
CLARK, DICY

8 Mar 1832- Thomas King, C.C.O.
8 Mar 1832- Benj. Stonecypher, J.P.
source: license- 1751-01/1-15
see also volume 3, page 106

HOLMES, ALLEN
and
RUMSEY, HESTERAN

8 Mar 1832- Thomas King, C.C.O.
8 Mar 1832- Benj. Laughridge, J.P.
source: license- 1751-02/3-72
see also volume 3, page 147

FLOOD, WILLIAM
and
SMITH, REBECCA

10 Mar 1832- Thomas King, C.C.O.
11 Mar 1832- Nathan Gunnels, J.P.
source: license- 1751-02/3-49
see also volume 3, page 101

CHILDERS, THOMAS
and
VICKRY, MILLY

11 Mar 1832- Thomas King, C.C.O.
11 Mar 1832- Dozier Thornton, M.G.
source: license- 1751-01/2-31
see also volume 3, page 114

KNOX, SAMUEL
and
SWIFT, MARY AN

27 Mar 1832- Thomas King, C.C.O.
3 Apr 1832- Asa Chandler, M.G.
source: license- 1751-02/4-53
see also volume 3, page 98

BELLAMY, PLEASANT
and
CHATHAM, SARAH J.

3 Apr 1832- Thomas King, C.C.O.
5 Apr 1832- Hiram Bennett, J.P.
source: license- 1751-01/1-10
see also volume 3, page 97

VAUGHAN, JOHN
and
BLACK, SARAH

5 Apr 1832- Thomas King, C.C.O.
6 Apr 1832- W'm Burroughs, J.P.
source: license- 1751-04/8-151
see also volume 3, page 100

BELL, ALISON
and
FREEMAN, MATILDA

8 Apr 1832- Thomas King, C.C.O.
8 Apr 1832- Joseph McEntire, J.P.
source: license- 1751-01/1-10
see also volume 3, page 113

AYERS, BAYKER
and
SHELNUT, ELIZABETH

19 Apr 1832- Thomas King, C.C.O.
19 Apr 1832- Job Hammond, J.P.
source: license- 1751-01/1-7
see also volume 3, page 107

MORGAN, JAMES
and
BURGESS, MARY

25 Apr 1832- Thomas King, C.C.O.
30 Apr 1832- Royal Bryan, J.P.
source: license- 1751-03/5-102
see also volume 3, page 102

HOOD, JAMES H.
and
COOK, EMILY

22 May 1832- Thomas King, C.C.O.
22 May 1832- Joseph McEntyre, J.P.
source: license- 1751-02/3-72
see also volume 3, page 107

DUELL, WILLIAM
and
FULGHAM, ELIZABETH

2 June 1832- Thomas King, C.C.O.
7 June 1832- Job Hammond, J.P.
source: license- 1751-01/2-45
see also volume 3, page 106

RAY, JEHU(? JOHN?)
and
HOWELL, SARAH

6 June 1832- Thomas King, C.C.O.
10 June 1832- Rob't Williams, J.P.
source: license- 1751-03/6-122
see also volume 3, page 96

MIZE, CLARKSON
and
PAGE, SALLY

6 June 1832- Thomas King, C.C.O.
7 June 1832- Littleton Meeks
source: license- 1751-03/5-101
see also volume 4, page 118

BURGESS, JOHN M.
and
MITCHELL, MARTHA S.

17 June 1832- Thomas King, C.C.O.
17 June 1832- William Burroughs, J.P.
source: license- 1751-01/1-19
see also volume 3, page 100

SMITH, WILEY
and
MURDOCK, PRUDENCE

21 June 1832- Thomas King, C.C.O.
28 June 1832- Samuel McCollum, J.P.
source: license- 1751-04/7-139
see also volume 3, page 95

UNDERWOOD, LITTLEBERRY
and
KEY, LOUISA

26 June 1832- Thomas King, C.C.O.
28 June 1832- Nathan Gunnels, J.P.
source: license- 1751-04/7-150
see also volume 3, page 115

BENNETT, PETER
and
COBB, ANNA

19 July 1832- Thomas King, C.C.O.
19 July 1832- William Burroughs
source: license- 1751-01/1-11
see also volume 3, page 105

KING, JAMES
and
NEAL, VIRGINIA N.

4 Aug 1832- Thomas King, C.C.O.
16 Aug 1832- Joseph McEntire, J.P.
source: license- 1751-02/4-83
see also volume 3, page 110

PAIR, MARCUS W.
and
KEESLER, HANNAH

14 Aug 1832- Thomas King, C.C.O.
14 Aug 1832- Robert Williams, J.P.
source: license- 1751-03/5-108
see also volume 3, page 114

FOWLER, JOHN A.
and
KEESLER, KATHARINE

28 Aug 1832- Thomas King, C.C.O.
4 Sept 1832- Robert Williams, J.P.
source: license- 1751-02/3-50
see also volume 3, page 125

HENDRICKS, GILFORD E.
and
CRIDER, SUSAN

28 Aug 1832- Thomas King, C.C.O.
30 Aug 1832- John Wilson, J.P.
source: license- 1751-02/3-67
see also volume 3, page 104

COX, MICHEL
and
THORNTON, MARY

17 Sept 1832- Thomas King, C.C.O.
20 Sept 1832- R. Thornton, M.G.
source: license- 1751-01/2-35
see also volume 3, page 111

WARWICK, ALLEN
and
HOLLEY, LOUISA H.

18 Sept 1832- Thomas King, C.C.O.
20 Sept 1832- W'm J. Parks, M.G.
source: license- 1751-04/8-157
see also volume 3, page 111

BOSEL, WILLIAM
and
BOND, ELIZA

... Sept 1832- Thomas King, C.C.O.
27 Sept 1832- Reuben Thornton, M.G.
source: license- 1751-01/1-14
see also volume 4, page 64

ROYSTER, WESLEY
and
MURDOCK, POLLY

1 Oct 1832- Thomas King, C.C.O.
11 Oct 1832- Sam'l McCollum, J.P.
source: license- 1751-03/6-126
see also volume 3, page 112

PHILLIPS, H.K.
and
PATERSON, NANCY

7 Oct 1832- Thomas King, C.C.O.
11 Oct 1832- James Attaway, J.P.
source: license- 1751-03/6-114
see also volume 3, page 110

DICKERSON, JOEL
and
SLATON, ELIZABETH

9 Oct 1832- Thomas King, C.C.O.
11 Oct 1832- G.L. Sandidge, J.I.C.
source: license- 1751-01/2-43
see also volume 3, page 110

LITT, KENNY
and
ROBINSTON, PATSEY

15 Oct 1832- Thomas King, C.C.O.
15 Oct 1832- Chesley Cawthon, J.P.
source: volume 3, page 126
(note: the Georgia Archives Inventory of
licenses indicates this license should
be in 1751-02/4-81. The compiler could
not locate it)

GARRISON, BARNABAS
and
CAUDELL, JANE

17 Oct 1832- Thomas King, C.C.O.
18 Oct 1832- John Catlett, J.P.
source: license- 1751-02/3-54
see also volume 3, page 121

CALAWAY, MARTIN
and
SCOTT, LUSIAAN

21 Oct 1832- Thomas King, C.C.O.
21 Oct 1832- Benj'n Loughridge, J.P.
source: license- 1751-01/2-21
see also volume 3, page 142

ALLEN, JOHN M.
and
MACKIE, MARTHA

23 Oct 1832- Thomas King, C.C.O.
23 Oct 1832- Joseph McEntire, J.P.
source: license- 1751-01/1-4
see also volume 3, page 112

BLACK, JAMES M.
and
COUCH, MARY M.

24 Oct 1832- Thomas King, C.C.O.
25 Oct 1832- W'm Burroughs, J.P.
source: license- 1751-01/1-12
see also volume 3, page 113

LANGSTON, THOMAS J.
and
NEAL, ELIZABETH

25 Oct 1832- Thomas King, C.C.O.
25 Oct 1832- Nathan Gunnels, J.P.
source: license- 1751-02/4-84
see also volume 3, page 123

COLLYER, MOSES
and
BARNETT(?), SUSAN

1 Nov 1832- Thomas King, C.C.O.
1 Nov 1832- M.W. Vandiver, M.G.
source: license- 1751-01/2-34
see also volume 3, page 124

GRAHAM, W'M R.
and
PAYNE, MALISA

3 Nov 1832- Thomas King, C.C.O.
8 Nov 1832- Hiram Bennett, J.P.
source: license- 1751-02/3-59
see also volume 3, page 113

GARDINER, SAMUEL
and
FORSYTH, NANCY

14 Nov 1832- Thomas King, C.C.O.
15 Nov 1832- David Garrison
source: license- 1751-02/3-53
see also volume 4, page 25

HUGHES, WILLIAM
and
JAMES, NICY

18 Nov 1832- Thomas King, C.C.O.
18 Nov 1832- Nathan Gunnels, J.P.
source: license- 1751-02/3-74
see also volume 3, page 116

PACK, JOHN R.
and
WALTERS, LEAR

20 Nov 1832- Thomas King, C.C.O.
20 Nov 1832- W'm King, J.P.
source: license- 1751-03/5-108
see also volume 3, page 122

COKER, JOSEPH
and
BRIDGES, CLOE

24 Nov 1832- Thomas King, C.C.O.
25 Nov 1832- W'm King, J.P.
source: license- 1751-02/2-33
see also volume 3, page 118

LOWREY, ELISHA
and
HAND, POLLY

10 Dec 1832- Thomas King, C.C.O.
13 Dec 1832- Rob't Pulliam, J.I.C.
source: license- 1751-02/4-88
see also volume 3, page 104

HOSEY, LEVI
and
DELPORT, HARRIETT

12 Dec 1832- Thomas King, C.C.O.
13 Dec 1832- Rob't Mitchell, J.P.
source: license- 1751-02/3-73
see also volume 3, page 104

VAUGHAN, WILLIAM
and
WILKINSON, MARY

19 Dec 1832- Thomas King, C.C.O.
20 Dec 1832- W'm Burroughs, J.P.
source: license- 1751-04/8-151
see also volume 3, page 103

REED, JAMES A.
and
CHILES, MARGARET

22 Dec 1832- Thomas King, C.C.O.
22 Dec 1832- W. Blankenship, J.P.
source: license- 1751-03/6-123
see also volume 3, page 127

BELLAMY, ASA
and
YARBROUGH, KATHARINE

24 Dec 1832- Thomas King, C.C.O.
27 Dec 1832- Hiram Bennett, J.P.
source: license- 1751-01/1-10
see also volume 3, page 112

SCOT, ALLEN
and
MC FARLAND, POLLEY

26 Dec 1832- Thomas King, C.C.O.
27 Dec 1832- Royal Bryan, J.P.
source: license- 1751-03/6-130
see also volume 3, page 129

WESTBROOK, JOEL M.
and
RILEY, LUCY

27 Dec 1832- Thomas King, C.C.O.
27 Dec 1832- Joseph McEntire, J.P.
source: license- 1751-04/8-160
see also volume 3, page 122

STOVALL, WILKINS
and
GARRETT, MAHALEY

16 Jan 1833- Thomas King, C.C.O.
17 Jan 1833- Royal Bryan, J.P.
source: license- 1751-04/7-144
see also volume 3, page 131

CHATHAM, WILLIAM
and
TATE, MARY

19 Jan 1833- Thomas King, C.C.O.
20 Jan 1833- Job Hammond, J.P.
source: license- 1751-01/2-29
see also volume 3, page 118

CARPENTER, JAMES
and
BARRETT, ELIZA H.

23 Jan 1833- Thomas King, C.C.O.
14 Feb 1833- S. Hymer, Minister
source: license- 1751-01/2-23
see also volume 3, page 126

ISBELL, ALLEN
and
BURTON, SARAH

25 Jan 1833- Thomas King, C.C.O.
27 Jan 1833- Sam'l Moore, J.P.
source: license- 1751-02/4-75
see also volume 3, page 116

SEWELL, FRANCIS
and
BLACKWELL, LUCY

30 Jan 1833- Thomas King, C.C.O.
31 Jan 1833- Job Hammond, J.P.
source: license- 1751-03/6-132
see also volume 3, page 118

ISBELL, JOHN
and
COCKERHAM, ELIZABETH

10 Feb 1833- Thomas King, C.C.O.
10 Feb 1833- W'm Burroughs, J.P.
source: license- 1751-02/4-75
see also volume 3, page 123

VAUGHAN, PERRY M.
and
MALDEN, VIRGINIA

11 Feb 1833- Thomas King, C.C.O.
12 Feb 1833- John Catlett, J.P.
source: license- 1751-04/8-151
see also volume 3, page 124

SMITH, ALFERD
and
CHAPPELEAR, CASSANDRA

18 Feb 1833- Thomas King, C.C.O.
18 Feb 1833- W'm Burroughs, J.P.
source: license- 1751-04/7-136
see also volume 3, page 131

MC MILLION, JOHN B.
and
HALL, ELIZABETH

3 Mar 1833- Thomas King, C.C.O.
3 Mar 1833- Job Bowers, J.P.
source: license- 1751-02/4-92
see also volume 3, page 120

KEASLER, HENRY
and
HALEY, NANCY

4 Mar 1833- Thomas King, C.C.O.
5 Mar 1833- Job Hammond, J.P.
source: license- 1751-02/4-80
see also volume 3, page 124

CURRY, JOHN
and
PERCIL, SUSAN

11 Mar 1833- Thomas King, C.C.O.
15 Mar 1833- C. Addison, J.P.
source: license- 1751-01/2-39
see also volume 3, page 126

BAKER, JOHN G.
and
MULLENIX, FRANKEY P.

12 Mar 1833- Thomas King, C.C.O.
12 Mar 1833- Royal Bryan, J.P.
source: license- 1751-01/1-8
see also volume 3, page 131

BRYAN, JESSE
and
HARBIN, SARAH

31 Mar 1833- Thomas King, C.C.O.
31 Mar 1833- Benj'n Loughridge, J.P.
source: license- 1751-01/1-18
see also volume 3, page 143

CHEEK, JOHN
and
DUNCAN, ANER

2 Apr 1833- Thomas King, C.C.O.
4 Apr 1833- John Wilson, J.P.
source: license- 1751-01/2-30
see also volume 3, page 125

VICKREY, JOSEPH H.
and
SANDERS, PATIENT

8 Apr 1833- Thomas King, C.C.O.
8 Apr 1833- W'm King, J.P.
source: license- 1751-04/8-154
see also volume 3, page 130

NORWOOD, WILLIAM
and
THOMPSON, ELVIRA

10 Apr 1833- Thomas King, C.C.O.
10 Apr 1833- Littleton Meeks, M.G.
source: license- 1751-03/5-106
see also volume 4, page 117

DAVIS, JEFFERSON
and
TAPP, MARY

12 Apr 1833- Thomas King, C.C.O.
14 Apr 1833- W'm R. Wellborn, M.G.
source: license- 1751-01/2-41
see also volume 4, page 117

PERRY, RICHARD
and
JACKSON, REBECA

24 Apr 1833- Thomas King, C.C.O.
24 Apr 1833- Littleton Meeks, M.G.
source: license- 1751-03/5-113
see also volume 4, page 118

HINSON, WILLIAM
and
RAMSEY, NANCY

26 Apr 1833- Thomas King, C.C.O.
26 Apr 1833- Rob't Williams, J.I.C.
source: license- 1751-02/3-70
see also volume 3, page 121

WHITTEN, JOHN R.
and
PHIPS, MARY

30 Apr 1833- Thomas King, C.C.O.
30 Apr 1833- W'm R. Wellborn, M.G.
source: license- 1751-04/8-164
see also volume 3, page 130

HOWARD, BENJAMIN
and
BRYAN, LUCINDA

10 May 1833- Thomas King, C.C.O.
10 May 1833- William Burroughs, J.P.
source: license- 1751-02/3-73
see also volume 3, page 122

PIERCE, MARTIN
and
BURGESS, NANCY

3 June 1833- Thomas King, C.C.O.
3 June 1833- James Stovall, J.P.
source: license- 1751-03/6-115
see also volume 3, page 130

MC ENTIRE, DANIEL
and
KIRK, SARAH

9 June 1833- Thomas King, C.C.O.
9 June 1833- Benj'n Laughridge, J.P.
source: license- 1751-02/4-91
see also volume 3, page 143

HUNNICUT, WILSON F.
and
HYATT, ELIZABETH

11 July 1833- Thomas King, C.C.O.
11 July 1833- Joseph McEntire, J.P.
source: license- 1751-02/3-74
see also volume 3, page 121

HOLBROOK, PLEASANT
and
HARBOUR, MARY

17 July 1833- Thomas King, C.C.O.
19 July 1833- A.E. Whitten, J.I.C.
source: license- 1751-02/3-71
see also volume 3, page 120

PICKENS, ALEXANDER
and
PICKENS, ELIZABETH

17 Aug 1833- Thomas King, C.C.O.
27 Aug 1833- Nelson Osbern, M.G.
source: license- 1751-03/6-115
see also volume 3, page 129

WILKERSON, THOMAS
and
ISBELL, CLARKEY

18 Aug 1833- Thomas King, C.C.O.
18 Aug 1833- James Stovall, J.P.
source: license- 1751-04/8-165
see also volume 3, page 132

PATERSON, THORNTON
and
ROBESON(?), MARY

25 Aug 1833- Thomas King, C.C.O.
25 Aug 1833- Benj'n Loughridge, J.P.
source: license- 1751-03/5-109
see also volume 3, page 145

MARTIN, MICAJAH
and
WILLIAMS, LUCY

14 Sept 1833- Thomas King, C.C.O.
16 Sept 1833- C. Addison, J.P.
source: license- 1751-03/5-95
see also volume 3, page 117

CARTER, WILLIAM R.
and
PAGE, SALLY

8 Oct 1833- Thomas King, C.C.O.
8 Oct 1833- S. Hymer, M.G.
source: license- 1751-01/2-25
see also volume 4, page 114

HAYNES, JAMES W.
and
REED, NANCY

10 Oct 1833, Thomas King, C.C.O.
10 Oct 1833- S. Hymer, M.G.
source: license- 1751-02/3-66
see also volume 4, page 32

WOOD, GILLUM
and
ROPER, LYDIA

13 Oct 1833- Thomas King, C.C.O.
13 Oct 1833- W'm Burroughs, J.P.
source: license- 1751-04/8-169
see also volume 3, page 119

BOWERS, EDY
and
GLOVER, JANE

14 Oct 1833- Thomas King, C.C.O.
15 Oct 1833- Job Bowers, J.P.
source: license- 1751-01/1-14
see also volume 3, page 138

SHEARLY, WILLIAM   17 Oct 1833- Thomas King, C.C.O.
    and   17 Oct 1833- C. Addison, J.P.
EVANS, ADALINE   source: license- 1751-04/7--133
                                 see also volume 3, page 128

WILLIAMS, JAMES   5 Nov 1833- Thomas King, C.C.O.
    and   7 Nov 1833- Geo. W. Key, M.G.
MEDDERS, ESTHER   source: license- 1751-04/8-166
                                 see also volume 3, page 117

JONES, DR. TERRELL H.   5 Nov 1833- Thomas King, C.C.O.
    and   7 Nov 1833- Reuben Thornton, M.G.
BUSH, JUDITH A.   source: license- 1751-02/4-78
                                 see also volume 3, page 127

BUSH, DANIEL   18 Nov 1833- Thomas King, C.C.O.
    and   21 Nov 1833- Reuben Thornton, M.G.
JONES, EMILY   source: license- 1751-01/1-20
                                 see also volume 3, page 119

BOSWELL, JAMES   20 Nov 1833- Thomas King, C.C.O.
    and   21 Nov 1833- James Stovall, J.P.
GRADDY, ELIZABETH   source: license- 1751-01/1-14
                                 see also volume 3, page 125

BAGWELL, ALBERT G.   28 Nov 1833- Thomas King, C.C.O.
    and   28 Nov 1833- W. Blankenship, J.P.
WALKER, REBECCA   source: license- 1751-01/1-8
                                 see also volume 3, page 129

MULKEY, JOHN   4 Dec 1833- Thomas King, C.C.O.
    and   5 Dec 1833- Robert Mitchell, J.P.
LEACH, ELIZABETH   source: license- 1751-03/5-104
                                 see also volume 3, page 127

WHEELER, RICHARD   5 Dec 1833- Thomas King, C.C.O.
    and   5 Dec 1833- C. Addison, J.P.
MILLS, CAROLINE   source: license- 1751-04/8--161
                                 see also volume 3, page 117

PURCEL, JARRET   12 Dec 1833- Thomas King, C.C.O.
    and   13 Dec 1833- C. Addison, J.P.
MABRY, MARY   source: license- 1751-03/6-120
                                 see also volume 3, page 119

POOLE, WILLIAM R.   12 Dec 1833- Thomas King, C.C.O.
    and   12 Dec 1833- F. Callaway, M.G.
STOVALL, SUSANAH   source: license- 1751-03/6-116
                                 see also volume 3, page 116

NORWOOD, ANDREW   18 Dec 1833- Thomas King, C.C.O.
    and   19 Dec 1833- Rob't Mitchell, J.P.
MITCHELL, ELIZABETH   source: license- 1751-03/5-106
                                 see also volume 3, page 128

HARPER, ANDREW K.   18 Dec 1833- Thomas King, C.C.O.
    and   20 Dec 1833- W'm R. Wellborn
LITTLE, ANNY Y.   source: license- 1751-02/3-63
                                 see also volume 3, page 134

GARNER, GEORGE, JR.
and
CLEVELAND, ARMINDA B.

23 Dec 1833- Thomas King, C.C.O.
26 Dec 1833- Matthew W. Vandivier, M.G.
source: license- 1751-02/3-53
see also volume 3, page 120

THORNTON, JEREMIAH J.
and
WALTERS, MARY

23 Dec 1833- Thomas King, C.C.O.
25 Dec 1833- Ruben Thornton, M.G.
source: license- 1751-04/7-149
see also volume 4, page 106

TEASLEY, WILLIAM
and
REED, ELMIRY

26 Dec 1833- Thomas King, C.C.O.
26 Dec 1833- Nelson Osbern, M.G.
source: license- 1751-04/7-146
see also volume 3, page 123

EPPERZON, CHARLES
and
HOUZE, CHARLOTTE

1 Jan 1834- Thomas King, C.C.O.
1 Jan 1834- John Catlett, J.P.
source: license- 1751-02/3-47

MARTIN, WILLIAM J.
and
MILLER, LUSE(? or C.... E.)

18 Jan 1834- Thomas King, C.C.O.
18 Jan 1834- Rob't Williams, J.I.C.
source: license- 1751-03/5-95
see also volume 3, page 115

WILBANKS, GILLAM
and
CALLIHAM, REBECKAH

26 Jan 1834- Thomas King, C.C.O.
26 Jan 1834- Benj. Stonecypher, J.P.
source: license- 1751-04/8-165
see also volume 3, page 133

PARKER, BENJAMIN B.
and
WILSON, SARAH

10 Feb 1834- Thomas King, C.C.O.
10 Feb 1834- S. Crandal, J.T.P.C.(?)
source: license- 1751-03/5-108
see also volume 3, page 135

DICKASON, JOHN R.
and
ADGE, ELIZABETH

12 Feb 1834- Thomas King, C.C.O.
12 Feb 1834- Benjamin Stonecypher, J.P.
source: license- 1751-01/2-43
see also volume 3, page 135

HARDY, JOHN
and
FREEMAN, ELIZABETH

9 Feb 1834- Thomas King, C.C.O.
20 Feb 1834- Henry David, M.G.
source: license- 1751-02/3-63
see also volume 3, page 144

WESTBROOK, WILLIAM L.
and
VAUCHN, MARIAH

24 Feb 1834- Thomas King, C.C.O.
30 Mar 1834- Robert Mitchell, J.P.
source: license- 1751-04/8-160
see also volume 3, page 141

WESTBROOK, STEPHEN B.
and
SHANNON, MARY

13 Mar 1834- Thomas King, C.C.O.
13 Mar 1834- Woodson Blankinship, J.P.
source: license- 1751-04/8-160
see also volume 3, page 142

RAY, WILLIAM
and
HOLCOMBE, MATILDA

18 Mar 1834- Thomas King, C.C.O.
18 Mar 1834- John A. Davis, M.G.
source: license- 1751-03/6-122
see also volume 3, page 141

WALTERS, GREEN C.
and
CARNES, SARAH

30 Mar 1834- Thomas King, C.C.O.
30 Mar 1834- John Burton, J.P.
source: license- 1751-04/8-156
see also volume 4, page 111

JENKINS, JESSE
and
AKINS, ELENDER

17 Apr 1834- Thomas King, C.C.O.
17 Apr 1834- Benj'n Laughridge, J.P.
source: license- 1751-02/4-77
see also volume 4, page 112

HOOPER, RICHARD
and
MILLER, ADENEA (?)

23 Apr 1834- Thomas King, C.C.O.
23 Apr 1834- Robert Williams, J.I.C.
source: license- 1751-02/3-72
see also volume 3, page 144

MEADOWS, WILLIAM
and
GOBER, ORPHA

16 May 1834- Thomas King, C.C.O.
27 May 1834- David Garrison, M.G.
source: license- 1751-03/5-98
see also volume 4, page 1

HILL, BENJAMIN R.
and
MAULDING, SALLY

10 June 1834- Thomas King, C.C.O.
10 June 1834- Harvey M. Mayes, J.P.
source: license- 1751-02/3-69
see also volume 3, page 138

HUNTER, WILLIAM M.
and
SMITH, SARAH

22 July 1834- Thomas King, C.C.O.
24 July 1834- Matthew W. Vandiver, M.G.
source: license- 1751-02/3-74

WELDON, WELBOURN
and
AYERS, ABIGAIL

26 July 1834- Thomas King, C.C.O.
27 July 1834- Samuel Moore, M.G.
source: license- 1751-04/8-159
see also volume 4, page 111

POWERS, ALEXANDER
and
HOWELL, NANCY

3 Aug 1834- Thomas King, C.C.O.
3 Aug 1834- R.A.R. Neal, J.P.
source: license- 1751-03/6-117
see also volume 3, page 136

AYCOCK, RICHARD L.
and
LEACH, RACHEL

17 Aug 1834- Thomas King, C.C.O.
17 Aug 1834- Woodson Blankenship, J.P.
source: license- 1751-01/1-7
see also volume 3, page 142

WHITFIELD, GRAY
and
MURRAY, ANNA

19 Aug 1834- Thomas King, C.C.O.
...... 1834- ....
source: license- 1751-04/8-163

SCOTT, JOEL
and
SMITH, VESTA

20 Aug 1834- Thomas King, C.C.O.
20 Aug 1834- John A, Davis, Minister
source: license- 1751-03/6-130
see also volume 3, page 147,148

STOVALL, DAVID C.
and
TURMAN, ALPHA

21 Sept 1834- Thomas King, C.C.O.
25 Sept 1834- S. Hymer, M.G.
source: license- 1751-04/7-143
see also volume 4, page 113

KITCHENS, JOSIAH
and
NORWOOD, NANCY

25 Sept 1834- Thomas King, C.C.O.
25 Sept 1834- L. Meeks, M.G.
source: license- 1751-02/4-83
see also volume 4, page 44

ANDERS, DANIEL
and
VESSELS, LUSINDA

6 Oct 1834- Thomas King, C.C.O.
6 Oct 1834- R.A.R. Neal, J.P.
source: license- 1751-01/1-5

MARTIN, CLUFF
and
JOLLY, ANNEZ(?)

10 Oct 1834- Thomas King, C.C.O.
12 Oct 1834- R.A.R. Neal, J.P.
source: license- 1751-03/5-95
see also volume 3, page 144

REED, JOSEPH
and
HUTCHENS, MARY M.(? E.?)

29 Oct 1834- Thomas King, C.C.O.
14 Dec 1834- Benj'n Laughridge, J.P.
source: license- 1751-03/6-123
see also volume 4, page 109

HARRISON, OLIVER
and
STONE, SUSAN

30 Oct 1834- Thomas King, C.C.O.
30 Oct 1834- Thomas Farmer, J.I.C.
source: license- 1751-02/3-64
see also volume 3, page 133

HILBURN, N.S.
and
BIRD, MARTHA H.

4 Nov 1834- Thomas King, C.C.O.
4 Nov 1834- W'm Shackelford, J.P.
source: license- 1751-02/3-69
see also volume 3, page 140

MC CALLA, JAMES R.
and
YANCEY, PELONIA A.E.

5 Nov 1834- Thomas King, C.C.O.
7 Nov 1834- R. McAlpin, M.G.
source: license- 1751-02/4-89
see also volume 3, page 139

HOOPER, GARLAND
and
PAYNE, ARTIMISA

5 Nov 1834- Thomas King, C.C.O.
5 Nov 1834- Robert Williams, J.I.C.
source: license- 1751-02/3-72
see also volume 3, page 137

GUEST, DAVID
and
HICKS, MATILLDY(?)

8 Nov 1834- Thomas King, C.C.O.
9 Nov 1834- Asa York, J.P.
source: license- 1751-02/3-60
see also volume 3, page 148

MABRY, ELI L.
and
SCOGGINS, MARTHA

14 Nov 1834- Thomas King, C.C.O.
15 Nov 1834- S.D. Thomason, J.P.
source: license- 1751-02/4-89
see also volume 3, page 134

MURPHEY, JAMES
and
GARNER, ANNA

29 Nov 1834- Thomas King, C.C.O.
30 Nov 1834- W'm Burroughs, J.P.
source: license- 1751-03/5-104
see also volume 3, page 139

LANKFORD, NOONAN
and
BURGESS, ELIZABETH

11 Dec 1834- Thomas King, C.C.O.
11 Dec 1834- Benj'n Laughridge, J.P.
source: license- 1751-02/4-84
see also volume 4, page 109

SHANNON, LEONARD
and
BRAWNER, CHARLOTTE

13 Dec 1834- Thomas King, C.C.O.
18 Dec 1834- W'm J. Parks, M.G.
source: license- 1751-04/7-133
see also volume 4, page 143

HOLBROOK, THOMAS P.
and
GLOVER, MARHY(?)

13 Dec 1834- Thomas King, C.C.O.
14 Dec 1834- Job Bowers, J.P.
source: license- 1751-02/3-71
see also volume 4, page 113

TURK, MILTON
and
CHAMBERS, ELIZABETH M.

13 Dec 1834- Thomas King, C.C.O.
16 Dec 1834- Harvy M. Mayes, J.P.
source: license- 1751-04/7-150
see also volume 4, page 6

BETENBAU, MICHAEL
and
HEMPHILL, CAROLINE

13 Dec 1834- Thomas King, C.C.O.
14 Dec 1834- W. Blankenship, J.P.
source: license- 1751-01/1-11
see also volume 3, page 136

BELL, JAMES
and
WOOD, WELTHYANN

16 Dec 1834- Thomas King, C.C.O.
18 Dec 1834- Royal Bryan, J.P.
source: license- 1751-01/1-10
see also volume 3, page 143

PURCELL, JACOB
and
GUEST, MARTHA

17 Dec 1834- Thomas King, C.C.O.
17 Dec 1834- Lewis Ballard, M.G.
source: license- 1751-03/6-120
see also volume 3, page 140

MINYARD, FLEMING
and
GUEST, MARY

17 Dec 1834- Thomas King, C.C.O.
14 Jan 1835- Asa York, J.P.
source: license- 1751-03/5-100
see also volume 3, page 137

KEY, TOLBERT
and
BURGESS, MRS. EFFA

19 Dec 1834- Thomas King, C.C.O.
21 Dec 1834- W'm R. Wellborn, M.G.
source: license- 1751-02/4-82
see also volume 3, page 135

HAYNES, MOSES
and
CARR(?), POSEY

23 Dec 1834- Thomas King, C.C.O.
23 Dec 1834- Job Bowers, J.P.
source: license- 1751-02/3-66
see also volume 4, page 124

MORRIS, EPPE
and
TURMAN, ELIZA

27 Dec 1834- Thomas King, C.C.O.
28 Dec 1834- Alvan Dean, J.I.C.
source: license- 1751-03/5-102
see also volume 3, page 140

CRAWFORD, MOSES B.
and
SMITH, NANCY

29 Dec 1834- Thomas King C.C.O.
29 Dec 1834- W'm Burroughs, J.P.
source: license- 1751-01/2-36
see also volume 3, page 147

HICKS, HARVEY
and
NIXON, SARAH

31 Dec 1834- Thomas King, C.C.O.
1 Jan 1835- Rob't Crump, J.P.
source: license- 1751-02/3-68
see also volume 3, page 136

JINKINS, RICHARD
and
PULLIAM, ALPHA

1 Jan 1835- Thomas King, C.C.O.
1 Jan 1835- W. Blankenship, J.P.
source: license- 1751-02/4-77
see also volume 3, page 145

HAYNES, ELI T.
and
HARBOUR, MARTHA

5 Jan 1835- Thomas King, C.C.O.
7 Jan 1835- D.L. Ballew(?), Elder,
            M.E. Church
source: license- 1751-02/3-66
see also volume 3, page 138

MITCHELL, JAMES
and
BONDS, LUCY

26 Jan 1835- Thomas King, C.C.O.
27(?) Jan 1835- Mathew W. Vandiver, M.G.
source: license- 1751-03/5-100
see also volume 3, page 141

CRIDER, JOHN
and
CRIDER, SOPHIA

4 Feb 1835- Thomas King, C.C.O.
8 Feb 1835- Thomas H. Murdock, J.P.
source: license- 1751-01/2-36
see also volume 3, page 146

CARTER, CHALES W.
and
HOOPER, ELIZABETH

5 Feb 1835- Thomas King, C.C.O.
5 Feb 1835- Benj. Loughridge, J.P.
source: license- 1751-01/2-25
see also volume 4, page 92

BARTON, DAVID(DANIEL?)
and
MITCHELL, WINNEY

5 Feb 1835- Thomas King, C.C.O.
5 Feb 1835- W'm Burroughs, J.P.
source: license- 1751-01/1-9
see also volume 3, page 146

BAKER, RUSSEL
and
PHILIPS, ARKADA

11 Feb 1835- Thomas King, C.C.O.
12 Feb 1835- Nelson Osbern, M.G.
source: license- 1751-01/1-8
see also volume 4, page 117

WALTERS, WILLIAM P.
and
BLACK, MARY B.

12 Feb 1835- Thomas King, C.C.O.
12 Feb 1835- W'm Burroughs, J.P.
source: license- 1751-04/8-156
see also volume 3, page 145

GARRISON, DAVID J.
and
MEADERS, NANCY

14 Feb 1835- Thomas King, C.C.O.
17 Feb 1835- David Garrison
source: license- 1751-02/3-54
see also volume 4, page 24

GARRETT, PENDLETON
and
HUTCHINS, FRANCIS

21 Feb 1835- Thomas King, C.C.O.
21 Feb 1835- W'm Burroughs, J.P.
source: license- 1751-02/3-54
see also volume 3, page 147

WRIGHT, WILLIAM C.
and
BRIDGES, DELILAH

14 Mar 1835- Thomas King, C.C.O.
17 Mar 1835- John B. Wade, M.G.
source: license- 1751-04/8-170
see also volume 3, page 148

RAMSEY, WADE H.
and
CRUMP, MRS. CLARY LILES

1 Apr 1835- Thomas King, C.C.O.
2 Apr 1835- Asa York, J.P.
source: license- 1751-03/6-122
see also volume 4, page 51

REED, JACOB P.
and
HAMMOND, TERRESA C.

1 Apr 1835- Thomas King, C.C.O.
2 Apr 1835- W. Magee, M.G.
source: license- 1751-03/6-123
see also volume 3, page 146

PERRY PATERICK
and
MEEKS, ELIZABETH

5 May 1835- Thomas King, C.C.O.
7 May 1835- W'm R. Wellborn, M.G.
source: license- 1751-03/5-113
see also volume 4, page 38

BELL, AARON
and
HARDIN, EVALINA

9 May 1835- Thomas King, C.C.O.
10 May 1835- John Burton, J.P.
source: license- 1751-01/1-10
see also volume 4, page 111

ENGLISH, HIRAM
and
MAULDLING, ELIZER

10 May 1835- Thomas King, C.C.O.
10 May 1835- John Catlett, J.P.
source: license- 1751-02/3-47
see also volume 4, page 115

BALDWIN, WILLIAM
and
WILKERSON, FANNY

12 May 1835- Thomas King, C.C.O.
12 May 1835- Benj'n Loughridge, J.P.
source: license- 1751-01/1-9

PARKS, OLIVER
and
FLEMING, MARTHA

15 May 1835- Thomas King, C.C.O.
15 May 1835- Harvy M. Mayes, J.P.
source: license- 1751-03/5-109
see also volume 4, page 115

MCDONALD, DAVID A.
and
QUAILES, HULDA

5 June 1835- Thomas King, C.C.O.
5 June 1835- L. Meeks, M.G.
source: license- 1751-02/4-90
see also volume 4, page 124

BARTON, WILLIAM E.
and
WALTERS, MARTHA ANN

6 June 1835- Thomas King, C.C.O.
21 June1835- Drury Hutchins
source: license- 1751-01/1-9
see also volume 4, page 107

BLAIR, JOHN
and
RICHIE, MARTHA

13 June 1835- Thomas King, C.C.O.
13 June 1835- John B. Word, J.P.
source: license- 1751-01/1-13
see also volume 4, page 112

ALLEN, CHARLES
and
WADE, LISA

24 June 1835- Thomas King, C.C.O.
24 June 1835- C. Addison, J.P.
source: license- 1751-01/1-4
see also volume 4, page 114

MITCHELL, JAMES C.
and
EDDINS, MARTHA A.

27 June 1835- Thomas King, C.C.O.
30 July 1835- Lewis Ballard, M.G.
source: license- 1751-03/5-100
see also volume 4, page 122

GORDEN, ALSTON
and
FLOOD, VIRGINIA

14 July 1835- Thomas King, C.C.O.
14 July 1835- S.D. Thomason, J.P.
source: license- 1751-02/3-58
see also volume 4, page 26

```
SCOTT, NIMROD                    28 July 1835- Thomas King, C.C.O.
  and                            29 July 1835- John A. Davis, M.G.
HAZE, NANCY                      source: license- 1751-03/6-130
                                 see also volume 4, page 116


BREWSTER, WILLIAM PINKNEY        6 Aug 1835- Thomas King, C.C.O.
  and                            6 Aug 1835- Asa York, J.P.
HIX, MRS. MEEKEY                 source: license- 1751-01/1-16
                                 see also volume 4, page 49


CARTER, JAMES S.                 18 Aug 1835- Thomas King, C.C.O.
  and                            18 Aug 1835- Benj. Laughridge, J.P.
MC ENTIRE, SUSANNAH              source: license- 1751-01/2-25
                                 see also volume 4, page 94


CLARK, DAVID                     26 Aug 1835- Thomas King, C.C.O.
  and                            27 Aug 1835- John B. Word, J.P.
DAVIS, NANCY T.                  source: license- 1751-01/2-32
                                 see also volume 4, page 115


HILL, WILLIAM R.                 1 Sept 1835- Thomas King, C.C.O.
  and                            2 Sept 1835- Josiah Murray, J.P.
SHERIDAN, NANCY                  source: licenses(2)- 1751-02/3-69
                                 see also volume 4, page 13


BURGESS, ELIAS M.                10 Sept 1835- Thomas King, C.C.O.
  and                            10 Sept 1835- W'm Burroughs, J.P.
MITCHELL, MARY                   source: license- 1751-01/1-19


WILKASON, W'M H.                 16 Sept 1835- Thomas King, C.C.O.
  and                            17 Sept 1835- S. Hymer, Min.
CHEEK, PLEASANT                  source: license- 1751-04/8-165
                                 see also volume 4, page 33, 34


KEY, THOMAS J.                   18 Sept 1835- Thomas King, C.C.O.
  and                            29 Sept 1835- McCarty Oliver, M.G.
LITTLE, MARTHA                   source: license- 1751-02/4-82
                                 see also volume 4, page 105


WILKINSON, ISAAC A.              20 Sept 1835- Thomas King, C.C.O.
  and                            20 Sept 1835- W'm Burroughs, J.P.
LEE, ELIZABETH                   source: license- 1751-04/8--165
                                 see also volume 4, page 123


ADAMS, JESSE                     24 Sept 1835- Thomas King, C.C.O.
  and                            24 Sept 1835- Daniel Mosley, J.P.
COLLYER, CHRISTIAN               source: license- 1751-01/1-2
                                 see also volume 4, page 113


MINYARD, WILLIAM                 26 Sept 1835- Thomas King, C.C.O.
  and                            27 Sept 1835- Solomon D. Thomason, J.P.
SMITH, SARAH                     source: license- 1751-03/5-100
                                 see also volume 4, page 8


CLARK, WILLIAM W.                27 Sept 1835- Thomas King, C.C.O.
  and                            14 Oct 1835- Daniel Mosley, J.P.
ADAMS, ELIZABETH                 source: license- 1751-01/2-32
                                 see also volume 4, page 112
```

PRUITT, JOHN W.
and
NEAL, SUSAN C.

28 Sept 1835- Thomas King, C.C.O.
1 Oct 1835- W.R. Welborn, M.G.
source: license- 1751-03/6-119
see also volume 4, page 124

FAGANS(?), J.Z.(?)
and
HADDEN(?), NANCY

8 Oct 1835- Thomas King, C.C.O.
8 Oct 1835- L. Meeks
source: license- 1751-02/3-48
see also volume 4, page 125

PATTERSON, ROBERT
and
STRANGE, ANN

11 Oct 1835- Thomas King, C.C.O.
11 Oct 1835- James L. Gillespie, J.P.
source: license- 1751-03/5-110
see also volume 4, page 110

PIERCE, WILLIAM
and
BRANAM, NANCY

11 Oct 1835- Thomas King, C.C.O.
11 Oct 1835- Dan'l Mosley, J.P.
source: license- 1751-03/6-115
see also volume 4, page 16

JONES, JOHN A.
and
FULGUM, PRICILLA

18 Oct 1835- Thomas King, C.C.O.
18 Oct 1835- Benj'n Laughridge, J.P.
source: license- 1751-02/4-78
see also volume 4, page 93

ASKEW, G.W.
and
WADE, LUCY

23 Oct 1835- Thomas King, C.C.O.
29 Oct 1835- Nelson Osbern, M.G.
source: license- 1751-01/1-6
see also volume 4, page 120

TURK, JOHN
and
LITTLE, MARY

24 Oct 1835- Thomas King, C.C.O.
27 Oct 1835- H.M. Mayes, J.P.
source: license- 1751-04/7-150
see also volume 4, page 7

MC JUNKIN, JOSEPH J.
and
COCKERHAM, MILLEY

30 Oct 1835- Thomas King, C.C.O.
3 Nov 1835- Noah Looney, J.I.C.
source: license- 1751-02/4-92
see also volume 4, page 120

HARBIN, WILLIAM
and
BOGGS, ELIZA JANE

1 Nov 1835- Thomas King, C.C.O.
1 Nov 1835- Noah Looney, J.I.C.
source: license- 1751-02/3-62
see also volume 4, page 116

STRANGE, JESSE
and
WILEY, MARY A.

17 Nov 1835- Thomas King, C.C.O.
19 Nov 1835- W'm R. Welborn, M.G.
source: volume 4, page 108

TOMPSON, ALFRED
and
HAYNES, HANNER

19 Nov 1835- Thomas King, C.C.O.
19 Nov 1835- Littleton Meeks, M.G.
source: license- 1751-04/7-148
see also volume 4, page 126

PAYNE, JACKSON C.
and
CARSON, MRS. LUCINDA

24 Nov 1835- Thomas King, C.C.O.
26 Nov 1835- Asa York, J.P.
source: license- 1751-03/5-111
see also volume 4, page 50,51

ADAMS, ISRAEL
and
DOBBS, MARTHA

1 Dec 1835- Thomas King, C.C.O.
1 Dec 1835- Lewis Ballard, M.G.
source: license- 1751-01/1-2

PRUET, PHILIP
and
THOMAS, MARY

7 Dec 1835- Thomas King, C.C.O.
7 Dec 1835- H.M. Mayes, J.P.
source: license- 1751-03/6-119
see also volume 4, page 27

BUSH, WILLIAM F.
and
JONES, HARRIETT B.

9 Dec 1835- Thomas King, C.C.O.
13 Dec 1835- W'm R. Wellborne, M.G.
source: license- 1751-01/1-20
see also volume 4, page 109

CARNES, WILLIAM
and
WRIGHT, HANNAH

12 Dec 1835- Thomas King, C.C.O.
20 Dec 1835- John B. Wade, M.G.
source: license- 1751-01/2-23
see also volume 4, page 126

DAVICE(? DAVID?), LITTLETON M.
and
WILLIAMS, MARY

13 Dec 1835- Thomas King, C.C.O.
13 Dec 1835- Benjamin Stonecypher, J.P.
source: license- 1751-01/2-40
see also volume 4, page 118

ESKEW, JOHN B.
and
MOLDER, ELIZABETH

14 Dec 1835- Thomas King, C.C.O.
17 Dec 1835- Levi Garrison, M.G.
source: license- 1751-02/3-47
see also volume 4, page 123

MINISH, RICHARD
and
MEDERS, MARTHA G.

16 Dec 1835- Thomas King, C.C.O.
17 Dec 1835- Henry David, M.G.
source: license- 1751-03/5-100
see also volume 4, page 110

HOSEY, BENNETT
and
WRIGHT, FRANCIS

17 Dec 1835- Thomas King, C.C.O.
17 Dec 1835- Robert Mitchell, J.P.
source: license- 1751-02/3-73
see also volume 4, page 116

MORRIS, THOMAS
and
TURMAN, MARY

19 Dec 1835- Thomas King, C.C.O.
20 Dec 1835- Alvan Dean, J.I.C.
source: license- 1751-03/5-102
see also volume 4, page 121

HAMILTON, WILLIAM B.
and
MCARTEY, ELIZABETH

26 Dec 1835- Thomas King, C.C.O.
5 Jan 1836- H.M. Mayes, J.P.
source: license- 1751-02/3-62
see also volume 4, page 12

JORDAN, JOHN
and
VILKEY, SYNTHA

29 Dec 1835- Thomas King, C.C.O.
4 Jan 1836- Job Bowers, J.P.
source: license- 1751-02/4-79
see also volume 4, page 114

STUBBS, JAMES F.
and
ADAMS, NANCY

5 Jan 1836- Thomas King, C.C.O.
6 Jan 1836- J. Allen, J.P.
source: license- 1751-04/7-144
see also volume 4, page 125

CALDWELL, WILLIAM W.
and
HARRISON, ELVIRA

7 Jan 1836- Thomas King, C.C.O.
7 Jan 1836- Humphrey Posey, M.G.
source: license- 1751-01/2-21
see also volume 4, page 122

BRYAN, ROBERT R.
and
SCULL, SUSAN

10 Jan 1836- Thomas King, C.C.O.
10 ... 1836- W'm Burroughs, J.P.
source: license- 1751-01/1-18
see also volume 4, page 122

SMITH, WILLIAM W.
and
CHATERCIAL(?), ELIZABET

17 Jan 1836- Thomas King, C.C.O.
17 Jan 1836- Benj'n Laughridge, J.P.
source: license- 1751-04/7-139
see also volume 4, page 92

PHILIPS, PASCHAL C.
and
WILKEY, MILISSA

20 Jan 1836- Thomas King, C.C.O.
22 Jan 1836- Ruben Thornton, M.G.
source: license- 1751-03/6-114
see also volume 4, page 110

WESTBROOK, MILTON
and
THOMASON, RACHEL

21 Jan 1836- Thomas King, C.C.O.
21 Jan 1836- Solomon D. Thomason, J.P.
source: license- 1751-04/8-160
see also volume 4, page 9

GILLESPIE, PATTERSON R.
and
MANGUM, RHODA

23 Jan 1836- Thomas King, C.C.O.
24 Jan 1836- W'm R. Wellborn, M.G.
source: license- 1751-02/3-56

PAYNE, JOHN C.
and
SHACKELFORD, LAWRY

24 Jan 1836- Thomas King , C.C.O.
24 Jan 1836- C. Addison, J.P.
source: license- 1751-03/5-112
see also volume 4, page 24

ALBRITTON, JAMES
and
BRYAN, NANCY

4 Feb 1836- Thomas King, C.C.O.
5 Feb 1836- W. Blankenship, J.P.
source: license- 1751-01/1-4
see also volume 4, page 125

FINCH, OSBERN
and
HOOPER, JOICY

7 Feb 1836- Thomas King, C.C.O.
7 Feb 1836- Benj. Loughridge, J.P.
source: license- 1751-02/3-48
see also volume 4, page 94

SHIRLEY, ABRAHAM
and
DOWNS, ELIZA

11 Feb 1836- Thomas King, C.C.O.
11 Feb 1836- W'm Burroughs, J.P.
source: license- 1751-04/7-134
see also volume 4, page 126

SMITH, JOSEPH N.
and
HOLLEY, MARTHA

16 Feb 1836- Thomas King, C.C.O.
16 Feb 1836- Christopher Addison, J.P.
source: license- 1751-04/7-138
see also volume 4, page 108

PATERSON, DUDLA R.
and
HUNT, SINTHEY

16 Feb 1836- Thomas King, C.C.O.
16 Feb 1836- Benj'n Laughridge, J.P.
source: license- 1751-03/5-110
see also volume 4, page 93,94

COLLINS, BENJAMIN
and
SMITH, SUSANAH

17 Feb 1836- Thomas King, C.C.O.
18 Feb 1836- John A. Davis, M.G.
source: license- 1751-01/2-34

THOMAS, MADISON H.
and
SHELTON, NANCY F.

18 Feb 1836- Thomas King, C.C.O.
28 Feb 1836- Harvey M. Mayes, J.P.
source: license- 1751-04/7-147
see also volume 4, page 18

PARKER, JOSEPH H.
and
HARRISON, ELIZABETH

20 Feb 1836- Thomas King, C.C.O.
3 Mar 1836- John B. Wade
source: license- 1751-03/5-108
see also volume 4, page 119

BOWEN, ANDREW W.
and
MC COLLOM, SARAH

2 Mar 1836- Thomas King, C.C.O.
10 Mar 1836- John Wilson, J.P.
source: license- 1751-01/1-14
see also volume 4, page 38

ECHOLS, SHAPLEIGH
and
SUMMERVILLE, SARAH

10 Mar 1836- Thomas King, C.C.O.
10 Mar 1836- Benj'n Laughridge, J.P.
source: license- 1751-02/3-46
see also volume 4, page 92,93

SMITH, WILLIAM
and
KING, LYDIA

22 Mar 1836- Thomas King, C.C.O.
22 Mar 1836- H.M. Mayes, J.P.
source: license- 1751-04/7-139
see also volume 4, page 27

ORRE, LEWIS
and
SLATON, LUCINDA

25 Mar 1836- Thomas King, C.C.O.
29 Mar 1836- H.M. Mayes, J.P.
source: license- 1751-03/5-107
see also volume 4, page 11

TONEY, WILLIAM C.
and
ANDREWS, JANE E.

30 Mar 1836- Thomas King, C.C.O.
30 Mar 1836- W'm R. Wellborn, M.G.
source: license- 1751-04/7-149
see also volume 4, page 123

HYDE, WILLIAM
and
MANLEY, NANCY

30 Mar 1836- Thomas King, C.C.O.
31 Mar 1836- Thomas H. Murdock, J.P.
source: license- 1751-02/3-74

HARBOUR, TALMAN
and
HARRISON, ADALINE

7 Apr 1836- Thomas King, C.C.O.
7 Apr 1836- Alvan Dean, J.I.C.
source: license- 1751-02/3-62
see also volume 4, page 119

WHITE, SAMUEL
and
SMITH, FA..TY

20 Apr 1836- Thomas King, C.C.O.
21 Apr 1836- Daniel Mosley, J.P.
source: license- 1751-04/8-162
see also volume 4, page 107

SEWEL, JAMES
and
BURGESS, CATHARINE

21 Apr 1836- Thomas King, C.C.O.
21 Apr 1836- Joseph McEntire
source: license- 1751-03/6-131
see also volume 4, page 23

BLANKENSHIP, BENJAMIN and POSEY, ABIGAL	23 Apr 1836-Thomas King, C.C.O. 24 Apr 1836- Noah Looney, J.I.C. source: license- 1751-01/1-13
HENDRICKS, JOHN C. and HOLBROOK, KATHARINE	15 May 1836- Thomas King, C.C.O. 21 Aug 1836- W'm R. Callen, J.P. source: license- 1751-02/3-67 see also volume 4, page 3
MARSHALL, STERLING and MABRY, NANCY	23 May 1836- Thomas King, C.C.O. 27(?) May 1836- Noah Looney, J.I.C. source: license- 1751-03/5-95 see also volume 4, page 121
STOVALL, GEORGE W. and GLENN, ELIZA P.W.	7 June 1836- Thomas King, C.C.O. 7 June 1836- Fred. D. Lowry source: license- 1751-04/7-143 see also volume 4, page 2
WHISONANT, HENRY and COLLENS, ARINDA	30 June 1836- Thomas King, C.C.O. 30 June 1836- Daniel Mosley, J.P. source: license- 1751-04/8-161 see also volume 4, page 25
CHILDS, WILLIAM and BAILEY, MARY	9 July 1836- Thomas King, C.C.O. 10 July 1836- John A. Davis, M.G. source: license- 1751-01/2-31 see also volume 4, page 18
ORR, ASA and HILL, LUCINDA	10 July 1836- Thomas King, C.C.O. 10 July 1836- Josiah Murray, J.P. source: license- 1751-03/5-107 see also volume 4, page 2
SMITH, JESSE and HOLCOMB, KATHARINE	13 Aug 1836- Thomas King, C.C.O. 14 Aug 1836- Daniel Mosley, J.P. source: license- 1751-04/7-137 see also volume 4, page 15
SCOTT, ARCHIBALD and HOLEBROOK, PARTHENY	24 Aug 1836- Thomas King, C.C.O. 25 Aug 1836- Noah Looney, J.I.C. source: license- 1751-03/6-130 see also volume 4, page 7,8
MAGEE, JOHN and WILLIAMS, RHODA C.	25 Aug 1836- Thomas King, C.C.O. 27 Aug 1836- S. Hymer, M.G. source: license- 1751-02/4-94 see also volume 4, page 41
ANDRES, CLEAVLAND and BENNET, MELISSA IRLE	28 Aug 1836- Thomas King, C.C.O. 28 Aug 1836- C. Addison, J.P. source: license- 1751-01/1-5 see also volume 4, page 19
WESTBROOK, WILEY F. and CHATHAM, MARY	1 Sept 1836- Thomas King, C.C.O. 1 Sept 1836- Alvan Dean, J.I.C. source: license- 1751-04/8-160 see also volume 4, page 14

NEESE, LEWIS and COKER, ADALINE	5 Sept 1836- Thomas King, C.C.O. 11 Sept 1836- Thomas H. Murdock, J.P. source: license- 1751-03/5-105 see also volume 4, page 3
PAYNE, WILLIAM and RAMSEY, ELIZABETH	6 Sept 1836- Thomas King, C.C.O. 16 Sept 1836- C. Addison, J.P. source: license- 1751-03/5-112 see also volume 4, page 9
LOWERY, JACKSON and HARRISON, CATHARINE	6 Sept 1836- Thomas King, C.C.O. 8 Sept 1836- John B. Wade source: license- 1751-02/4-88 see also volume 4, page 22
CARLAN, JOHN B. and ANDERS, ELIZER	14 Sept 1836- Thomas King, C.C.O. 14 Sept 1836- H.M. Mayes, J.P. source: license- 1751-01/2-22 see also volume 4, page 26
JOLLY, SAMUEL and TILLER, ANNY	2 Oct 1836- Thomas King, C.C.O. 2 Oct 1836- Isaac M. David, J.P. source: license- 1751-04/7-145 see also volume 4, page 25
THOMPSON, JONATHAN and BEAL, ELIZABETH	8 Oct 1836- Thomas King, C.C.O. 8 Oct 1836- Daniel Mosley, J.P. source: license- 1751-04/7-148 see also volume 4, page 72
FULLBRIGHT, DAVID and MILLER, ELIZABETH	10 Oct 1836- Thomas King, C.C.O. 10 Oct 1836- Noah Looney, J.I.C. source: license- 1751-02/3-52 see also volume 4, page 5,6
BRAWNER, WASHINGTON, M. and TOWNS, NANCY	11 Oct 1836- Thomas King, C.C.O. 13 Oct 1836- Ja's L. Gillespie, J.P. source: license- 1751-01/1-15 see also volume 4, page 17
HENDRICKS, WILLIAM and LEADFORD, MRS. CATHARINE	13 Oct 1836- Thomas King, C.C.O. 13 Oct 1836- S.D. Thomason, J.P. source: license- 1751-02/3-67 see also volume 4, page 8,9
EDWARDS, EDWARD H. and HOOPER, EMELIA	16 Oct 1836- Thomas King, C.C.O. 16 Oct 1836- Benj'n Loughridge, J.P. source: license- 1751-02/3-46
HAYNES, ELIJAH and CONE(?), POLLY	17 Oct 1836- Thomas King, C.C.O. 18 Oct 1836- Job Bowers, J.P. source: license- 1751-02/3-66 see also volume 4, page 20
OZMENT, JOSEPH R. and LATNER, ELIZABETH H.	24 Oct 1836- Thomas King, C.C.O. 26 Oct 1836- Job Bowers, J.P. source: license- 1751-03/5-107 see also volume 4, page 21

STOE, WILLIAM
and
SMITH, MARY

6 Nov 1836- Thomas King, C.C.O.
6 Nov 1836- Daniel Mosley, J.P.
source: license- 1751-03/7-142
see also volume 4, page 72

WHITE, JOSHUA M.
and
HIGGINS, ELIZABETH

6 Nov 1836- Thomas King, C.C.O.
6 Nov 1836- C. Addison, J.P.
source: license- 1751-04/6-162
see also volume 4, page 15

TAYLOR, SPENCER
and
HOLCOMB, CINTHEY

11 Nov 1836- Thomas King, C.C.O.
13 Nov 1836- John A. Davis, M.G.
source: license- 1751-04/7-145
see also volume 4, page 12,13

NEESE, ANDREW
and
SHELL, JANE

20 Nov 1836- Thomas King, C.C.O.
24 Nov 1836- Nelson Osbern, M.G.
source: license- 1751-03/5-105
see also volume 4, page 17

HOLBROOK, BERRIAN
and
COX, MARY J.

27 Nov 1836- Thomas King, C.C.O.
4 Dec 1836- Job Bowers, J.P.
source: license- 1751-02/3-71
see also volume 4, page 27

STOVALL, JOSEPH
and
BROWN, MARY

28 Nov 1836- Thomas King, C.C.O.
28 Nov 1836- Job Bowers, J.P.
source: license- 1751-04/7-143
see also volume 4, page 14,15

GOBER, GEORGE, JR.
and
HOLBROOK, MAHALA

1 Dec 1836- Thomas King, C.C.O.
1 Dec 1836- Alvan Dean, J.I.C.
source: license- 1751-02/3-57
see also volume 4, page 3,4

ALLEN, RICHARD, JR.
and
SLAYTON, MARTHA

2 Dec 1836- Thomas King, C.C.O.
6 Dec 1836- James L. Gillespie, J.P.
source: license- 1751-01/1-4
see also volume 4, page 11,12

SEWELL, MARION
and
DAVID, PILLINA W.

7 Dec 1836- Thomas King, C.C.O.
8 Dec 1836- Joseph McEntire, J.P.
source: license- 1751-03/6-132
see also volume 4, page 23

DEMSEY, BERRYMAN S.
and
ASCA, RUTHA

12 Dec 1836- Thomas King, C.C.O.
15 Dec 1836- John B. Wade
source: license- 1751-01/2-45
see also volume 4, page 24

KESLER, DAVID
and
SILLMAN, ARMINDA

13 Dec 1836- Thomas King, C.C.O.
15 Dec 1836- C. Addison, J.P.
source: license- 1751-02/4-82
see also volume 4, page 12

PAYN, OBADIAH C.
and
AYERS, ELIZA

13 Dec 1836- Thomas King, C.C.O.
13 Dec 1836- C. Addison, J.P.
source: license- 1751-03/5-112
see also volume 4, page 7

SEGARS, SAMUEL
and
PAYNE, HARRIETT

13 Dec 1836- Thomas King, C.C.O.
13 Dec 1836- C. Addison, J.P.
source: license- 1751-03/6-131
see also volume 4, page 6

NEAL, DAVID J.
and
DAVID, NANCY H.

13 Dec 1836- Thomas King, C.C.O.
15 Dec 1836- W'm R. Callen, J.P.
source: license- 1751-03/5-105
see also volume 4, page 16

CAMP, GILES A.
and
SMITH, SYNTHA

15 Dec 1836- Thomas King, C.C.O.
15 Dec 1836- Daniel Mosley, J.P.
source: license- 1751-01/2-21
see also volume 4, page 84

AYERS, JESSE P.
and
PAYNE, SARAH

19 Dec 1836- Thomas King, C.C.O.
19 Dec 1836- C. Addison, J.P.
source: license- 1751-01/1-7
see also volume 4, page 10

TURMAN, JAMES
and
SMITH, MARTHA

20 Dec 1836- Thomas King, C.C.O.
24 Dec 1836- Tho's H. Murdock, J.P.
source: license- 1751-04/7-150
see also volume 4, page 10

LITTLE, JOHN H.
and
HOLLEY, EMMILY M.

22 Dec 1836- Thomas King, C.C.O.
22 Dec 1836- Job Hammond, J.P.
source: license- 1751-02/4-86
see also volume 4, page 13

JENKINS, LEWIS
and
GARNER, SARAH

25 Dec 1836- Thomas King, C.C.O.
25 Dec 1836- Noah Looney, J.I.C.
source: license- 1751-02/4-77
see also volume 4, page 4

FULGIM, JESSE P.
and
JONES, ELIZABETH

29 Dec 1836- Thomas King, C.C.O.
29 Dec 1836- Benj'n Loughridge, J.P.
source: license- 1751-02/3-52
see also volume 4, page 93

WAY, WILLIAM
and
CHEEK, PRISCILLA

1 Jan 1837- Thomas King, C.C.O.
1 Jan 1837- Job Bowers, J.P.
source: license- 1751-04/8-158
see also volume 4, page 19

GARRISON, THOMAS S.
and
WICKHAM, MARIAH

12 Jan 1837- Thomas King, C.C.O.
12 Jan 1837- John Catlett, J.P.
source: license- 1751-02/3-54
see also volume 4, page 1

SEWELL, MARION
and
BLACK, SUSANNAH

26 Jan 1837- Thomas King, C.C.O.
2 Feb 1837- David Vaughan, J.P.
source: license- 1751-03/6-132
see also volume 4, page 15,16

HARRISON, TERREL L.
and
HOOPER, CLEMENTIN' C.

8 Feb 1837- Thomas King, C.C.O.
9 Feb 1837- Noah Looney, J.I.C.
source: license- 1751-02/3-64
see also volume 4, page 16,17

WRIGHT, JAMES W.
and
VERNER, ELIZABETH

18 Feb 1837- Thomas King, C.C.O.
9 Mar 1837- John B. Wade, M.G.
source: license- 1751-04/8-170
see also volume 4, page 13,14

TAYLOR, M.D.J.
and
THOMAS, ARMINDA C.

21 Feb 1837- Thomas King, C.C.O.
21 Feb 1837- W'm J. Parks, M.G.
source: license- 1751-04/7-145
see also volume 4, page 21

HARRIS, ALLEN
and
MANLY, POLLY

7 Mar 1837- Thomas King, C.C.O.
9 Mar 1837- Job Bowers, J.P.
source: license- 1751-02/3-63
see also volume 4, page 21

BLACKWELL, HENSLEY
and
SEWELL, ELIZABETH

9 Mar 1837- Thomas King, C.C.O.
9 Mar 1837- Noah Looney, J.I.C.
source: license- 1751-01/1-12
see also volume 4, page 1

HOLLEY, JAMES R.
and
BANKS, SARYANN E.

15 Mar 1837- Thomas King, C.C.O.
16 Mar 1837- Noah Looney, J.I.C.
source: license- 1751-02/3-72
see also volume 4, page 5

MURDOCK, CARY C.
and
DUNAHOO, MARY ANN

25 Mar 1837- Thomas King, C.C.O.
26 Mar 1837- John A. Davis, M.G.
source: license- 1751-03/5-104
see also volume 4, page 10,11

GOBER, ROBERT H.
and
NEAL, FRANCES

4 Apr 1837- Thomas King, C.C.O.
20 Apr 1837- H.P. Pitchford, G.M.
source: license- 1751-02/3-57
see also volume 4, page 2

STOVALL, HENREY F.
and
AKINS, CARLINE

15 Apr 1837- Thomas King, C.C.O.
16 Apr 1837- Thomas Farmer, J.I.C.
source: license- 1751-04/7-143
see also volume 4, page 10,11

STONECYPHER, JOSEPH
and
PATTERSON, ELIZABETH

20 Apr 1837- Thomas King, C.C.O.
20 Apr 1837- H.M. Patterson, J.P.
source: license- 1751-01/2-39
see also volume 4, page 33

BAILEY, THOMPSON
and
NORWOOD, DELILA

30 Apr 1837- Thomas King, C.C.O.
..........-..........
source: license- 1751-01/1-8
see also volume 4, page 6

CHATHAM, JOHN W.
and
LACY, RHODA

3 May 1837- Thomas King, C.C.O.
4 May 1837- Noah Looney, J.I.C.
source: license- 1751-01/2-29
see also volume 4, page 20

NEESE, LEWIS
and
ALBRITTON, ELIZABETH

24 May 1837- Thomas King, C.C.O.
25 May 1837- Thomas H. Murdock, J.P.
source: license- 1751-03/5-105
see also volume 4, page 4

PORTER, JOHN
and
ADAMS, MEHALA

31 May 1837- Thomas King, C.C.O.
1 June 1837- Milton P. Hudson, J.P.
source: license- 1751-03/6-117
see also volume 4, page 22

GOODE, GEORGE W.
and
BAKER, MARTHA

1 June 1837- Thomas King, C.C.O.
1 June 1837- James L. Gillespie, J.P.
source: license- 1751-02/3-58
see also volume 4, page 20

RISENOR, THOMAS
and
MALONE, EMILY

1 June 1837- Thomas King, C.C.O.
1 June 1837- W'm Burroughs, J.P.
source: license- 1751-03/6-125
see also volume 4, page 26

TOWNS, CAPEL
and
SHANON, AVIS W.

6 June 1837- Thomas King, C.C.O.
7 June 1837- Ja's L. Gillespie, J.P.
source: license- 1751-04/7-149
see also volume 4, page 18

GROOVER, MILTON
and
SOMERS, SUSAN

17 June 1837- Thomas King, C.C.O.
22 June 1837- Nelson Osbern, M.G.
source: license- 1751-02/3-60
see also volume 4, page 8

THOMASON, WILLIS B.
and
STONE, CATHARINE H.

18 July 1837- Thomas King, C.C.O.
19 July 1837- James Smith, J.P.
source: license- 1751-04/7-148
see also volume 4, page 5

NEESE, JACOB
and
SEWEL, MANERVE

25 July 1837- Thomas King, C.C.O.
27 July 1837- H. Pitchford, M.G.
source: license- 1751-03/5-105
see also volume 4, page 22

BALEY, AMSTARD
and
CLEAVLAND, ALPHA

27 July 1837- Thomas King, C.C.O.
27 July 1837- David Simmons, M.G.
source: license- 1751-01/1-9
see also volume 4, page 28

HAINS, JOHN W.
and
THORNTON, CATHARINE F.

1 Aug 1837- Thomas King, C.C.O.
1 Aug 1837- Littleton Meeks
source: license- 1751-02/3-61
see also volume 4, page 133

WALTERS, ANDREW J.M.
and
ROWLAND, MARTHA

6 Aug 1837- Thomas King, C.C.O.
6 Aug 1837- W'm Burroughs, J.P.
source: license- 1751-04/8-158
see also volume 4, page 45

QUAILS, ROBERT
and
HILL, MARY

10 Aug 1837- Thomas King, C.C.O.
10 Aug 1837- L. Meeks, M.G.
source: license- 1751-03/6-121
see also volume 4, page 38,39

JORDAN, JAMES, JR.
and
VICKRY, MARY

23 Aug 1837- Thomas King, C.C.O.
24 Aug 1837- Job Bowers, J.P.
source: license- 1751-02/4-79
see also volume 4, page 46

GORDEN, HENRY
and
MC FARRON, MARY

23 Aug 1837- Thomas King, C.C.O.
27 Aug 1837- Joseph McEntire, J.P.
source: license- 1751-02/3-58
see also volume 4, page 19

DAVIS, ROBERT
and
MANLY, LETTY

26 Aug 1837- Thomas King, C.C.O.
26 Aug 1837- John A. Davis, M.G.
source: license- 1751-01/2-41

JONES, PEYTON R.
and
SCULL, CATHARINE

5 Sept 1837- Thomas King, C.C.O.
5 Sept 1837- E.W. Morris, J.I.C.
source: license- 1751-02/4-78
see also volume 4, page 23

TONEY, CHARLES
and
MIZE, SARAH

12 Sept 1837- Thomas King, C.C.O.
13 Sept 1837- H.P. Pitchford, M.G.
source: license- 1751-04/7-149
see also volume 4, page 28

SHACKLEFORD, JAMES L.
and
PAYNE, ELVIRA

26 Sept 1837- Thomas King, C.C.O.
28 Sept 1837- M.W. Vandivier, M.G.
source: license- 1751-04/7-133
see also volume 4, page 28

ROGERS, JOHN
and
THOMAS, SARAH

15 Oct 1837- Thomas King, C.C.O.
16 Oct 1837- R.A.R. Neal, J.I.C.
source: license- 1751-03/6-126
see also volume 4, page 54

HUBBARD, LEWIS
and
VICKERY, DELILA

20 Oct 1837- Thomas King, C.C.O.
23 Oct 1837- Job Bowers, J.P.
source: license- 1751-02/3-74
see also volume 4, page 39

GOBER, JOHN
and
KING, ELIZABETH

22 Oct 1837- Thomas King, C.C.O.
22 Oct 1837- Ja's L. Gillespie, J.P.
source: license- 1751-02/3-57
see also volume 4, page 35

HARRISON, JOHN T.
and
BALDWIN, ANNA

27 Oct 1837- Thomas King, C.C.O.
2 Nov 1837- James R. Smith, M.G.
source: license- 1751-02/3-64
see also volume 4, page 37,38

SEEGERS, JOHN
and
CAUDLE, ELIZA T.

28 Oct 1837- Thomas King, C.C.O.
29 Oct 1837- Ja's L. Gillespie, J.P.
source: license- 1751-03/6-131
see also volume 4, page 42

STOVALL, WILLIAM
and
JORDAN, MARY ANN

9 Nov 1837- Thomas King, C.C.O.
9 Nov 1837- W'm Burroughs, J.P.
source: license- 1751-04/7-144
see also volume 4, page 34,35

WATERS, LEWIS
and
SCOTT, MARTHA

9 Nov 1837- Thomas King, C.C.O.
9 Nov 1837- Daniel Mosley, J.P.
source: license- 1751-04/8-158
see also volume 4, page 73,74

LITTEL, JAMES M.
and
HEADEN, LOUSANNA

11 Nov 1837- Thomas King, C.C.O.
11 Nov 1837- L. Meeks
source: license- 1751-02/4-86
see also volume 4, page 45

ALLEN, WILLIAM D.
and
RAMSEY, RHODA

12 Nov 1837- Thomas King, C.C.O.
12 Nov 1837- C. Addison, J.P.
source: license- 1751-01/1-4
see also volume 4, page 34

CLARK, JOHN T.
and
DEVALL, IMALY E.

13 Nov 1837- Thomas King, C.C.O.
14 Nov 1837- Philip Mathews, M.G.
source: license- 1751-01/2-32
see also volume 4, page 32

ALLEN, ALFRED S.
and
KNOX, NANCY

14 Nov 1837- Thomas King, C.C.O.
16 Nov 1837- H.P. Pitchford, M.G.
source: license- 1751-01/1-4
see also volume 4, page 31

SMITH, EZEKIEL
and
JONES, SARAH

16 Nov 1837, Thomas King, C.C.O.
19 Nov 1837- H.P. Pitchford, M.G.
source: license- 1751-04/7-136
see also volume 4, page 30

GOBER, WILLIAM J.
and
KING, SARAH

19 Nov 1837- Thomas King, C.C.O.
19 Nov 1837- James L. Gillespie, J.P.
source: license- 1751-02/3-57
see also volume 4, page 40

BURTON, ABRAHAM
and
CAWTHON, HARRIETT

23 Nov 1837- Thomas King, C.C.O.
23 Nov 1837- David Simmons, M.G.
source: license- 1751-01/1-20
see also volume 4, page 29

FLOOD, JOHN
and
WESTBROOK, VISA

25 Nov 1837- Thomas King, C.C.O.
26 Nov 1837- Robert Mitchell, J.P.
source: license- 1751-02/3-49
see also volume 4, page 31

BURTON, WILLIAM
and
BURTON, MARTHA

25 Nov 1837- Thomas King, C.C.O.
30 Nov 1837- David Simmons, M.G.
source: license- 1751-01/1-20
see also volume 4, page 29

GARNER, MARTIN G.
and
GOBER, ELIZABETH

27 Nov 1837- Thomas King, C.C.O.
5 Dec 1837- Ja's Hargrove, O.M.
source: license- 1751-02/3-53
see also volume 4, page 43,44

FOWLER, GEORGE D.
and
ADAMS, SARAH H.

28 Nov 1837- Thomas King, C.C.O.
30 Nov 1837- H.P. Pitchford, M.G.
source: license- 1751-02/3-50
see also volume 4, page 31,32

LAWRENCE, JOSEPH
and
RENOLDS, MILLY

30 Nov 1837- Thomas King, C.C.O.
30 Nov 1837- James L. Gillespie, J.P.
source: license- 1751-02/4-85
see also volume 4, page 40

PARKS, JOHNSON
and
TONEY, BELINDA

1 Dec 1837- Thomas King, C.C.O.
1 Dec 1837- James L. Gillespie, J.P.
source: license- 1751-03/5-109
see also volume 4, page 40

GARRISON, MARTIN
and
ARTHUR, TRIPHENAH

3 Dec 1837- Thomas King, C.C.O.
3 Dec 1837- James L. Gillespie, J.P.
source: license- 1751-02/3-54
see also volume 4, page 43

CHAMBERS, THOMAS
and
COKER, ELIZABETH

5 Dec 1837- Thomas King, C.C.O.
5 Dec 1837- Job Bowers, J.P.
source: license- 1751-01/2-27
see also volume 4, page 42

BLAIR, HUGH
and
STONE, JULEY

12 Dec 1837- Thomas King, C.C.O.
19 Dec 1837- Thomas Farmer, J.I.C.
source: license- 1751-01/1-13
see also volume 4, page 33

BOND, EPHRAIM M.
and
ROYSTON, HESTERANN

12 Dec 1837- Thomas King, C.C.O.
14 Dec 1837- Noah Looney, J.I.C.
source: license- 1751-01/1-13
see also volume 4, page 32,33

COX, MATTHEW
and
WHITE, REBECCA

21 Dec 1837- Thomas King, C.C.O.
21 Dec 1837- L. Meeks, M.G.
source: license- 1751-01/2-35
see also volume 4, page 41

KELLY, JOHN
and
BROWN, ELIZA

22 Dec 1837- Thomas King, C.C.O.
22 Dec 1837- John Wilson, J.P.
source: license- 1751-02/4-81
see also volume 4, page 30

VICKRY, ELIAS
and
HUBBARD, MORIAH

23 Dec 1837- Thomas King, C.C.O.
24 Dec 1837- Job Bowers, J.P.
source: license- 1751-04/8-154
see also volume 4, page 42

ALLEN, BENJAMIN
and
GLENN, ARMINDA

26 Dec 1837- Thomas King, C.C.O.
26 Dec 1837- J.C. Hooper, J.P.
source: license- 1751-01/1-4
see also volume 4, page 37

JOHNSON, JAMES R.
and
TINSLEY, DESA M.

28 Dec 1837- Thomas King, C.C.O.
28 Dec 1837- E.M. Burgess, J.P.
source: license- 1751-02/4-77
see also volume 4, page 44,45

MILLER, SAMUEL
and
CRUMP, PERMELIA

28 Dec 1837- Thomas King, C.C.O.
28 Dec 1837- C. Addison, J.P.
source: license- 1751-03/5-99
see also volume 4, page 35,36

SCOGGINS, WILLIAM A.
and
GASAWAY, LU NDY

5(?) Jan 1838- Thomas King, C.C.O.
7 Jan 1838- Noah Looney, J.I.C.
source: license- 1751-03/6-129
see also volume 4, page 28,29

RICE, NOAH
and
FORD, SARAI

6 Jan 1838- Thomas King, C.C.O.
7 Jan 1838- Henry David, M.G.
source: license- 1751-03/6-124
see also volume 4, page 53

BELLAMY, GILBERT F.
and
THOMASON, SAREPTAY

7 Jan 1838- Thomas King, C.C.O.
8 Jan 1838- E.W. Morris, J.I.C.
source: license- 1751-01/1-10
see also volume 4, page 34

GILLESPIE, MILTON W.
and
BRAWNER, MELISSA H.

9 Jan 1838- Thomas King, C.C.O.
9 Jan 1838- W'm R. Wellborn, V.D.M.
source: license- 1751-02/3-56
see also volume 4, page 36

ANDERS, JOHN
and
ABBIT, DEBA

10 Jan 1838- Thomas King, C.C.O.
11 Jan 1838- W'm R. Callen, J.P.
source: license- 1751-01/1-5
see also volume 4, page 78

ISBELL, ALLEN
and
SHACKLEFORD, CINTHA

10 Jan 1838- Thomas King, C.C.O.
11 Jan 1838- Drury Hutchins, M.G.
source: license- 1751-02/4-75
see also volume 4, page 45,46

WARD, ANDREW J.
and
CRUMP, MARYAN

16 Jan 1838- Thomas King, C.C.O.
16 Jan 1838- Asa Payne, J.P.
source: license- 1751-04/8-157
see also volume 4, page 37

BIRD, JOHN SHEW
and
ALLEN, MARY

18 Jan 1838- Thomas King, C.C.O.
18 Jan 1838- Noah Looney, J.I.C.
source: license- 1751-01/1-12
see also volume 4, page 41

CAPE, MARION
and
CHAMBERS, LENE

18 Jan 1838- Thomas King, C.C.O.
18 Jan 1838- Littleton Meeks, M.G.
source: license- 1751-01/2-22
see also volume 4, page 46

REMP(RENESS?,RENEP?), DANIEL
and
FULLER, NANCY P.

18 Jan 1838- Thomas King, C.C.O.
18 Jan 1838- Benj. Stonecypher, J.P.
source: license- 1751-03/6-124
see also volume 4, page 39

PRESLEY, DANIEL
and
ARMSTRONG, MATILDA

1 Feb 1838- Thomas King, C.C.O.
1 Feb 1838- Noah Looney, J.I.C.
source: license- 1751-03/6-118
see also volume 4, page 29,30

SMITH, JESSE M.
and
BURGESS, MARTHA

6 Feb 1838- Thomas King, C.C.O.
6 Feb 1838- E.M. Burgess, J.P.
source: license- 1751-04/7-137
see also volume 4, page 43

NEAL, ROBERT A.R.
and
KING, NANCY E.

13 Feb 1838- Thomas King, C.C.O.
13 Feb 1838- W'm J. Parks, M.G.
source: license- 1751-03/5-105
see also volume 4, page 35

95

PITCHFORD, WILLIAM G.   20 Feb 1838- Thomas King, C.C.O.
and   20 Feb 1838- H.P. Pitchford, M.G.
WEMMS, ELIZABETH   source: license- 1751-03/6-115
                               see also volume 4, page 36

MANLEY, RICHARD   24 Feb 1838- Thomas King, C.C.O.
and   24 Feb 1838- Tho's H. Murdock, J.P.
WILKENSON, MARGET   source: license- 1751-02/4-04
                              see also volume 4, page 48,49

DODD, WILEY   1 Mar 1838- Thomas King, C.C.O.
and   1 Mar 1838- L. Meeks, M.G.
CHALMERS, JANE   source: license- 1751-01/2-44
                              see also volume 4, page 47

WILLIS, FIELDEN T.   2 Mar 1838- Thomas King, C.C.O.
and   2 Mar 1838- Jno. M. Stovall, J.P.
RUMSEY, CLOIA   source: license- 1751-04/8-168
                              see also volume 4, page 79

BAKER, JOSHUA   6 Mar 1838- Thomas King, C.C.O.
and   6 Mar 1838- James L. Gillespie, J.P.
REED, CHARLOTTE A.   source: license- 1751-01/1-8
                              see also volume 4, page 87

HOOPER, WASHINGTON H.   6 Mar 1838- Thomas King, C.C.O.
and   6 Mar 1838- E.M. Burgess, J.P.
HANCOCK, FRANCES   source: license- 1751-02/3-72
                              see also volume 4, page 44

BRYAN, ROYAL   11 Mar 1838- Thomas King, C.C.O.
and   11 Mar 1838- W'm Burroughs, J.P.
HENNINGS, HARRIETT S.C.   source: volume 4, page 56,57

HAMPTON, WILLIAM   12 Mar 1838- Thomas King, C.C.O.
and   12 Mar 1838- James L. Gillespie, J.P.
KELLER, MILDRETT   source: license- 1751-02/3-62
                              see also volume 4, page 66

DYAR, GEORGE W.   12 Apr 1838- Thomas King, C.C.O.
and   15 Apr 1838- David Simmons, M.G.
BLACK, MARY   source: license- 1751-01/2-45
                              see also volume 4, page 69

TABOR, FRANCIS A.   12 Apr 1838- Thomas King, C.C.O.
and   12 Feb 1838- Robert Crump, J.I.C.
BELLE, MARTHA   source: license- 1751-04/7-145
                              see also volume 4, page 49

REEDER, ANDREW P.   28 Apr 1838- Thomas King, C.C.O.
and   10 May 1838- David Simmons, Pastor of
SWIFT, HARRIETT   the Baptist Church
                              source: license- 1751-03/6-124
                              see also volume 4, page 48

VAUGHAN, JOHN   11 May 1838- Thomas King, C.C.O.
and   13 May 1838- John A. Davis, M.G.
CHILDS, MIRICA   source: license- 1751-04/8-151
                              see also volume 4, page 47

CHAPPLEAR, JAMES H.   15 May 1838- Thomas King, C.C.O.
   and   15 May 1838- Jon. M. Stovall, J.P.
WHITWORTH, DORITHY   source: license- 1751-01/2-28
                             see also volume 4, page 56

JONES, JAMES D.   15 May 1838- Thomas King, C.C.O.
   and   20 May 1838- Reuben Thornton, M.G.
NEAL, MARTHA E.   source: license- 1751-02/4-78
                             see also volume 4, page 51

WHITWORTH, WILLIAM   20 May 1838- Thomas King, C.C.O.
   and   20 May 1838- E.M. Burgess, J.P.
CHAPPELEAR, ORPHA C.   source: license- 1751-04/8-164
                             see also volume 4, page 56

CASH, HOWARD   23 May 1838- Thomas King, C.C.O.
   and   23 May 1838- W'm Burroughs, J.P.
ADCOCK, LOUISA   source: license- 1751-01/2-25
                             see also volume 4, page 47,48

MASON, JAMES   23 May 1838- Thomas King, C.C.O.
   and   27 May 1838- W'm R. Wellborn, V.D.M.
RODGERS, FRANCIS   source: license- 1751-03/5-96
                             see also volume 4, page 54
                                                    • -

WILBANKS, MARSHAL   3 June 1838- Thomas King, C.C.O.
   and   3 June 1838- E.M. Burgess, J.P.
KELLY, MARYAN S.   source: license- 1751-04/8-165
                             see also volume 4, page 53

LANKFORD, JOHN   7 June 1838- Thomas King, C.C.O.
   and   7 June 1838- Jo'n M. Stovall, J.P.
DAVIS, CLARYANN   source: license- 1751-02/4-85
                             see also volume 4, page 55,56

POTTS, JONATHAN   2 July 1838- Thomas King, C.C.O.
   and   2 July 1838- Reuben Thornton, M.G.
GUNTER, TEMPY   source: license- 1751-03/6-117
                             see also volume 4, page 55

HUBBARD, FRANCIS   23 July 1838- Thomas King, C.C.O.
   and   25 July 1838- Job Bowers, J.P.
SANDERS, MARY   source: license- 1751-02/3-74
                             see also volume 4, page 51,52

SALMONS, OLIVER   27 Aug 1838- Thomas King, C.C.O.
   and   5 Sept 1838- Job Bowers, J.P.
CLEVELAND, ELIZABETH   source: license- 1751-04/7-140
                             see also volume 4, page 50

COKER, ALSEA T.   4 Sept 1838- Thomas King, C.C.O.
   and   9 Sept 1838- Tho's H. Murdock, J.P.
NEESE, MARY   source: license- 1751-01/2-33
                             see also volume 4, page 50

PERRY, THOMAS R.   5 Sept 1838- Thomas King, C.C.O.
   and   13 Sept 1838- Isaac M. David, J.P.
MEDDERS, JULY M.   source: license- 1751-03/5-113
                             see also volume 4, page 56

MC CALL, JAMES M.
and
BAIRD, MARY ANN

6 Sept 1838- Thomas King, C.C.O.
11 Sept 1838- J.C. Hooper, J.P.
source: license- 1751-02/4-89
see also volume 4, page 52

COLLY, JAMES(?)
and
FOWLER, ANNA

12 Sept 1838- Thomas King, C.C.O.
13 Sept 1838- W'm R. Callen, J.P.
source: license- 1751-01/2-34
see also volume 4, page 78

DAYMON, JOHN
and
NORWOOD, ADALINE

22(23?) Sept 1838- Thomas King, C.C.O.
23 Sept 1838- Noah Looney, J.I.C.
source: license- 1751-01/2-42
see also volume 4, page 52

FREEMAN, HUDSON
and
RILEY, EDNA

1 Oct 1838- Thomas King, C.C.O.
25 Oct 1838- Isaac M. David, J.P.
source: license- 1751-02/3-51
see also volume 4, page 54

SEWELL, LEVI
and
ADERHOLD, ELIZABETH

17 Oct 1838- Thomas King, C.C.O.
18 Oct 1838- Noah Looney, J.I.C.
source: license- 1751-03/6-132
see also volume 4, page 48

MC EVER, BRICE
and
JONES, SYNTHA H.

27 Oct 1838- Thomas King, C.C.O.
28 Oct 1838- Noah Looney, J.I.C.
source: license- 1751-02/4-91
see also volume 4, page 52,53

WARMACK, JOHNSON
and
BOND, SARAH

31 Oct 1838- Thomas King, C.C.O.
1 Nov 1838- John A. Davis, M.G.
source: license- 1751-04/8-157
see also volume 4, page 55

QUILLIAM, OSBORN P.
and
MEADOWS, GINSEY W.

13 Nov 1838- Thomas King, C.C.O.
15 Nov 1838- W'm J. Parks, M.G.
source: license- 1751-03/6-121
see also volume 4, page 55

PRATER, WILLIAM
and
BRYAN, DOBIA D.

24 Nov 1838- Thomas King, C.C.O.
24 Nov 1838- Littleton Meeks, M.G.
source: license- 1751-03/6-117
see also volume 4, page 75,76

VICKERY, THOMAS
and
PEEK, WINNEY

10 Dec 1838- Thomas King, C.C.O.
16 Dec 1838- Tho's H. Highsmith, J.P.,
            Elbert Co.
source: license- 1751-04/8-153
see also volume 4, page 77

MINYARD, JAMES
and
SMITH, MARY

13 Dec 1838- Thomas King, C.C.O.
13 Dec 1838- Noah Looney, J.I.C.
source: license- 1751-03/5-100
see also volume 4, page 53

JOHNSON, HENRY
and
DONAHOO, ELEANOR

14 Dec 1838- Thomas King, C.C.O.
16 Dec 1838- Tho's H. Murdock, J.P.
source: license- 1751-02/4-77
see also volume 4, page 80

CAMP, EDWARD M.
and
JINKINS, MASCY S.

19 Dec 1838- Thomas King, C.C.O.
19 Dec 1838- Daniel Mosley, J.P.
source: license- 1751-01/2-21
see also volume 4, page 75

MINYARD, JEPTHA
and
SCOGGINS, ELIZABETH

20 Dec 1838- Thomas King, C.C.O.
20 Dec 1838- Noah Looney, J.I.C.
source: license- 1751-03/5-100
see also volume 4, page 76,77

AARON, JOHN R.
and
MATHIS, MILLISSA

20 Dec 1838- Thomas King, C.C.O.
30 Dec 1838- Isaac M. David, J.P.
source: license- 1751-01/1-1
see also volume 4, page 88

LANGSTON, REUBEN J.
and
YARBROUGH, SARAH

24 Dec 1838- Thomas King, C.C.O.
27 Dec 1838- Noah Looney, J.I.C.
source: license- 1751-02/4-84
see also volume 4, page 63

SMITH, RUSSEL T.
and
CRIDER, SARAH

24 Dec 1838- Thomas King, C.C.O.
26 Dec 1838- Job Bowers, J.P.
source: license- 1751-04/7-139
see also volume 4, page 84,85

WILLIAMS, JAMES
and
CHANDLER, MARY

10 Jan 1839- Thomas King, C.C.O.
10 Jan 1839- David Simmons, M.G.
source: license- 1751-04/8-166
see also volume 4, page 90

HAMBEY, J.F.L.
and
BURGESS, SARAH

11 Jan 1839- Thomas King, C.C.O.
13 Jan 1839- Noah Looney, J.I.C.
source: license- 1751-02/3-62
see also volume 4, page 69

OVEBEY, JOSEPH (O.?)
and
WILLIAMS, JANE L.

15 Jan 1839- Thomas King, C.C.O.
17 Jan 1839- Nimrod Andrews, J.P.
source: license- 1751-03/5-107
see also volume 4, page 62

ENGLISH, WESLEY
and
SHAW, ELIZABETH

19 Jan 1839- Charles Baker, J.P. for
           Thomas King,(C.C.O.)
27 Jan 1839- Daniel Mosley, J.P.
source: license- 1751-02/3-47
see also volume 4, page 90

WALTERS, RUFUS K.
and
CAUTHEN, RODY

22 Jan 1839- Thomas King, C.C.O.
31 Jan 1839- D. Hutchins, M.W.G.
source: license- 1751-04/8-156
see also volume 4, page 66,67

CRUMP, MEMERY
and
BANKS, MARY

5 Feb 1839- Thomas King, C.C.O.
5 Feb 1839- Nelson Osbern, M.G.
source: license- 1751-01/2-39
see also volume 4, page 63

PAYNE, LITTLETON M.
and
GUEST, SARAH

16 Mar 1839- Thomas King, C.C.O.
20 Mar 1839- C. Addison, J.P.
source: license- 1751-03/5-112
see also volume 4, page 83,84

SEGERS, JAMES
and
JACKSON, LOVEDAY

29 Apr 1839- Thomas King, C.C.O.
30 Apr 1839- Reuben J. Langston, J.P.
source: license- 1751-03/6-131
see also volume 4, page 86

JACKSON, RANDAL L.
and
SMITH, ANSALINE

30 Apr 1839- "King" , C.C.O.
30 Apr 1839- Littleton Meeks, M.G.
source: license- 1751-02/4-76
see also volume 4, page 76

SMITH, MILES
and
JACKSON, MAHULDA

4 May 1839- Thomas King, C.C.O.
5 May 1839- Reuben Langston, J.P.
source: license- 1751-04/7-138
see also volume 4, page 83

INGRAM, JOHN
and
MC CARTER, MALINDA

16 May 1839- Thomas King, C.C.O.
16 May 1839- Robert Mitchell, J.P.
source: license- 1751-02/4-75
see also volume 4, page 62

PACK, JAMES
and
WILLIAMSON, ELISA

24 May 1839- Thomas King, C.C.O.
30 May 1839- Joel Haley, J.P.
source: license- 1751-03/5-108
see also volume 4, page 69

AYERS, JESSE F.
and
SUMMERS, MRS. TENA

4 June 1839- Thomas King, C.C.O.
4 June 1839- Asa York, J.P.
source: license- 1751-01/1-7
see also volume 4, page 64

NORWOOD, CROXTON
and
TONEY, LEWRANEY

16 June 1839- Thomas King, C.C.O.
16 June 1839- Littleton Meeks, M.G.
source: license- 1751-03/5-106
see also volume 4, page 75

BURGESS, JOHN M.
and
ASKEW, MARY

30 June 1839- Thomas King, C.C.O.
30 June 1839- W'm Burroughs, J.P.
source: license- 1751-01/1-19
see also volume 4, page 67

SWIFT, JOHNITHON D.
and
KNOX, FRANCIS S.

11 July 1839- Thomas King, C.C.O.
11 July 1839- John W. Lewis, Minister
source: license- 1751-04/7-144
see also volume 4, page 65

RIGHT, ROBERT
and
CALAHAM, SARAH

17 July 1839- Thomas King, C.C.O.
17 July 1839- Daniel Mosley, J.P.
source: license- 1751-04/8-170
see also volume 4, page 89,90

CROMER, HIRAM
and
GOBER, SARAH

23 July 1839- Thomas King, C.C.O.
25 July 1839- Joel Haley, J.P.
source: license- 1751-01/2-37
see also volume 4, page 68

ADERHOLD, JOHN H.
and
STUBS, CATHARINE H.

29 July 1839- Thomas King, C.C.O.
30 July 1839- R.A.R. Neal, J.I.C.
source: license- 1751-01/1-3
see also volume 4, page 81

WALTERS, JESSE
and
CAWTHON, RHODA

8(18?) Sept 1839- Thomas King, C.C.O.
18 Sept 1839- W'm Burroughs, J.P.
source: license- 1751-04/8-158
see also volume 4, page 77

GREEN, CALEB
and
BRYAN, NANCY

12 Sept 1839- Thomas King, C.C.O.
12 Sept 1839- Daniel Moseley, J.P.
source: license- 1751-02/3-59
see also volume 4, page 74

SCOGGINS, DAVID
and
HENSON, NANCY

16 Sept 1839- Thomas King, C.C.O.
17 Sept 1839- Asa York, J.P.
source: license- 1751-03/6-129
see also volume 4, page 81

WHISENANT, PETER
and
COLLENS, MARY

19 Sept 1839- Thomas King, C.C.O.
19 Sept 1839- Daniel Mosley, J.P.
source: license- 1751-04/8-161
see also volume 4, page 73

JUSTICE, STEPHEN
and
HOUSE, ELIZABETH

20 Sept 1839- Thomas King, C.C.O.
24 Sept 1839- William Turk, J.P.
source: license- 1751-02/4-79
see also volume 4, page 71

COLLINS, CHARLES O.
and
SMITH, MURSY

23 Sept 1839- Thomas King, C.C.O.
25 Sept 1839- Daniel Mosley, J.P.
source: license- 1751-01/2-34
see also volume 4, page 73

POOLE, JOHN M.
and
STOVALL, REBECCA W.

24 Sept 1839- Thomas King, C.C.O.
24 Sept 1839- R.A.R. Neal, J.I.C.
source: license- 1751-03/6-116
see also volume 4, page 64

CARNES, WELLES
and
HERRING, CLARISSA

26 Sept 1839- Thomas King, C.C.O.
29(27?) Sept 1839- John B. Wade, P.G.
source: license- 1751-01/2-23
see also volume 4, page 89

MANLEY, DANIEL J.(?)
and
BLACKWELL, NANCY

26 Sept 1839- Thomas King, C.C.O.
26 Sept 1839- Thomas H. Murdock, J.P.
source: license- 1751-02/4-94
see also volume 4, page 63

KING, THOMAS
and
EVIT, SARY

1 Oct 1839- Thomas King, C.C.O.
3 Oct 1839- Daniel Mosley, J.P.
source: license- 1751-02/4-83
see also volume 4, page 88

ATTAWAY, FREEMAN H.
and
WILLIAMS, SARAH H.

6 Oct 1839- Thomas King, C.C.O.
6 Oct 1839- Tho's H. Murdock, J.P.
source: license- 1751-01/1-6
see also volume 4, page 74

HUGHES, WILLIAM
and
JOLLY, MARY

19 Oct 1839- Thomas King, C.C.O.
20 Oct 1839- Jacob Strickland, J.P.
source: license- 1751-02/3-74
see also volume 4, page 68

SKIPER, WILIS and BARNETT, MARTHA	30 Oct 1839- Thomas King, C.C.O. 30 Oct 1839- Daniel Mosley, J.P. source: license- 1751-04/7-135 see also volume 4, page 65
WARTERS, LUTHER and CAMP, ANN	30 Oct 1839- Thomas King, C.C.O. 30 Oct 1839- David Vaughan, J.P. source: license- 1751-04/8-157 see also volume 4, page 82
BURGESS, REUBEN C. and CANE, REBECCA A.	4 Nov 1839- Thomas King, C.C.O. 7 Nov 1839- Pleasant F. Burgess, M.G. source: license- 1751-01/1-19 see also volume 4, page 83
CHEEK, ROWLAND B. and TURMAN, HULDA	8 Nov 1839- Thomas King, C.C.O. 10 Nov 1839- Thomas H. Murdock, J.P. source: license- 1751-01/2-30 see also volume 4, page 68
SMITH, DAVID and MC FARLAND, MARTHA	12 Nov 1839- Thomas King, C.C.O. 12 Nov 1839- Noah Looney, J.I.C. source: license- 1751-04/7-136 see also volume 4, page 80,81
REED, JOHN L. and KNOX, MRS. ELIZY	21 Nov 1839- Thomas King, C.C.O. 21 Nov 1839- John M. Stovall, J.P. source: license- 1751-03/6-123 see also volume 4, page 90,91
CHEEK, BURGESS, H. and MILNER, HANNAH	23 Nov 1839- Thomas King, C.C.O. 27 Nov 1839- Job Bowers, J.P. source: license- 1751-01/2-30 see also volume 4, page 82
RUCKER, ELLET and SANDERS, LIZBETH	27 Nov 1839- Thomas King, C.C.O. 27 Nov 1839- A.W. Bell, J.P. source: license- 1751-03/6-127 see also volume 4, page 80
BENNETT, WILLIAM and GLENN, CATHARINE	14 Dec 1839- Thomas King, C.C.O. 15 Dec 1839- Asa York, J.P. source: license- 1751-01/1-11 see also volume 4, page 79
NEWMAN, REUBEN and ABBOT, LUVINDA(?)	22 Dec 1839- Thomas King, C.C.O. 22 Dec 1839- Minyard Sanders, J.P. source: license- 1751-03/5-106 see also volume 4, page 85,86
PARKS, FLOYD and FLEMING, MALISA	25 Dec 1839- Thomas King, C.C.O. 25 Dec 1839- W'm J. Parks, M.G. source: license- 1751-03/5-109 see also volume 4, page 85
STRIBLING, THOMAS F. and REED, ELMIRA P.	26 Dec 1839- Thomas King, C.C.O. 26 Dec 1839- Noah Looney, J.I.C. source: license- 1751-04/7-144 see also volume 4, page 61

SMITH, JAMES A.
and
SIMS, MAHULDA

31 Dec 1839- Thomas King, C.C.O.
2 Jan 1840- Daniel Mosley, J.P.
source: license- 1751-04/7-137
see also volume 4, page 91

WRIGHT, BEDNEGO F.
and
JENKINS, MARY E.

8 Jan 1840 Thomas King, C.C.O.
9 Jan 1840 - Daniel Mosley, J.P.
source: license- 1751-04/8-170
see also volume 4, page 85

MITCHEL, DAVID W.
and
MORGAN, CISSIAH

11 Jan 1840- Thomas King, C.C.O.
14 Jan 1840- Daniel Mosley, J.P.
source: license- 1751-03/5-100
see also volume 4, page 91

SMITH, JESSE
and
ENGLISH, MARTHA

23 Jan 1840- Thomas King, C.C.O.
23 Jan 1840- Daniel Mosley, J.P.
source: license- 1751-04/7-137
see also volume 4, page 78,79

YOUNG, THOMAS M.
and
HACKETT, ELLEN C.

23 Jan 1840- Thomas King, C.C.O.
28 Jan 1840- A.W. Ross, M.G.
source: license- 1751-04/8-171
see also volume 4, page 71

HALEY, WILLIAM
and
CROMER, BARBARY

1 Feb 1840- Thomas King, C.C.O.
4 Feb 1840- Joel Haley, J.P.
source: license- 1751-02/3-61
see also volume 4, page 70

PARKS, FLEMING
and
ASTON(?), MARTHA H.

1 Feb 1840- Thomas King, C.C.O.
13 Feb 1840- Isaac M. David, J.P.
source: license- 1751-03/5-109
see also volume 4, page 58,59

NORVELL, HUGH
and
GLOVER, MARYANN

2 Feb 1840- Thomas King, C.C.O.
2 Feb 1840- Minyard Sanders, J.P.
source: license- 1751-03/5-106
see also volume 4, page 86

WESTBROOK, THOMPSON
and
CHATHAM, CYNTHA

6 Feb 1840- Thomas King, C.C.O.
6 Feb 1840- Green B. Holbrook, J.P.
source: license- 1751-04/8-160
see also volume 4, page 71,72

RAY, CHARLES M.
and
GLOVER, SARAH ANN

18 Feb 1840- Thomas King, C.C.O.
18 Feb 1840- Minyard Sanders, J.P.
source: license- 1751-03/6-123
see also volume 4, page 86

WADE, JOHN H.
and
RILEY, POLEY

21 Feb 1840- Thomas King, C.C.O.
23 Feb 1840- Isaac M. David, J.P.
source: license- 1751-04/8-155
see also volume 4, page 59

SEWELL, WOODSON
and
ADERHOLD, CATHARINE

27 Feb 1840- Thomas King, C.C.O.
27 Feb 1840- R.A.R. Neal, J.I.C.
source: license- 1751-03/6-132
see also volume 4, page 70

AYRES, HENRY D.
and
AYRES, CATHARINE A.

24 Apr 1840- Thomas King, C.C.O.
26 Apr 1840- William Ash, J.P.
source: license- 1751-01/1-7
see also volume 4, page 58

POOL, GEORGE W.
and
CROW, NANCY

23 Apr 1840- Thomas King, C.C.O.
26 Apr 1840- W'm B. Gillespie, J.P.
source: license- 1751-03/6-116
see also volume 4, page 66

BIARDEN, JOHN
and
HUDSON, CHARLOTTE M.

2 June 1840- Thomas King, C.C.O.
2 June 1840- Minyard Sanders, J.P.
source: license- 1751-01/1-12
see also volume 4, page 89

HIDE, WILLIAM
and
PARKS, MARY

11 June 1840- Thomas King, C.C.O.
11 June 1840- W'm B. Gillespie, J.P.
source: license- 1751-02/3-68
see also volume 4, page 82,83

HUBBARD(?), PARTIN(?)
and
CHEEK, ELIZABETH

11 July 1840- Thomas King, C.C.O.
12 July 1840- John A. Davis, M.G.
source: license- 1751-02/3-74
see also volume 4, page 65

HAWKINGS, JAMES M.
and
STRANGE, MARY A.

12 July 1840- Thomas King, C.C.O.
12 July 1840- W'm B. Gillespie, J.P.
source: license- 1751-02/3-65
see also volume 4, page 67

PATTERSON, TRYON
and
PREWETT, ELIZA

18 July 1840- Thomas King, C.C.O.
18 July 1840- Littleton Meeks
source: license- 1751-03/5-110
see also volume 4, page 87

MEEKS, NACEY D.
and
AYRES, ELIZABETH NARCISA ANN

18 Aug 1840- Thomas King, C.C.O.
23 Aug 1840- James Smith, J.P.
source: license- 1751-03/5-98
see also volume 4, page 143

MASSEY, EPHRAIM
and
SARTAIN, MARY ANN

12 Sept 1840- Thomas King, C.C.O.
1 Oct 1840- W'm B. Gillespie, J.P.
source: license- 1751-03/5-96
see also volume 4, page 60

RAY, ALFIRD
and
WALTERS, JULIAN

18 Sept 1840- Thomas King, C.C.O.
18 Sept 1840- W'm Burroughs, J.P.
source: license- 1751-03/6-123
see also volume 4, page 59

PHILIPS, THOMAS A.T.
and
SEWELL, ARMINDA

21 Sept 1840- Thomas King, C.C.O.
24 Sept 1840- Nelson Osbern, M.G.
source: license- 1751-03/6-114
see also volume 4, page 92

CARY, WILLIAM
and
PRESLEY, SARY CAROLINE

8 Oct 1840- Thomas King, C.C.O.
8 Oct 1840- Robert Mitchell, J.P.
source: license- 1751-01/2-25
see also volume 4, page 87,88

JONES, ALFRED S.   14 Oct 1840- Thomas King, C.C.O.
and   15 Oct 1840- Nelson Osbern, J.P.
REED, MARY   source: license- 1751-02/4-78
                                see also volume 4, page 62

HEMPHILL, JOHN   27 Oct 1840- Thomas King, C.C.O.
and   27 Oct 1840- Thomas H. Murdock, J.P.
BEARD, NANCY   source: license- 1751-02/3-67
                                see also volume 4, page 60

WILLIAMS, ROBERT P.   11 Nov 1840- Thomas King, C.C.O.
and   19 Nov 1840- A. Pennington, M.G.
VERNER, ESTER   source: license- 1751-04/8-167
                                see also volume 4, page 61

NEESE, ANDREW   11 Nov 1840- Thomas King, C.C.O.
and   13 Nov 1840- A. Pennington, M.G.
ADAMS, JULIA ANN   source: license- 1751-03/5-105
                                see also volume 4, page 60,61

DODD, JEREMIAH   30 Nov 1840- Thomas King, C.C.O.
and   2 Dec 1840- A.W. Bell, Esq'r(?)
WESTBROOKS, MARY M.   source: license- 1751-01/2-44
                                see also volume 4, page 139

MC CURDY, ARCHIBALD J.   3 Dec 1840- Thomas King, C.C.O.
and   3 Dec 1840- Littleton Meeks
SANDERS, ELIZABETH E.   source: license- 1751-02/4-90
                                see also volume 4, page 88,89

STRANGE, JAMES H.   4 Dec 1840- Thomas King, C.C.O.
and   15 Dec 1840- John B. Wade, M.G.
JONES, SUSAN ELIZABETH   source: volume 4, page 95

BOND, LINDSEY   14 Dec 1840 Thomas King, C.C.O.
and   19 Dec 1840- Job Bowers, J.P.
PRESLEY, ELIZA J.   source: volume 4, page 100

ROWLAND, JAMES W.   17 Dec 1840- Thomas King, C.C.O.
and   17 Dec 1840- W'm Burroughs, J.P.
WALTERS, POLLEY   source: license- 1751-03/6-126
                                see also volume 4, page 57

PULLIAM, HOMER VIRGIL   17 Dec 1840- Thomas King, C.C.O.
and   17 Dec 1840- R.A.R. Neal, J.I.C.
PATRICK, MARTHA BURNETTA   source: license- 1751-03/6-120
                                see also volume 4, page 58

BLACK, DAVID M.   19 Dec 1840(sic)- Thomas King, C.C.O.
and   20 Dec 1841(sic)- John A. Davis, M.G.
HOLCOMB, JANE   source: license- 1751-01/1-12
                                see also volume 4, page 106

PULLIAM, JOSEPH P.   22 Dec 1840- Thomas King, C.C.O.
and   22 Dec 1840- W'm Burroughs, J.P.
FULBRIGHT, MAY   source: license- 1751-03/6-120
                                see also volume 4, page 57

KEELING, MOSES M.
and
SCOTT, PHEBY

4 Jan 1841- Thomas King, C.C.O.
7 Jan 1841- Daniel Mosley, J.P.
source: volume 4, page 96

WELLS, WILLIAM
and
ROE, ANNY(?)

6 Jan 1841- Thomas King, C.C.O.
6 Jan 1841- Job Bowers, J.P.
source: volume 4, page 100

CAMP, JOHN W.
and
WATERS, MARYAN

7 Jan 1841- Thomas King, C.C.O.
7 Jan 1841- David Vaughan, J.P.
source: volume 4, page 102

BOND, WILLIS D.
and
PHILLIPS, HANAH M.

11 Jan 1841- Thomas King, C.C.O.
12 Jan 1841- Rob't Mitchell, J.P.
source: volume 4, page 101

WILEY, WESLEY C.
and
SANDERS, MARTHA

17 Jan 1841- Thomas King, C.C.O.
17 Jan 1841- W'm B. Gillespie, J.P.
source: volume 4, page 96

PRITCHETT, HENRY
and
SEGARS, ELIZABETH

21 Jan 1841- Thomas King, C.C.O.
21 Jan 1841- W'm B. Gillespie, J.P.
source: volume 4, page 97

STEFLE(STUFLE?), JAMES
and
VICKERY, RACHEL

27 Jan 1841- Thomas King, C.C.O.
28 Jan 1841- John B. Wade, M.G.
source: volume 4, page 95

GARNER, DERREL
and
POOL, MARTHA

2 Feb 1841- Thomas King, C.C.O.
4 Feb 1841- Nelson Osbern, M.G.
source: volume 4, page 104

SMITH, JAMES D.
and
SCALES, ELIZABETH

9 Feb 1841- Thomas King, C.C.O.
9 Feb 1841- Tho's H. Murdock, J.P.
source: volume 4, page 99

WADKINS, WILLIAM J.
and
ROBERTSON, ELIZA

21 Feb 1841- Thomas King, C.C.O.
21 Feb 1841- W'm B. Gillespie, J.P.
source: volume 4, page 99

BRYAN, BENJAMIN K.
and
JORDAN, ATLANTEH(?) O.

21 Feb 1841- Thomas King, C.C.O.
21 Feb 1841- W'm Burroughs, J.P.
source: license- 1751-01/1-18
see also volume 4, page 144

BRIDGES, WILSON
and
COKER, MARY

22 Feb 1841- Thomas King, C.C.O.
23 Feb 1841- Job Bowers, J.P.
source: volume 4, page 102

MOSLEY, ANDERSON
and
CRAWFORD, RACHAEL

25 Feb 1841- Thomas King, C.C.O.
25 Feb 1841- John H. Patrick, J.I.C.
source: volume 4, page 105

STEPHENS, STEPHEN B.
and
BELL, MARYAN

4 Mar 1841- Thomas King, C.C.O.
4 Mar 1841- Thomas Morris, J.I.C.
source: volume 4, page 104

MURDOCK, CHARLES C.
and
CRIDER, MARTHA S.

14 Mar 1841- Thomas King, C.C.O.
14 Mar 1841- John A. Davis, M.G.
source: volume 4, page 103

CHEEK, JAMES S.
and
ATTAWAY, FRANCES T.

14 Mar 1841- Thomas King, C.C.O.
14 Mar 1841- Job Bowers, J.P.
source: license- 1751-01/2-30
see also volume 4, page 145

GLOVER, JOSEPH P.
and
BROWN, JULIAN

16 Mar 1841- Thomas King, C.C.O.
18 Mar 1841- John B. McMillen, J.I.C.
source: volume 4, page 103

STARRITT, WILLIAM
and
GAINES, SUSANNAH

16 Mar 1841- Thomas King, C.C.O.
16 Mar 1841- Tho's H. Murdock, J.P.
source: volume 4, page 101

WHORTEN, JOSEPH
and
JEANS, LUCINDA

18 Mar 1841- Thomas King, C.C.O.
18 Mar 1841- W'm B. Gillespie, J.P.
source: volume 4, page 98

CARSON, JAMES
and
GARNER, MARY

25 Mar 1841- Thomas King, C.C.O.
25 Mar 1841- Green B. Holbrook, J.P.
source: volume 4, page 98

JACKSON, ADREW(?ADRENE?) J.
and
LAURENCE, NANCY

1 Apr 1841- Thomas King, C.C.O.
1 Apr 1841- Isaac B. Laurence, J.P.
source: license- 1751-02/4-76
see also volume 4, page 130

HUBBARD, TOLIVER W.
and
MC LANE, JEMIMA

4 Apr 1841(sic)- Thomas King, C.C.O.
2 Apr 1841(sic)- Green B. Holbrook, J.P.
source: volume 4, page 97

ACRE, A. LINTON
and
MARTIN, IRENA

18 Apr 1841- Thomas King, C.C.O.
18 App 1841- Isaac B. Laurence, J.P.
source: license- 1751-01/1-1
see also volume 4, page 133,134

CAUDLE, GREEN
and
POOL(E), FRANCES

9 May 1841- Thomas King, C.C.O.
9 May 1841- W'm B. Gillespie, J.P.
source: license- 1751-01/2-26
see also volume 4, page 137

HOOD, STEPHEN R.
and
SEWELL, JANE

23 May 1841- Thomas King, C.C.O.
23 May 1841- John P. Jolly, J.P.
source: license- 1751-02/3-72
see also volume 4, page 136

CASH, JOSEPH
and
HOOPER, MILLY

1 June 1841- Thomas King, C.C.O.
1 June 1841- John A. Davis, M.G.
source: license- 1751-01/2-25
see also volume 4, page 206

LOTHERDG, BENJAMIN
and
FULLBRIGHT, MARY

25 June 1841- Thomas King, C.C.O.
25 June 1841- Isaac B. Laurence, J.P.
source: license- 1751-02/4-88
see also volume 4, page 131

PAYNE(?), MADISON
and
HOBSON(?), MATILDA

27 June 1841- Thomas King, C.C.O.
27 June 1841- W'm Burroughs, J.P.
source: license- 1751-03/5-112
see also volume 4, page 134

BING, JAMES
and
FINCH, MARTHA

27 June 1841- Thomas King, C.C.O.
27 June 1841- Zechariah Thomas, J.P.
source: license- 1751-01/1-12
see also volume 4, page 138

CAPE, F.F.
and
MC DONALD, SISCILLY E.

13 July 1841- Thomas King, C.C.O.
13 July 1841- Isaac B. Laurence, J.P.
source: license- 1751-01/2-22
see also volume 4, page 131,132

WOOTEN, AARON
and
MANLEY, ELIZABETH

14 July 1841- Thomas King, C.C.O.
16 July 1841- Tho's H. Murdock, J.P.
source: license- 1751-04/8-169
see also volume 4, page 130

KNOX, EPHRAIM M.
and
ALLEN, MARY M.

2 Aug 1841- Thomas King, C.C.O.
3 Aug 1841- Eli Bennett, M.G.
source: license- 1751-02/4-83
see also volume 4, page 142

MANLY, WILLIAM G.
and
EATON, AMANDA L.

13 Aug 1841- Thomas King, C.C.O.
15 Aug 1841- John B. McMillion, J.I.C.
source: license- 1751-02/4-94
see also volume 4, page 135,136

WADE, HENRY H.
and
ROUSE, REBECCA

9 Sept 1841- Thomas King, C.C.O.
9 Sept 1841- Stephen R. Hood, J.P.
source: license- 1751-04/8-155
see also volume 4, page 144

PAYNE, FRANCIS M.
and
GULLY, ALPHA F.O.

19 Sept 1841- Thomas King, C.C.O.
19 Sept 1841- John B. Wade, P.G.
source: license- 1751-03/5-111
see also volume 4, page 142

LOVIN, SANDFORD
and
BAKER, MARIAH

21 Sept 1841- Thomas King, C.C.O.
21 Sept 1841- Isaac B. Laurence, J.P.
source: license- 1751-02/4-88
see also volume 4, page 151,152

PARKS, HENRY
and
BOZWELL, SARAH

29 Sept 1841- Thomas King, C.C.O.
30 Sept 1841- Sam'l Orr, J.P.
source: license- 1751-03/5-109
see also volume 4, page 150

CAUDELL, DAVID
and
CROW, SARAH

30 Sept 1841- Thomas King, C.C.O.
30 Sept 1841- Isaac B. Laurence, J.P.
source: license- 1751-01/2-26
see also volume 4, page 152

BLANKINSHIP, JOHN
and
PAYNE, CAROLINE

15 Oct 1841- Thomas King, C.C.O.
17 Oct 1841- Noah Looney, J.P.
source: license- 1751-01/1-13
see also volume 4, page 127

BELL, JOSEPH
and
MINYARD, EMALINE

18 Oct 1841- Thomas King, C.C.O.
20 Oct 1841- Noah Looney, J.P.
source: license- 1751-01/1-10
see also volume 4, page 135

BRYAN, MARTIN
and
JOHNSTON, MARTHA

22 Oct 1841- Thomas King, C.C.O.
22 Oct 1841- Zechariah Thomas, J.P.
source: license- 1751-01/1-18
see also volume 4, page 137-138

WATSON, WHITFIELD
and
MURRAY, SUSAN

22 Oct 1841- Thomas King, C.C.O.
22 Oct 1841- Isaac B. Laurence, J.P.
source: license- 1751-04/8-158
see also volume 4, page 151

MATHEWS, WILLIAM
and
NEAL, MRS. TABITHA

28 Oct 1841- Thomas King, C.C.O.
2 Nov 1841- Henry David, M.G.
source: license- 1751-03/5-96
see also volume 4, page 166

COOPER, TEMPLE F.
and
PATRICK, UNITY L.

3 Nov 1841- Thomas King, C.C.O.
3 Nov 1841- Noah Looney, J.P.
source: license- 1751-01/2-35
see also volume 4, page 141,142

HUDSON, MILTON P.
and
BOSWELL, ELIZABETH A.

8 Nov 1841- Thomas King, C.C.O.
11 Nov 1841- Pleasant F. Burgess, M.G.
source: license- 1751-02/3-74
see also volume 4, page 150,151

LANGSTON, ASA
and
MAYES, JANE

10 Nov 1841- Thomas King, C.C.O.
10 Nov 1841- Minyard Sanders, J.P.
source: license- 1751-02/4-84
see also volume 4, page 138,139

GOULDSBY, CHARLES
and
HAZY, SCIENTIFIC

18 Nov 1841- Thomas King, C.C.O.
18 Nov 1841- Noah Looney, J.P.
source: license- 1751-02/3-59
see also volume 4, page 137

STOVALL, JOHN
and
MILLNER, JUDITH

22 Nov 1841- Thomas King, C.C.O.
22 Nov 1841- Job Bowers, J.P.
source: license- 1751-04/7-143
see also volume 4, page 145

ALBRITTON, ISAAC G.
and
SUELL, JUDA L.

22 Nov 1841- Thomas King, C.C.O.
25 Nov 1841- W'm Burroughs, J.P.
source: license- 1751-01/1-4
see also volume 4, page 127,128

VICKORY, WILLIAM
and
CRAFT, SARAH ANN

9 Dec 1841- Thomas King, C.C.O.
9 Dec 1841- John B. Wade, P.G.
source: license- 1751-04/8-154
see also volume 4, page 128,129

SANDIDGE, COLUMBUS F.
and
PULLIAM, ELENOR E.

14 Dec 1841- Thomas King, C.C.O.
14 Dec 1841- Rob't A.R. Neal, J.I.C.
source: license- 1751-03/6-128
see also volume 4, page 149

VICKERY, THOMAS
and
HERING, MARY ELIZABETH

15 Dec 1841- Thomas King, C.C.O.
30 Dec 1841- Tho's W. Childers, J.P.
source: license- 1751-04/8-153
see also volume 4, page 148,149

MC DOOGLE, AARON
and
CARTER, SARY

15 Dec 1841- Thomas King, C.C.O.
9 Jan 1842- Tho's W. Childers, J.P.
source: license- 1751-02/4-90
see also volume 4, page 154,155

PAYNE, JESSE M.
and
SARTIN, MAHALA C.

20 Dec 1841- Thomas King, C.C.O.
23 Dec 1841- W'm B. Gillespie, J.P.
source: license- 1751-03/5-111
see also volume 4, page 153,154

DELPORT, JAMES
and
RILEY, ELIZABETH

21 Dec 1841- Thomas King, C.C.O.
22 Dec 1841- W'm T. Crow, J.P.
source: license- 1751-01/2-43
see also volume 4, page 140

WEEMS, PLEASANT
and
WESTBROOK, ISBELA

23 Dec 1841- Thomas King, C.C.O.
23 Dec 1841- R.A.R. Neal, J.I.C.
source: license- 1751-04/8-159
see also volume 4, page 129

MOSS, RICHARD K.
and
VARNER, SARAH C.

27 Dec 1841- Thomas King, C.C.O.
5 Jan 1842- John A. Davis, M.G.
source: license- 1751-03/5-103
see also volume 4, page 129,130

FREEMAN, JHONATHAN
and
RILEY, MORIER

30 Dec 1841- Thomas King, C.C.O.
30 Dec 1841- John P. Jolly, J.P.
source: license- 1751-02/3-51
see also volume 4, page 132,133

MASSY, JOHN W.
and
SMITH, AILSEY

1 Jan 1842- Thomas King, C.C.O.
2 Jan 1842- David Carson, M.G.
source: license- 1751-03/5-96
see also volume 4, page 140,141

GLYNN, ANDREW
and
BRIGES, MARY

2 Jan 1842- Thomas King, C.C.O.
2 Jan 1842- Noah Looney, J.P.
source: license- 1751-02/3-57
see also volume 4, page 139,140

SLATON, WILLIAM
and
MIZE, EDEA ADLINE(?)

6 Jan 1842- Thomas King, C.C.O.
6 Jan 1842- Samuel Orr, J.P.
source: license- 1751-04/7-135
see also volume 4, page 149

JONES, CHARLES WESLEY
and
KING, ELSEY CARLINE

12 Jan 1842- Thomas King, C.C.O.
12 Jan 1842- Samuel Orr, J.P.
source: license- 1751-02/4-78
see also volume 4, page 150

CHATHAM, THOMAS H.
and
JONES, MARTHA A.

17 Jan 1842- Thomas King, C.C.O.
19 Jan 1842- W'm B. Gillespie, J.P.
source: license- 1751-01/2-29
see also volume 4, page 152,153

SHOCKLEY, KIRNEY K. (?)
and
MANGUM, BETHENA

17 Jan 1842- Thomas King, C.C.O.
23 Jan 1842- W'm J. Parks, M.G.
source: license- 1751-04/7-134
see also volume 4, page 192,193

BING, GEORGE A.
and
HOOPER, MARY

27 Jan 1842- Thomas King, C.C.O.
27 Jan 1842- Zechariah Thomas, J.P.
source: license- 1751-01/1-12
see also volume 4, page 164

FARMER, WILLIAM H.
and
MC FARLAND, RHODA

1 Feb 1842- Thomas King, C.C.O.
6 Feb 1842- David Simmons, M.G.
source: license- 1751-02/3-48
see also volume 4, page 179,180

CLARK, FRANCIS
and
ROE, AMANDA

9 Feb 1842- Thomas King, C.C.O.
10 Feb 1842- Job Bowers, J.P.
source: license- 1751-01/2-32
see also volume 4, page 128

PARKS, OSBORN B.
and
LEGG, JOICY B.

9 Feb 1842- Thomas King, C.C.O.
10 Feb 1842- Ja's Hargrove, M.G.
source: license- 1751-03/5-109
see also volume 4, page 147

BAKER, WYLY
and
MASSY, HESTER

11 Feb 1842- Thomas King, C.C.O.
13 Feb 1842- Isaac B. Laurence, J.P.
source: license- 1751-01/1-8
see also volume 4, page 155

SEWELL, CHRISTOPHER
and
CASEY, MATILDA

24 Feb 1842- Thomas King, C.C.O.
24 Feb 1842- Nelson Osbern, M.G.
source: license- 1751-03/6-132
see also volume 4, page 143 ,144

TEMPLES, JOHN
and
BROWN, MARGARETT A.

5 Apr 1842- Thomas King, C.C.O.
5 Apr 1842- Noah Loony, J.P.
source: license- 1751-04/7-146
see also volume 4, page 147,148

MC DONALD, JAMES M.
and
MASSY, TREPHENA

5 Apr 1842- Thomas King, C.C.O.
5 Apr 1842- James F.W. Freeman, M.G.
source: license- 1751-02/4-90
see also volume 4, page 146,147

HUDSON, WILLIAM C.
and
HOODLOW, MARY ANN

8 Apr 1842- Thomas King, C.C.O.
8 Apr 1842- Job Bowers, J.P.
source: license- 1751-02/3-74
see also volume 4, page 148

HENLEY, JOHN S.
and
MC ENTIRE, MINERVA C.

13 Apr 1842- Thomas King, C.C.O.
14 Apr 1842- Jesse Childers, M.G.
source: license- 1751-02/3-68
see also volume 4, page 141

SPEARS, SIMS
and
MITCHELL, MARIAN

.... 1842- Thomas King, C.C.O.
17 Apr 1842- W'm T. Crow, J.P.
source: license- 1751-04/7-141
see also volume 4, page 166

ADRIAN, DAVID W.
and
MC KIE, MARY

9 May 1842- Thomas King, C.C.O.
9 May 1842- William Turk, J.I.C.
source: license- 1751-01/1-3
see also volume 4, page 154

VAUGHAN, JOSHUA
and
WILEY, MARY

4 June 1842- Thomas King, C.C.O.
4 June 1842- W'm Burroughs, J.P.
source: license- 1751-04/8-151
see also volume 4, page 147

WESTBROOK, STEPHEN F.
and
MOLDER, VINA

14 July 1842- Thomas King, C.C.O.
14 July 1842- Noah Looney, J.P.
source: license- 1751-04/8-160
see also volume 4, page 153

LEUALLAN, JOSEPH, Sr.
and
WATSON, ELIZABETH

14 July 1842- Thomas King, C.C.O.
14 July 1842- Isaac B. Laurence. J.P.
source: license- 1751-02/4-85
see also volume 4, page 164

WESTBROOKS, WASHINGTON
and
COOK, CYNTHIA

17 July 1842- Thomas King, C.C.O.
17 July 1842- S.R. Hood, J.P.
source: license- 1751-04/8-160
see also volume 4, page 159

MORGAN, JOHN
and
HAMILTON, PARRINA

30 July 1842- Thomas King, C.C.O.
30 July 1842- Samuel Orr, J.P.
source: license- 1751-03/5-102
see also volume 4, page 146

HAYNES, STEPHEN
and
STONE, ELIZABETH

29 Aug 1842- Thomas King, C.C.O.
30 Sept 1842- Job Bowers, J.P.
source: license- 1751-02/3-66
see also volume 4, page 145,146

SCALES, WILLIAM G.
and
CROW, FRANCESS J.A.

28 Sept 1842- Thomas King, C.C.O.
29 Sept 1842- Littleton Meeks, M.G.
source: license- 1751-03/6-129
see also volume 4, page 153

BOWERS, THOMAS W,
and
GLOVER, ALPHA A.

5 Oct 1842- Thomas King, C.C.O.
6 Oct 1842- Job Bowers, J.P.
source: license- 1751-01/1-14
see also volume 4, page 157

BURNS, WILLIAM B.
and
NEAL, ARMINDA E.

10 Oct 1842- Thomas King, C.C.O.
11 Oct 1842- R.A.R. Neal, J.I.C.
source: license- 1751-01/1-20
see also volume 4, page 163,164

BLACKWELL, RUSSEL
and
SMITH, ELIZABETH

20 Oct 1842- Thomas King, C.C.O.
20 Oct 1842- R.A.R. Neal, J.I.C.
source: license- 1751-01/1-12
see also volume 4, page 155,156

ADAMS, JOHN J.
and
REYNOLDS, SUSANNAH M.

25 Oct 1842- Thomas King, C.C.O.
27 Oct 1842- Eli Bennett, M.G.
source: license- 1751-01/1-2
see also volume 4, page 158

SMITH, JAMES
and
SMITH, MARY

31 Oct 1842- Thomas King, C.C.O.
31 Oct 1842- L.M. Mitchell, J.I.C.
source: license- 1751-04/7-137
see also volume 4, page 166,167

GARRISON, THOMAS W.
and
FORSYTH, MALINDA

7 Nov 1842- Thomas King, C.C.O.
8 Nov 1842- Thomas Mize(?), J.P.
source: license- 1751-02/3-54
see also volume 4, page 162

GRIFFIN, HARDY
and
EPPERSON, KATHARINE

15 Nov 1842- Thomas King, C.C.O.
15 Nov 1842- W'm B. Gillespie, J.P.
source: license- 1751-02/3-60
see also volume 4, page 168,169

AYERS, JEDEDIAH
and
O'BARR, ELIZA

17 Nov 1842- Thomas King, C.C.O.
17 Nov 1842- H.F. Chandler, J.P.
source: license- 1751-01/1-7
see also volume 4, page 187

HEATON, HENRY O.
and
ADERHOLD, MARY

19 Nov 1842- Thomas King, C.C.O.
20 Nov 1842- R.A.R. Neal, J.I.C.
source: license- 1751-02/3-67
see also volume 4, page 155

PATTERSON, SAMUEL
and
PATTERSON, FRANCES M.

22 Nov 1842- Thomas King, C.C.O.
22 Nov 1842- W'm B. Gillespie, J.P.
source: license- 1751-03/5-110
see also volume 4, page 158

FREEMAN, DAVID
and
PREWETT, MARY

5 Dec 1842 (sic)- Thomas King, C.C.O.
6 Jan 1042(sic)- John P. Jolly, J.P.
source: license- 1751-02/3-51
see also volume 4, page 133

WRIGHT, PRIER H.
and
GULLEY, ELIZA B.

14 Dec 1842- Thomas King, C.C.O.
15 Dec 1842- John B. Wade, P.G.
source: license- 1751-04/8-170
see also volume 4, page 156

PRICKETT, JOHN N.
and
CLARKSON, JANE

15 Dec 1842- Thomas King, C.C.O.
17 Jan 1843- Stephen R. Hood, J.P.
source: license- 1751-03/6-119
see also volume 4, page 158,159

HAYNES, JAMES
and
SMITH, JANE

21 Dec 1842- Thomas King, C.C.O.
28 Dec 1842- Henry Tyler, M.G.- Elbert Co.
source: license- 1751-02/3-66
see also volume 4, page 161

COX, CLEMENT W.
and
YEARGAN, NANCY

22 Dec 1842- Thomas King, C.C.O.
22 Dec 1842- Zechariah Thomas, J.P.
source: license- 1751-01/2-35
see also volume 4, page 161

EPPERSON, JAMES W.
and
BOSWELL, FATAMA

23 Dec 1842- Thomas King, C.C.O.
23 Dec 1842- W'm B. Gillespie, J.P.
source: license- 1751-02/3-47
see also volume 4, page 165

FINCH, THOMAS
and
RUMSEY, ELIZA B.

25 Dec 1842- Thomas King, C.C.O.
25 Dec 1842- Z. Thomas, J.P.
source: license- 1751-02/3-48
see also volume 4, page 162,163

MASSEY, JAMES
and
ACRE, MARYAN

25 Dec 1842- Thomas King, C.C.O.
25 Dec 1842- Isaac B. Laurence
source: license- 1751-03/5-96
see also volume 4, page 159,160

LOTHEREDGE, JACOB
and
CANADY, ELLEN

25 Dec 1842- Thomas King, C.C.O.
25 ... 1842- Isaac B. Laurence, J.P.
source: license- 1751-02/4-88
see also volume 4, page 160

COKER, ISAIAH
and
CRIDER, JANE

2 Jan 1843- Thomas King, C.C.O.
7 Jan 1843- John A. Davis, M.G.
source: license- 1751-01/2-33
see also volume 4, page 190

WORD, JAMES D.
and
THOMPSON, SARRY D.

8 Jan 1843- Thomas King, C.C.O.
8 Jan 1843- Isaac B. Laurence, J.P.
source: license- 1751-04/8-170
see also volume 4, page 160

YEARGAN, FRANKLIN
and
FINCH, CATHARINE

14 Jan 1843- Thomas King, C.C.O.
14 Jan 1843- Zechariah Thomas, J.P.
source: license- 1751-04/8-171
see also volume 4, page 191

YEARGAN, WILLIAM D.
and
WILLIAMS, SARAH

14 Jan 1843- Thomas King, C.C.O.
14 Jan 1843- Zechariah Thomas, J.P.
source: license- 1751-04/8-171
see also volume 4, page 190

SMITH, ISAM
and
BURGESS, LOUCINDA

15 Jan 1843- Thomas King, C.C.O.
15 Jan 1843- Zechariah Thomas, J.P.
source: license- 1751-04/7-136
see also volume 4, page 180

WILLIAMS, NATHAN R.
and
CUMMINS, MELINDA

18 Jan 1843- Thomas King, C.C.O.
19 Jan 1843- John B. McMillian, J.I.C.
source: license- 1751-04/8-167
see also volume 4, page 165

COBB, SAMUEL
and
PAYNE, ELIZABETH E.

9 Feb 1843- Thomas King, C.C.O.
9 Feb 1843- R.A.R. Neal, J.I.C.
source: license- 1751-01/2-33
see also volume 4, page 156,157

VAUGHAN, WILLIAM H.
and
PRESLAR, MELINDA

11 Feb 1843- Thomas King, C.C.O.
12 Feb 1843- W'm B. Gillespie, J.P.
source: license- 1751-04/8-151
see also volume 4, page 157,158

GARNER, WILLIAM
and
JACKSON, SUSANAH

12 Feb 1843- Thomas King, C.C.O.
14 Feb 1843- Zechariah Thomas, J.P.
source: license- 1751-02/3-53
see also volume 4, page 188,189

ORR, THOMAS
and
HAGEWOOD, HESTERAN

14 Feb 1843- Thomas King, C.C.O.
14 Feb 1843- W'm B. Gillespie, J.P.
source: license- 1751-03/5-107
see also volume 4, page 168

CAZEE, GEORGE
and
PREWIT, LEAH

14 Feb 1843- Thomas King, C.C.O.
15 Feb 1843- John B. Wade, P.G.
source: license- 1751-01/2-26
see also volume 4, page 163

TYLER, REUBEN L.
and
PARKER, SELEY M.

6 Mar 1843- Thomas King, C.C.O.
9 Mar 1843- Robert Stripling, M.G.
source: license- 1751-04/7-150
see also volume 4, page 178

JONES, ROBERT
and
DUNSON, NANCY

18 Mar 1843- Thomas King, C.C.O.
19 Mar 1843- Minyard Sanders, J.P.
source: license- 1751-02/4-78
see also volume 4, page 169

GARNER, WILLIAM
and
CANE, ANN

21 Mar 1843- Thomas King, C.C.O.
21 Mar 1843- Zechariah Thomas, J.P.
source: license- 1751-02/3-53
see also volume 4, page 186,187

WHITFIELD, WILLIAM B.
and
GORDEN, ELIZABETH

9 Apr 1843- Thomas King, C.C.O.
9 Apr 1843- Samuel Orr, J.P.
source: license- 1751-04/8-163
see also volume 4, page 172

PICKHAM, GEORGE L.
and
CAPE, SARRY M.

11 Apr 1843- Thomas King, C.C.O.
11 Apr 1843- Tho's Mize, J.P.
source: license- 1751-03/6-115
see also volume 4, page 165,166

CROMER, DAVID
and
FOWLER, SUSAN

12 Apr 1843- Thomas King, C.C.O.
13 Apr 1843- W'm T. Crow, J.P.
source: license- 1751-01/2-37
see also volume 4, page 167,168

FARRAR, LEWIS
and
SMITH, MARGARETT

16 Apr 1843- Thomas King, C.C.O.
16 Apr 1843- M.W. Vandiver, M.G.
source: license- 1751-02/3-48
see also volume 4, page 162

HOLSENBAKE, JEPTHA
and
SMITH, ELIZABETH J.

11 May 1843- Thomas King, C.C.O.
11 May 1843- W'm Burroughs, J.P.
source: license- 1751-02/3-72
see also volume 4, page 174

ELEXANDER, JAMES
and
CHEEK, PRISCILLAR

1 June 1843- Thomas King, C.C.O.
1 June 1843- John B. Wade, P.G.
source: license- 1751-01/1-4
see also volume 4, page 171

BAITS, WILLIAM
and
LACY, CANDACE

3 June 1843- Thomas King, C.C.O.
4 June 1843- Job Bowers, J.P.
source: license- 1751-01/1-8
see also volume 4, page 167

LORD, SIMEON
and
CHANDLER, ELIZABETH

1 July 1843- Thomas King, C.C.O.
4 July 1843- John P. Jolly, J.P.
source: license- 1751-02/4-88
see also volume 4, page 170

AYRES, MORGAN
and
WEST, LUCY A.

4 July 1843- Thomas King, C.C.O.
4 July 1843- Isaac B. Laurence, J.P.
source: license- 1751-01/1-7
see also volume 4, page 175, 176

HAYES, JACOB
and
HENDRICKS, NANCY

10 July 1843- Thomas King, C.C.O.
10 July 1843- Job Bowers, J.P.
source: license- 1751-02/3-66
see also volume 4, page 189

DAVIS, YOUNG
and
SWIFT, NANCY

18 July 1843- Thomas King, C.C.O.
20 July 1843- ?   Chambers
source: license- 1751-01/2-41
see also volume 4, page 169

MARSHALL, ANDREW J.
and
MOORE, MARY ANN A.

7 Aug 1843- Thomas King, C.C.O.
8 Aug 1843- Nelson Osbern, M.G.
source: license- 1751-03/5-95
see also volume 4, page 169, 170

GARNER, JAMES
and
BALDWIN, KEZIRE

13 Aug 1843- Thomas King, C.C.O.
13 Aug 1843- Z. Thomas, J.F.
source: license- 1751-02/3-53
see also volume 4, page 188,18

WEEMS, JACOB
and
STUBBS, MATILDA C.

14 Aug 1843- Thomas King, C.C.O.
15 Aug 1843- G.B. Holbrook, J.P.
source: license- 1751-04/8-159
see also volume 4, page 171

BURTON, PETER E.
and
CHANDLER, NANCY M.

16 Aug 1843- Thomas King, C.C.O.
17 Aug 1843- David Simmons, M.G.
source: license- 1751-01/1-20
see also volume 4, page 178

SEWEL, JOHN
and
PULLIAM, FRANCES

31 Aug 1843- Thomas King, C.C.O.
31 Aug 1843- David Vaughan, J.P.
source: license- 1751-03/6-131
see also volume 4, page 170

CHILDS, JOHN
and
WHITLOWE, NELLY

9 Sept 1843- Thomas King, C.C.O.
10 Sept 1843- John A. Davis, M.G.
source: license- 1751-01/2-31
see also volume 4, page 187

SISSON, THOMAS S.
and
BUSH, LOUISA A.

9 Sept 1843- Thomas King, C.C.O.
15 Sept 1843- R.A.R. Neal, J.I.C.
source: license- 1751-04/7-135
see also volume 4, page 170,171

PREWITT, WILLIAM H.
and
WADE, ANNA R.

12 Sept 1843- Thomas King, C.C.O.
13 Sept 1843- Henry Cosper, P.G.
source: license- 1751-03/6-118
see also volume 4, page 172

PREWITT, ELY
and
FREEMAN, PLINEY

21 Sept 1843- Thomas King, C.C.O.
21 Sept 1843- John Lacy, M.G.
source: license- 1751-03/6-118
see also volume 4, page 198

SMITH, JOHN R.
and
RANDAL, ELIZA

21 Sept 1843- Thomas King, C.C.O.
21 Sept 1843- Zechariah Thomas, J.P.
source: license- 1751-04/7-138
see also volume 4, page 189

FREEMAN, WESLEY
and
PREWETT, LIVINEY

21 Sept 1843- Thomas King, C.C.O.
21 Sept 1843- John Lacy, M.G.
source: license- 1751-02/3-51
see also volume 4, page 197

CASH, STEPHEN
and
CAUDELL, NANCY

11 Oct 1843- Thomas King, C.C.O.
12 Oct 1843- Isaac B. Laurence, J.P.
source: license- 1751-01/2-25
see also volume 4, page 176 and 191 ,192

VANDIVER, BENJAMIN P.
and
BROWN(?BRONEN?), MARY

19 Oct 1843- Thomas King, C.C.O.
19 Oct 1843- Jacob Burris, M.G.
source: license- 1751-04/8-151
see also volume 4, page 193,194

WHITFIELD, WILLIAM
and
CRUMP, HANNOR

26 Oct 1843- Thomas King, C.C.O.
29 Oct 1843- Isaac B. Laurence, J.P.
source: license- 1751-04/8-163
see also volume 4, page 188

CHATHAM, LEMUEL
and
BELLAMY, LOVEVINA

27 Oct 1843- Thomas King, C.C.O.
29 Oct 1843- David Carson, M.G.
source: license- 1751-01/2-29
see also volume 4, page 172,173

BAGWELL, JOHN J.M.
and
HARRISON, ADALINE B.

31 Oct 1843- Thomas King, C.C.O.
31 Oct 1843- Noah Looney, J.P.
source: license- 1751-01/1-8
see also volume 4, page 175

REED, JAMES
and
GAINS, ELIZABETH

4 Nov 1843- Thomas King, C.C.O.
4 Nov 1843- Nelson Osbern, M.G.
source: license- 1751-03/6-123
see also volume 4, page 178,179

WILLIAMS, JOHNSON
and
LANKFORD, MARY

9 Nov 1843- Thomas King, C.C.O.
9 Nov 1843- Zechariah Thomas, J.P.
source: license- 1751-04/8-166
see also volume 4, page 188

ASHLEY, THOMAS
and
WORD, DELILAH

9 Nov 1843- Thomas King, C.C.O.
12 Nov 1843- Ephraim C. Eddins, J.P.
source: license- 1751-01/1-6
see also volume 4, page 194

TYLER, ALLEN
and
COFFIN(?), NANCY

11 Nov 1843- Thomas King, C.C.O.
16 Nov 1843- Robert Stripling, M.G.
source: license- 1751-04/7-150
see also volume 4, page 174

HAWKINS, BENNET
and
MITCHELL, JULIAN

17 Nov 1843- Thomas King, C.C.O.
30 Nov 1843- R.A.R. Neal
source: license- 1751-02/3-65
see also volume 4, page 173,174

HOSEY, DANIEL
and
WEST, MILLA

6 Dec 1843- Thomas King, C.C.O.
7 Dec 1843- J.H. Mitchell, J.P.
source: license- 1751-02/3-73
see also volume 4, page 173

HILL, HARRY M.
and
WILLIAMS, MARTHA

7 Dec 1843- Thomas King, C.C.O.
7 Dec 1843- Isaac B. Laurence, J.P.
source: license- 1751-02/3-69
see also volume 4, page 186

SMITH, JOHN C.
and
SLAYTON, CARYAN

10 Dec 1843- Thomas King, C.C.O.
10 Dec 1843- Samuel Orr, J.P.
source: license- 1751-04/7-138
see also volume 4, page 185

SCALES, MERREL P.
and
BAIRD, NANCY C.

12 Dec 1843- Thomas King, C.C.O.
12 Dec 1843- J.W. Farmer, M.G.
source: license- 1751-03/6-129
see also volume 4, page 175

CLEVELAND, WILLIAM E.
and
CHANLER, ANNA

21 Dec 1843- Thomas King, C.C.O.
21 Dec 1843- John B. Wade, P.G.
source: license- 1751-01/2-32
see also volume 4, page 179

VAUGHAN, ASA
and
FULBRIGHT. SUSAN

21 Dec 1843- Thomas King, C.C.O.
21 Dec 1843- David Vaughan, J.P.
source: license- 1751-04/8-151
see also volume 4, page 186

CAUTHON, LARKAN
and
CARPENTER, MARTHA H.

24 Dec 1843- Thomas King, C.C.O.
24 Dec 1843- John B. Wade, P.G.
source: license- 1751-01/2-26
see also volume 4, page 181

GREEN, ROBERT
and
JOHNSON, SARAH

24 Dec 1843- Thomas King, C.C.O.
24 Dec 1843- Zachariah Thomas, J.P.
source: license- 1751-02/3-59
see also volume 4, page 184,185

HUDSON, JAMES P.
and
MALONE, SARAH JANE

30 Dec 1843- Thomas King, C.C.O.
31 Dec 1843- W'm Turk, J.I.C.
source: license- 1751-02/3-74
see also volume 4, page 180

ROLLEN, THOMAS
and
BRIDGES, SELAH

31 Dec 1843- Thomas King, C.C.O.
31 Dec 1843- John B. Wade, P.G.
source: license- 1751-03/6-126
see also volume 4, page 185,186

MOSS, WILLIAM W.
and
WADE, MARY E.

1 Jan 1844- Thomas King, C.C.O.
2 Jan 1844- Henry Cosper, M.G.
source: license- 1751-03/5-103
see also volume 4, page 177

WILLIAMS, JOHN E.
and
STEPHENSON, HANNAH

6 Jan 1844- Thomas King, C.C.O.
7 Jan 1844- Eppy White, J.P.- Elbert Co.
source: license- 1751-04/8-166
see also volume 4, page 184

ANDERSON, THOMAS F.
and
BALLEW, JANE

6 Jan 1844- Thomas King, C.C.O.
11 Jan 1844- Littleton Meeks, M.G.
source: license- 1751-01/1-5
see also volume 4, page 177,178

HUDSON, FRANCIS A.
and
RAMSEY, RACHEL C.

20 Jan 1844- Thomas King, C.C.O.
23 Jan 1844- William Turk, J.I.C.
source: license- 1751-02/3-74
see also volume 4, page 181

PRITCHETT, JESSE
and
LECROY, MARY

21 Jan 1844- Thomas King, C.C.O.
21 Jan 1844- Isaac B. Laurence, J.P.
source: license- 1751-03/6-119
see also volume 4, page 208

LARD, JESSE
and
MAC DOUGAL, MARY

4 Feb 1844- Thomas King, C.C.O.
4 Feb 1844- John B. Wade, P.G.
source: license- 1751-02/4-85
see also volume 4, page 182,183

HAYS, HENDRICKS
and
MOSS, METILDA

10 Feb 1844- Thomas King, C.C.O.
11 Feb 1844- John A. Davis, M.G.
source: license- 1751-02/3-66
see also volume 4, page 176

ALEXANDER, JOHN M.
and
GUNNELS, SARAH FRANCIS

14 Feb 1844- Thomas King, C.C.O.
15 Feb 1844- W'm J. Parks, M.G.
source: license- 1751-01/1-4
see also volume 4, page 194,195

SMITH, WILLIAM S.
and
MOSS, ALISABETH H.(?)

29 Feb 1844- Thomas King, C.C.O.
29 Feb 1844- John A. Davis, M.G.
source: license- 1751-04/7-139
see also volume 4, page 177

LITTLE, CRAWFORD H.
and
NEAL, LUCINDA C.

21 Mar 1844- Thomas King, C.C.O.
21 Mar 1844- Henry David, M.G.
source: license- 1751-02/4-86
see also volume 4, page 212

```
DAVIS, COOPPER B.              23 Mar 1844- Thomas King, C.C.O.
    and                        23 Mar 1844- John A. Davis, M.G.
THOMAS, SARY                   source: license- 1751-01/2-41
                              see also volume 4, page 205


SEGERS, MARTIN                24 Mar 1844- Thomas King, C.C.O.
    and                        24 Mar 1844- Isaac B. Laurence, J.P.
BRADLY, MARRY                 source: license- 1751-03/6-131
                              see also volume 4, page 212


WARE, ASA J.                  27 Mar 1844- Thomas King, C.C.O.
    and                        28 Mar 1844- S.R. Hood, J.P.
HOOD, MARY A.                 source: license- 1751-04/8-157
                              see also volume 4, page 183


WARD, EDWARD                   1 Apr 1844- Thomas King, C.C.O.
    and                        1 Apr 1844- Isaac B. Laurence, J.P.
SHERDEN, MANDA OLIVY          source: license- 1751-04/8-157
                              see also volume 4, page 200


MINIARD, THOMAS               4 Apr 1844- Thomas King, C.C.O.
    and                        4 Apr 1844- Job Bowers, J.P.
SMITH, PENELOPE               source: license- 1751-03/5-100
                              see also volume 4, page 196


DAVIS, VAN, JR.              11 Apr 1844- Thomas King, C.C.O.
    and                       11 Apr 1844- Zachariah Thomas, J.P.
THOMAS, SUSANNAH             source: volume 4, page 308


HOSEY, ISAAC                 20 Apr 1844- Thomas King, C.C.O.
    and                       21 Apr 1844- J.H. Mitchell, J.P.
HOODLOW, SARAH A.            source: license- 1751-02/3-73
                              see also volume 4, page 235


ANDERSON, THOMAS F.          25 Apr 1844- Thomas King, C.C.O.
    and                       25 Apr 1844- Sanford Vandiver, M.G.
BUSH, JOYSEY                 source: license- 1751-01/1-5
                              see also volume 4, page 182


GILLESPIE, JAMES L.           3 May 1844- Thomas King, C.C.O.
    and                        8 May 1844- John B. Chappell
MEDERS, MARY E.              source: license- 1751-02/3-56
                              see also volume 4, page 183


PARKS, GEORGE W.              8 May 1844- Thomas King, C.C.O.
    and                        9 May 1844- Green B. Holbrook, J.P.
COFFEE(?), MILLY             source: license- 1751-03/5-109
                              see also volume 4, page 181 ,182


CAIN, WILLIAM T.             12 May 1844- Thomas King, C.C.O.
    and                       12 May 1844- David Vaughan, J.P.
BAIRD, SOPHRONA             source: license- 1751-01/2-21
                              see also volume 4, page 206


NICKLELSON, DAVID M.         18 May 1844- Thomas King, C.C.O.
    and                       19 May 1844- W'm T. Crow, J.P.
FOWLER, LUCINDA C.           source: license- 1751-03/5-106
                              see also volume 4, page 192
```

MEADERS, JAMES L.
and
REYNOLDS, MARY E.

30 May 1844(sic)- Thomas King, C.C.O.
7 May 1844(sic)- John B. Chappell
source: license- 1751-03/5-98
see also volume 4, page 183,184

HAYES, SOLATHIEL
and
TUCKER, NANCY JANE

4 July 1844- Thomas King, C.C.O.
4 July 1844- Job Bowers, J.P.
source: license- 1751-02/3-66
see also volume 4, page 195

SMITH, JOHN C.
and
BRUCE, ELIZABETH

9 July 1844- Thomas King, C.C.O.
10 July 1844- Rob't A.R. Neal, J.I.C.
source: license- 1751-04/7-138
see also volume 4, page 191

MASEY, JAMES E.
and
AARON, NANCYAN

16 July 1844- Thomas King, C.C.O.
21 July 1844- John H. Payne, J.P.
source: license- 1751-03/5-96
see also volume 4, page 235

COCKER, IZAAH
and
CRIDER, ALISABETH

27 July 1844- Thomas King, C.C.O.
27 July 1844- John A. Davis, M.G.
source: license- 1751-01/2-33
see also volume 4, page 204

GORDAN, WILLIAM
and
FLOOD, CELESTHUS E.D.

1 Aug 1844- Thomas King, C.C.O.
1 Aug 1844- Samuel Orr, J.P.
source: license- 1751-02/3-58
see also volume 4, page 217

PULIAM, BENJAMIN R.
and
CORTHAN, ORPHA

7 Aug 1844- Thomas King, C.C.O.
7 Aug 1844- David Vaughan, J.P.
source: license- 1751-03/5-113
see also volume 4, page 196,197

TUCKER, ALFRED S.
and
HENDRICK, ELIZABETH

24 Aug 1844- Thomas King, C.C.O.
25 Aug 1844- Job Bowers, J.P.
source: license- 1751-04/7-149
see also volume 4, page 195

GABLE, HARMON
and
KEESLER, BETHA

11 Sept 1844- Thomas King, C.C.O.
15 Sept 1844- John H. Little, J.P.
source: license- 1751-02/3-53
see also volume 4, page 210

CAMERON, WILLIAM
and
PAIR, MARY

12 Sept 1844- Thomas King, C.C.O.
12 Sept 1844- John H. Little, J.P.
source: license- 1751-01/2-21
see also volume 4, page 210

SEGERS, ELIGA
and
MARTIN, CAROLINE

15 Sept 1844- Thomas King, C.C.O.
15 Sept 1844- Isaac B. Laurence, J.P.
source: license- 1751-03/6-131
see also volume 4, page 213

MARLIN(?MARTIN?), ANDREW
and
BROWN, POLLY

16 Sept 1844- Thomas King, C.C.O.
16 Sept 1844- Isaac B. Laurence, J.P.
source: license- 1751-03/5-95
see also volume 4, page 209

BATES, JAMES
and
CHEEK, PRISCILLA

19 Sept 1844- Thomas King, C.C.O.
19 Sept 1844- Job Bowers, J.P.
source: license- 1751-01/1-9
see also volume 4, page 196

HIX, JAMES
and
MARTIAL, NANCY E.

20 Sept 1844- Thomas King, C.C.O.
20 Sept 1844- R.A.R. Neal, J.I.C.
source: license- 1751-02/3-70
see also volume 4, page 193

BURTON, BENJAMIN H.
and
KING, JANE C.

21 Sept 1844- Thomas King, C.C.O.
22 Sept 1844- R.A.R. Neal, J.I.C.
source: license- 1751-01/1-20
see also volume 4, page 193

HARRISON, CLARK
and
GARNER, LUCINDA

17 Oct 1844- Thomas King, C.C.O.
17 Oct 1844- Zachariah Thomas, J.P.
source: volume 4, page 305

SMITH, WILLIAM G.
and
RANDAL, ELIZABETH

20 Oct 1844- Thomas King, C.C.O.
20 Oct 1844- Zachariah Thomas, J.P.
source: volume 4, page 305

BRYAN, PLEASANT
and
DENMAN, NANCY

23 Oct 1844- Thomas King, C.C.O.
24 Oct 1844- Zachariah Thomas, J.P.
source: volume 4, page 308

SHELL, LEMUEL
and
VERNER, SARAH JANE

24 Oct 1844- Thomas King, C.C.O.
24 Oct 1844- John B. Wade, P.G.
source: license- 1751-04/7-133
see also volume 4, page 201

BROWN, ROBERT
and
LAURENCE(?), RACHEL

27 Oct 1844- Thomas King, C.C.O.
27 Oct 1844- Isaac B. Laurence, J.P.
source: license- 1751-01/1-17
see also volume 4, page 211

PENDERGRASS, EDWIN
and
PARKS, ELIZABETH C.

4 Nov 1844- Thomas King, C.C.O.
7 Nov 1844- Ja's Hargrove, M.G.
source: license- 1751-03/5-113
see also volume 4, page 203

BRAWNER, JEFFERS H.
and
WILEY, ARMINDA C.

2 Dec 1844- Thomas King, C.C.O.
5 Dec 1844- John H. Payne, J.P.
source: license- 1751-01/1-15
see also volume 4, page 201

SCOTT, JOHN
and
MOSS, NANCY

3 Dec 1844- Thomas King, C.C.O.
7 Dec 1844- J.A. Davis, M.G.
source: license- 1751-03/6-130
see also volume 4, page 205

HOUSE, GEORGE C.
and
HOUSE, BALSORY

7 Dec 1844- Thomas King, C.C.O.
8 Dec 1844- Minyard Sanders, J.P.
source: license- 1751-02/3-73
see also volume 4, page 237

WILIS, B.F.
and
HOLEY, MARY E.

10 Dec 1844- Thomas King, C.C.O.
10 Dec 1844- J.W. Glenn, J.I.C.
source: license- 1751-04/8-168
see also volume 4, page 198

MURRAY, WILLIAM
and
WATSON, SUSAN

12 Dec 1844- Thomas King, C.C.O.
12 Dec 1844- Isaac B. Laurence, J.P.
source: license- 1751-03/5-104
see also volume 4, page 214

HARBOUR, ELI J.
and
STOVALL, MARY

12 Dec 1844- Thomas King, C.C.O.
15 Dec 1844- John H. Little, J.P.
source: volume 4, page 213

HIGGINS, HENRY
and
MIZE(? MAYES?), MARGARIT

13 Dec 1844- Thomas King, C.C.O.
13 Dec 1844- Nathan Williams, J.P.
source: license- 1751-02/3-69
see also volume 4, page 214

HOSEY, BENNET
and
BRITT, ELIZABETH

14 Dec 1844- Thomas King, C.C.O.
15 Dec 1844- William T. Crow, J.P.
source: license- 1751-02/3-73
see also volume 4, page 221

WILLIAMS, NATHAN
and
SCARBOROUGH, JANE

26 Dec 1844- Thomas King, C.C.O.
26 Dec 1844- Frederick Scarborough, J.P.
source: license- 1751-04/8-167
see also volume 4, page 219

TURK, WILLIAM H.
and
ASH, ISABELLA S.

27 Dec 1844- Thomas King, C.C.O.
2 Jan 1845- H.C. Carter, V.D.M.
source: license- 1751-04/7-150
see also volume 4, page 200

LEUALLEN, JACKSON
and
ACRE, LOUVISA

9 Jan 1845- Thomas King, C.C.O.
9 Jan 1845- Isaac B. Laurence, J.P.
source: license- 1751-02/4-85
see also volume 4, page 211

WILLBANKS, HENRY M.
and
SANDERS, SARAH C.

9 Jan 1845- Thomas King, C.C.O.
9 Jan 1845- Littleton Meeks
source: license- 1751-04/8-165
see also volume 4, page 207

WILLIAMS, ROBERT P.
and
VERNER, JANE

14 Jan 1845- Thomas King, C.C.O.
15 Jan 1845- John B. Wade, P.G.
source: license- 1751-04/8-167
see also volume 4, page 207

SMALLWOOD, MARK
and
HYDE, NANCY

16 Jan 1845- Thomas King, C.C.O.
16 Jan 1845- Isaac B. Laurence, J.P.
source: license- 1751-04/7-135
see also volume 4, page 199

CARNES, SAMUEL
and
LOONEY, MARY

19 Jan 1845- Thomas King, C.C.O.
19 Jan 1845- John B. Wade, P.G.
source: license- 1751-01/2-23
see also volume 4, page 202

AYERS, LEWIS
and
ADAMS, MARY

22 Jan 1845- Thomas King, C.C.O.
23 Jan 1845- Nelson Osbern, M.G.
source: license- 1751-01/1-7
see also volume 4, page 199,200

PRUITT, SAMUEL
and
BOND, MILLEY

24 Jan 1845- Thomas King, C.C.O.
31 Jan 1845- John Lacy, M.G.
source: license- 1751-03/6-119
see also volume 4, page 209

WILBANKS, JAMES
and
PRICKETT, JULIA A.

27 Jan 1845- Thomas King, C.C.O.
30 Jan 1845- Ja's Hargrove, M.G.
source: license- 1751-04/8-165
see also volume 4, page 197

BURROUGHS, HENRY F.
and
CORTHON, MARTHA

6 Feb 1845- Thomas King, C.C.O.
6 Feb 1845- David Vaughan, J.P.
source: license- 1751-01/1-20
see also volume 4, page 208

COKER, JACOB F.
and
NEESE, ELIZABETH

14 Feb 1845- Thomas King, C.C.O.
16 Feb 1845- David Vaughan, J.P.
source: license- 1751-01/2-33
see also volume 4, page 204

CARNES, RICHARD
and
LOONY, LEAH

15 Feb 1845- Thomas King, C.C.O.
16 Feb 1845- John B. Wade, P.G.
source: license- 1751-01/2-23
see also volume 4, page 203

BRAY, HILLMAN
and
PHILLIPS, NANCY

17 Feb 1845- Thomas King, C.C.O.
17 Feb 1845- A. Johnson, J.P.
source: license- 1751-01/1-15
see also volume 4, page 198,199

INGRAM, LITTLETON
and
CAMARINE, CATHARINE

22 Feb 1845- Thomas King, C.C.O.
22 Feb 1845- W'm T. Crow, J.P.
source: license- 1751-02/4-75
see also volume 4, page 223

VICKERY, WILLIAM
and
STIEFIL, SUSAN

25 Feb 1845- Thomas King, C.C.O.
27 Feb 1845- Job Bowers, J.P.
source: license- 1751-04/8-153
see also volume 4, page 222

SKELTON, JOEL
and
RUCKER, MARTHA E.

27 Feb 1845- Thomas King, C.C.O.
27 Feb 1845- John B. Wade, P.G.
source: license- 1751-04/7-135
see also volume 4, page 202

ANDREWS, DAVID
and
MC CARTER, SUSANNAH

7 Mar 1845- Thomas King, C.C.O.
9 Mar 1845- Minyard Sanders, J.P.
source: license- 1751-01/1-5
see also volume 4, page 222

ASKEA, SAMUEL
and
ALEXANDER, MARY ELIZABETH

1 Apr 1845- Thomas King, C.C.O.
1 Apr 1845- John B. Wade, P.G.
source: license- 1751-01/1-6

CHEEK, CHARLES W.
and
BATES, ADALINE

4 Apr 1845- Thomas King, C.C.O.
4 Apr 1845- Job Bowers, J.P.
source: license- 1751-01/2-30
see also volume 4, page 223

RIDLEY, JOAB
and
PORTER, ELIZABETH

8 May 1845(sic)- Thomas King, C.C.O.
8 May 1846(sic)- Minyard Sanders, J.P.
source: license- 1751-03/6-125
see also volume 4, page 241

PARKS, HARWELL H.
and
QUILLIAN, SARAH ANN

22 May 1845- Thomas King, C.C.O.
22 May 1845- Ja's Hargrove, M.G.
source: license- 1751-03/5-109
see also volume 4, page 219

JACKSON, TILLMAN
and
PRESLAR, LOUVISA

8 June 1845- Thomas King, C.C.O.
8 June 1845- Isaac B. Laurence, J.P.
source: license- 1751-02/4-76
see also volume 4, page 227

MITCHELL, JOHN L.
and
HOPGOOD, NANCY

26 June 1845- Thomas King, C.C.O.
26 June 1845- W'm T. Crow, J.P.
source: license- 1751-03/5-100
see also volume 4, page 224

BATES, BRYANT
and
CUMMINS, MARY

24 July 1845- Thomas King, C.C.O.
24 July 1845- Job Bowers, J.P.
source: license- 1751-01/1-9
see also volume 4, page 217

WHITE, THO'S JEFFERSON
and
SANDERS, MARTHA CAROLINE TALETHA

24 July 1845- Thomas King, C.C.O.
24 July 1845- Tho's Holland, Minister
source: license- 1751-04/8-162
see also volume 4, page 220

HOLBROOK, FRANKLIN M.
and
DAWSON, ELIZABETH

28 July 1845- Thomas King, C.C.O.
31 July 1845- John G. York, J.I.C.
source: license- 1751-02/3-71
see also volume 4, page 218

GOODSON, WILLIAM
and
ENGLISH, ELIZAR

3 Aug 1845- Thomas King, C.C.O.
3 Aug 1845- William J. Wiley, J.P.
source: license- 1751-02/3-58
see also volume 4, page 224

VAUGHAN, CALVIN
and
BURGESS, NANCY T.

6 Aug 1845- Thomas King, C.C.O.
6 Aug 1845- Levi Sewell, J.P.
source: license- 1751-04/8-151
see also volume 4, page 220

TIMMONS, WILLIAM B.
and
AYRES, JULYAN

7 Aug 1845- Thomas King, C.C.O.
7 Aug 1845- John B. Wade, P.G.
source: license- 1751-04/7-149
see also volume 4, page 221

SHALS, MADISON
and
FREEMAN, FRANKEY

27 Aug 1845- Thomas King, C.C.O.
28 Aug 1845- John P. Jolly, J.P.
source: license- 1751-04/7-133
see also volume 4, page 221

ORR, SAMUEL
and
MC DONALD, CHRISTIAN E.

28 Aug 1845- Thomas King, C.C.O.
28 Aug 1845- William Turk, J.I.C.
source: license- 1751-03/5-107
see also volume 4, page 222

MASSEY, JAMES
and
TOWNS, FRANCES H.(? A?)

9 Sept 1845- Thomas King, C.C.O.
9 Sept 1845- Alexander Langston, J.P.
source: license- 1751-03/5-96

WESTBROOK, B.A.
and
HOOD, ELIZABETH

11 Sept 1845- Thomas King, C.C.O.
14 Sept 1845- Isham H. Goss, M.G.
source: license- 1751-04/8-160
see also volume 4, page 219

REED, GEORGE L.
and
WATER (? WATS?), MARTHA ANN

18 Sept 1845- Thomas King, C.C.O.
18 Sept 1845- David Vaughan, J.P.
source: license- 1751-03/6-123
see also volume 4, page 218

RAY, GEORGE A.
and
MIZE, MINEVY CLEMENTIN

2 Oct 1845- Thomas King, C.C.O.
2 Oct 1845- Minyard Sanders, J.P.
source: license- 1751-03/6-122
see also volume 4, page 214,215

HOOPER, RICHARD L.
and
MARTIN, MARY

5 Oct 1845- Thomas King, C.C.O.
5 Oct 1845- Isaac B. Laurence, J.P.
source: license- 1751-02/3-72
see also volume 4, page 226

WATSON, JAMES V.
and
WORD, ELIZABETH

9 Oct 1845- Thomas King, C.C.O.
12 Oct 1845- John G. York, J.I.C.
source: license- 1751-04/8-158
see also volume 4, page 238

HARRIS, WALTER (? WALTON?)
and
STRICTLAND, CLARISSA

11 Oct 1845- Thomas King, C.C.O.
11 Oct 1845- John P. Jolley, J.P.
source: volume 4, page 236

AARON, JOHN F.
and
ASHWORTH, MARTHA

12 Oct 1845- Thomas King, C.C.O.
12 Oct 1845- William J. Wiley, J.P.
source: license- 1751-01/1-1
see also volume 4, page 216

MIZE, WILLIAM B.
and
HOUSE (? HERIN?), MATILDA AN

16 Oct 1845- Thomas King, C.C.O.
16 Oct 1845- Tho's Mize, J.P.
source: license- 1751-03/5-101
see also volume 4, page 249

BRYAN, THOMAS A.
and
DAVISON (DAWSON?), EMALINE

17 Oct 1845- Thomas King, C.C.O.
17 Oct 1845- Zachariah Thomas, J.P.
source: volume 4, page 306,307

SMITH, THOMAS A.
and
SLATON, KISEY(?)

19 Oct 1845- Thomas King, C.C.O.
19 Oct 1845- W'm J. Wiley, J.P.
source: license- 1751-04/7-139
see also volume 4, page 216

SHANNON, JOHN H.
and
ALEXANDER, CYNTHIA A

22 Oct 1845-.H. Burton, Ck.O.C.
23 Oct 1845- W'm J. Parks, M.G.
source: license- 1751-04/7-133

GOOSBY, JUDGE A.P.
and
ALFRED, CAMELY

28 Oct 1845- Thomas King, C.C.O.
28 Oct 1845- Isaac B. Laurence, J.P.
source: license- 1751-02/3-58
see also volume 4, page 225

BEAIRD, HENNERY W.
and
HICKS, MARTHA (MRS.?)

30 Oct 1845- Thomas King, C.C.O.
30 Oct 1845- Nelson Osbern, M.G.
source: license- 1751-01-1-10
see also volume 4, page 215

PRITCHETT, MICAGAH
and
BAKER, EMILY

2 Nov 1845- Thomas King, C.C.O.
2 Nov 1845- I.B. Laurence, J.P.
source: license- 1751-03/6-119
see also volume 4, page 226

KITCHENS, ORTHANILE
and
WHORTON, MARYAN

8 Nov 1845- Thomas King, C.C.O.
9 Nov 1845- James L. Gillespie, J.P.
source: license- 1751-02/4-83
see also volume 4, page 229,230

WEEMS, FREEMAN
and
SMITH, MARY

8 Nov 1845- Thomas King, C.C.O.
9 Nov 1845- Green B. Holbrook, J.P.
source: license- 1751-04/8-159

MILLER, JAMES M.
and
STRANGE, HARRIETT

10 Nov 1845- Thomas King, C.C.O.
13 Nov 1845- James L. Gillespie, J.P.
source: license - 1751-03/5-99
see also volume 4, page 230,231

WALTERS, JOHN
and
ADAMS, PALLAAN

12 Nov 1845- Thomas King, C.C.O.
13 Nov 1845- John B. Wade, P.G.
source: license- 1751-04/8-156
see also volume 4, page 231

SHERIDAN, DAVID W.
and
HILL, ADALINE

13 Nov. 1845- Thomas King, C.C.O.
13 Nov 1845- Allen T. Garrison, J.P.
source: license- 1751-04/7-134
see also volume 4, page 320

QUILLIAN, FLETCHER A.
and
MEADERS, MELISSA

13 Nov 1845- Thomas King, C.C.O.
13 Nov 1845- W'm J. Parks, M.G.
source: license- 1751-03/6-121

FITZPATRICK, JAMES P.
and
DAVID, NANCY J.

15 Nov 1845- Thomas King, C.C.O.
20 Nov 1845- Elba Collins, J.P.
source: license- 1751-02/3-49
see also volume 4, page 296

AARON, GEORGE W.
and
CHATHAM, ALMEDA

25 Nov 1845- Thomas King, C.C.O.
25 Nov 1845- John G. York, J.I.C.
source: license- 1751-01/1-1
see also volume 4, page 238

SHANNON, SAMUEL
and
DAILY, MARY

11 Dec 1845- Thomas King, C.C.O.
11 Dec 1845- James Quillian, O.M.
source: license- 1751-04/7-133
see also volume 4, page 274

VICKRY, JAMES
and
SCOTT, ELIZABETH CAROLINE

17 Dec 1845- Thomas King, C.C.O.
18 Dec 1845- John B. Wade, P.G.
source: license- 1751-04/8-154
see also volume 4, page 228

PEAK, JACKSON
and
BRIDGES, SARAH ANN

17 Dec 1845- Thomas King, C.C.O.
21 Dec 1845- John B. Wade, P.G.
source: license- 1751-03/5-113
see also volume 4, page 231

CAUDELL, DANIEL
and
BRADLEY, SALLY

31 Dec 1845- Thomas King, C.C.O.
31 Dec 1845- Isaac B. Laurence, J.P.
source: license- 1751-01/2-26
see also volume 4, page 228

CHANDLER, JABES E.
and
PORTER, ROADY

12 Jan 1846- Thomas King, C.C.O.
29 Jan 1836- John Lacy, M.G.
source: license- 1751-01/2-27
see also volume 4, page 240

MARSHEL, JAMES A.
and
HIX, ELIZABETH

24 Jan 1846- Thomas King, C.C.O.
25 Jan 1846- Isaac M. Aderhold, J.I.C.
source: license- 1751-03/5-95

CASH, HOWARD
and
MC CRACKEN, CINTHA

3 Feb 1846- Thomas King, C.C.O.
3 Feb 1846- I.B. Laurence, J.P.
source: license- 1751-01/2-25
see also volume 4, page 227

RAE, CHARLES W.G.
and
HALL, DICIA ELVIRA

1 Mar 1846- Thomas King, C.C.O.
1 Mar 1846- John B. Wade, M.G.
source: license- 1751-03/6-123
see also volume 4, page 225

HOLLAND, BENJAMIN
and
CAWTHON, ELIZABETH

19 Mar 1846- Thomas King, C.C.O.
19 Mar 1846- John B. Wade, M.G.
source: license- 1751-02/3-72
see also volume 4, page 230

RHOADS, WILLIAM S.
and
RAY, ELIZABETH SUSANNA

22 Mar 1846- Thomas King, C.C.O.
22 Mar 1846- Minyard Sanders, J.P.
source: license- 1751-03/6-124
see also volume 4, page 243

CHAPMAN, JAMES M.
and
HEADEN, OLLIA F.

24 Mar 1846- Thomas King, C.C.O.
25 Mar 1846- Jno. E. Rives, M.G.
source: license- 1751-01/2-28
see also volume 4, page 228

BREWER, HENRY M.
and
SPARKS, L..ZAAN A.

12 Apr 1846- Thomas King, C.C.O.
12 Apr 1846- John A. Davis, M.G.
source: license- 1751-01/1-16
see also volume 4, page 240

GUEST, RUSSEL
and
GINN, CHARLOTTE S.F.

29 Apr 1846- Thomas King, C.C.O.
30 Apr 1846- John G. York, J.I.C.
source: license- 1751-02/3-60
see also volume 4, page 269

CHEEK, LARKIN S.
and
AUSTIN, MARY JANE ELIZABETH

27 June 1846- D. Dumas, D.C.C.O.
28 June 1846- L.B. Underwood, J.P.
source: license- 1751-01/2-30
see also volume 4, page 261

SMITH, RUSSEL J.
and
ASHWORTH, CYNTHIA

11 July 1846- Thomas King, C.C.O.
12 July 1846- James L. Gillespie, J.P.
source: license- 1751-04/7-138
see also volume 4, page 252

GORDON, WILLIAM
and
TONEY, MANERVEY

18 July 1846- Thomas King, C.C.O.
21 July 1846- James L. Gillespie, J.P.
source: license- 1751-02/3-58
see also volume 4, page 244

PHILLIPS, FRANCIS
and
COKER, CHARLOTTE

7 Aug 1846- Thomas King, C.C.O.
7 Aug 1846- Job Bowers, J.P.
source: license- 1751-03/6-114
see also volume 4, page 245

DAVIS, THOMAS D.
and
MARTIN, ELIZA EMELINE

9 Aug 1846- Thomas King, C.C.O.
9 Aug 1846- Isaac B. Laurence, J.P.
source: license- 1751-01/2-41
see also volume 4, page 248

GULLY, RICHARD L.
and
WADE, NANCY E.P.

11 Aug 1846- Thomas King, C.C.O.
11 Aug 1846- Lem'l R. Wiggins, M.G.
source: license- 1751-02/3-60
see also volume 4, page 239

WESTBROOKS, SAMPSON L.
and
BLANKENSHIP, MARY

14 Aug 1846- Thomas King, C.C.O.
16 Aug 1846- Isaac M. Aderhold, J.I.C.
source: license- 1751-04/8-160
see also volume 4, page 244

OSBERN, HARRISON W.
and
PHILIPS, GATSY

17 Aug 1846- Thomas King, C.C.O.
18 Aug 1846- Lem'l R. Wiggins, M.G.
source: license- 1751-03/5-107

CHANDLER, CLEMENT Q.
and
ADAMS, MARY A.

19 Aug 1846- Thomas King, C.C.O.
19 Aug 1846- John H. Patrick, J.I.C.
source: license- 1751-01/2-27
see also volume 4, page 232

PARKS, WILLIAM
and
HAYNES, SARAH

3 Sept 1846- Thomas King, C.C.O.
3 Sept 1846- Job Bowers, J.P.
source: license- 1751-03/5-109
see also volume 4, page 233

SANDERS, LEWIS
and
EATON, SARAH

6 Sept 1846- Thomas King, C.C.O.
6 Sept 1846- John B. Wade, M.G.
source: license- 1751-03/6-128
see also volume 4, page 245

129

GARNER, GEORGE W.
and
GARNER, MARTHA

6 Sept 1846- Thomas King, C.C.O.
6 Sept 1846- Zechariah Thomas, J.P.
source: license- 1751-02/3-53
see also volume 4, page 236

BREWER, JACKSON M.
and
MOSS, MARY

10 Sept 1846- Thomas King, C.C.O.
10 Sept 1846- John A. Davis, M.G.
source: license- 1751-01/1-16
see also volume 4, page 243

CHEEK, JOHN M.D.
and
GLOVER, ELIZABETH ANN

14 Sept 1846- Thomas King, C.C.O.
14 Sept 1846- Job Bowers, J.P.
source: license- 1751-01/2-30
see also volume 4, page 233

STARE, LEWIS
and
LATTNER, SATYRY J.

19 Sept 1846- Thomas King, C.C.O.
20 Sept 1846- Nelson Osbern, M.G.
source: license- 1751-04/7-141
see also volume 4, page 229

ASH, WILLIAM M.
and
TURK, CYNTHA J.

21 Sept 1846- Thomas King, C.C.O.
22 Sept 1846- H.C. Carter, V.D.M.
source: license- 1751-01/1-6
see also volume 4, page 257

NEWTON, HENERY
and
ASH, JANE C.

21 Sept 1846- Thomas King, C.C.O.
22 Sept 1846- H.C. Carter, V.D.M.
source: license- 1751-03/5-106
see also volume 4, page 258

HUBBARD, ZENUS
and
VICKERY, SINTHY

22 Sept 1846- Thomas King, C.C.O.
24 Sept 1846- Job Bowers, J.P.
source: license- 1751-02/3-74
see also volume 4, page 234

PORTER, EPPERSON
and
CHANDLER, SARAH

27 Sept 1846- Thomas King, C.C.O.
27 Sept 1846- John P. Jolly, J.P.
source: license- 1751-03/6-117
see also volume 4, page 242

BRIDGES, WILLIAM J.
and
WILLIAMS, MATILDA

3 Oct 1846- Thomas King, C.C.O.
3 Oct 1846- Job Bowers, J.P.
source: license- 1751-01/1-16
see also volume 4, page 234

BRUCE, DAVID L.
and
CRAWFORD, MARTHA MINERVA

4 Oct 1846- Thomas King, C.C.O.
8 Oct 1846- David Simmons, M.G.
source: license- 1751-01/1-18
see also volume 4, page 242

WHISENANT, JOHN NICHOLAS
and
SMITH, SUSANNAH

5 Oct 1846- Thomas King, C.C.O.
6 Dec 1846- John A. Davis, M.G.
source: license- 1751-04/8-169
see also volume 4, page 256

WALTERS, ALFRED F.
and
CRAFT, POLLY

7 Oct 1846- Thomas King, C.C.O.
7 Oct 1846- Job Bowers, J.P.
source: license- 1751-04/8-158
see also volume 4, page 232

OSBERN, JOHN W.   7 Oct 1846- Thomas King, C.C.O.
    and   8 Oct 1846- J.W. Carroll, M.G.
LATTNER, REBECAH   source: license- 1751-03/5-107
                                see also volume 4, page 237

BEALL, WILLIAM J.   17 Oct 1846- Thomas King, C.C.O.
    and   18 Oct 1846- James L. Gillespie, J.P.
WESTBROOK, SARAH T.   source: license- 1751-01/1-10
                                see also volume 4, page 252

CHATHAM, ISHAM   29 Oct 1846- Thomas King, C.C.O.
    and   29 Oct 1846- John G. York, J.I.C.
PAYNE, RODY   source: license- 1751-01/2-29
                                see also volume 4, page 239

BARTON, DAVID O.   7 Nov 1846- Thomas King, C.C.O.
    and   8 Nov 1846- David Simmons, M.G.
PATRICK, AURA   source: license- 1751-01/1-9
                                see also volume 4, page 241

CHEEK, BURGESS H.   8 Nov 1846- Thomas King, C.C.O.
    and   8 Nov 1846- David Vaughan, J.P.
PRICHED, MARTHA   source: license- 1751-01/2-30
                                see also volume 4, page 250

WEBB, JOHN   8 Nov 1846- Thomas King, C.C.O.
    and   8 Nov 1846- J.E. McCarter, J.P.
ROYSTON, NANCY   source: license- 1751-04/8-159
                                see also volume 4, page 270

RICHARDSON, JAMES G.   8 Nov 1846- Thomas King, C.C.O.
    and   8 Nov 1846- J.B. Wade, M.G.
CARTER, MARY   source: license- 1751-03/6-124
                                see also volume 4, page 253

NORWOOD, ANDREW   15 Nov 1846- Thomas King, C.C.O.
    and   15 Nov 1846- John H. Patrick, J.I.C.
RICE, POLLY   source: license- 1751-03/5-106
                                see also volume 4, page 254

WESTBROOKS, BARTLEY A.   17 Nov 1846- Thomas King, C.C.O.
    and   17 Nov 1846- Minyard Sanders, J.P.
CARTER, CASSA   source: license- 1751-04/8-160
                                see also volume 4, page 251

HILL, BENJAMIN C.   4 Dec 1846- Thomas King, C.C.O.
    and   4 Dec 1846- Allen T. Garrison, J.P.
COOPER, ELENOR   source: license- 1751-02/3-69
                                see also volume 4, page 320

KEESLER, DANIEL   5 Dec 1846- Thomas King, C.C.O.
    and   6 Dec 1846- Richard Wheeler, J.P.-
KELLER, POLLY ANN   Habersham Co.
                                source: license- 1751-02/4-80
                                see also volume 4, page 250

HOLLEY, JOHN A.   7 Dec 1846- Thomas King, C.C.O.
    and   8 Dec 1846- John G. York, J.I.C.
FREEMAN, MARY F.   source: license- 1751-02/3-72
                                see also volume 4, page 249

BOSWELL, JOHN C.
and
HUTSON, SARY M.

8 Dec 1846- Thomas King, C.C.O.
8 Dec 1846- John P. Jolly, J.P.
source: license- 1751-01/1-14
see also volume 4, page 283

BRYAN, FRANCIS C.
and
SMITH, SARAH E.

18 Dec 1846- Thomas King, C.C.O.
24 Dec 1846- Tho's Pulliam, J.P.
source: license- 1751-01/1-18
see also volume 4, page 259

ARENDALL, NATHAN L.
and
ASH, JANE B.

19 Dec 1846- Thomas King, C.C.O.
20 Dec 1846- John H. Little, J.P.
source: license- 1751-01/1-6
see also volume 4, page 254

COCKRUM, ROBERT
and
SHERRIDEN(? SHIPPELLEN?),
MALINDA A.

26 Dec 1846- Thomas King, C.C.O.
31 Dec 1846- Tho's Mize, J.P.
source: license- 1751-01/2-33
see also volume 4, page 262

ATKINSON, MARION
and
CROW, PERLINA A.

1 Jan 1847- Thomas King, C.C.O.
3 Jan 1847- David Carson, M.G.
source: license- 1751-01/1-6
see also volume 4, page 251

CHAMBERS, JOHN E.
and
TURK, MARGARET M.

4 Jan 1847- Thomas King, C.C.O.
5 Jan 1847- W'm J. Parks, M.G.
source: license- 1751-01/2-27
see also volume 4, page 257

HUBBARD, LEVI
and
ROE, ELIZABETH

7 Jan 1847- Thomas King, C.C.O.
7 Jan 1847- Job Bowers, J.P.
source: license- 1751-02/3-74
see also volume 4, page 263

HOLLEY, WILLIAM
and
FREEMAN, SARAH G.P.

9 Jan 1847- Thomas King, C.C.O.
10 Jan 1847- W'm J. Parks, M.G.
source: license- 1751-02/3-72
see also volume 4, page 256

BLACK, JOHN G.A.
and
WALTERS, MARY ANN

10 Jan 1847- Thomas King, C.C.O.
11 Jan 1847- David Vaughan, J.P.
source: license- 1751-01/1-12
see also volume 4, page 260

NEAL, JOHN M.
and
MARTIN, CINTHA

11 Jan 1847- Thomas King, C.C.O.
14 Jan 1847- W'm J. Parks, M.G.
source: license- 1751-03/5-105
see also volume 4, page 259

FORD, JAMES
and
JONES, MARTHA A.

12 Jan 1847- Thomas King, C.C.O.
12 Jan 1847- John B. Wade, M.G.
source: license- 1751-02/3-49
see also volume 4, page 246

SEWELL, JAMES
and
BLACK, ELIZABETH

14 Jan 1847- Thomas King, C.C.O.
14 Jan 1847- David Vaughan, J.P.
source: license- 1751-03/6-132
see also volume 4, page 258

AYRES, JAMES C.
and
DAVIS, MARYANN

19 Jan 1847- Thomas King, C.C.O.
21 Jan 1847- John A. Davis, M.G.
source: license- 1751-01/1-7
see also volume 4, page 260

SMITH, BAILEY
and
RAMSEY, ELIZABETH

19 Jan 1847- Thomas King, C.C.O.
19 Jan 1847- John P. Jolly, J.P.
source: license- 1751-04/7-136
see also volume 4, page 282

WARD, LEVY
and
ALLRED, EMILY

21 Jan 1847- Thomas King, C.C.O.
21 Jan 1847- I.B. Laurence, J.P.
source: license- 1751-04/8-157
see also volume 4, page 262

PRATER, JAVERS
and
SHELTON, MARGARET

24 Jan 1847- Thomas King, C.C.O.
24 Jan 1847- Alfred Smith, J.P.
source: license- 1751-03/6-117
see also volume 4, page 255

PRATER, THOMAS
and
SHELTON, MARY

24 Jan 1847- Thomas King, C.C.O.
24 Jan 1847- Alfred Smith, J.P.
source: license- 1751-03/6-117
see also volume 4, page 255

CLEVELAND, THOMAS G.
and
SANDERS, REBECCA

25 Jan 1847- Thomas King, C.C.O.
28 Jan 1847- H.F. Chandler, J.P.
source: license- 1751-01/2-32
see also volume 4, page 295

MANGUM, GILFORD M.
and
SHOCKLY, ELIZABETH U.C.

26 Jan 1847- Thomas King, C.C.O.
26 Jan 1847- James L. Gillespie, J.P.
source: license- 1751-02/4-94
see also volume 4, page 247

LANKFORD, JOHN
and
HYDE(?), SARAH

29 Jan 1847- Thomas King, C.C.O.
29 Jan 1847- Zachariah Thomas, J.P.
source: volume 4, page 307

BOSWELL, JASPER N.
and
PRICKETT, SARAH M.

3 Feb 1847- Thomas King, C.C.O.
3 Feb 1847- John P. Jolly, J.P.
source: license- 1751-01/1-14
see also volume 4, page 283

DEBENPORT, MATTHEW
and
BEARDIN, CHARLOTTE M.

11 Feb 1847- Thomas King, C.C.O.
11 Feb 1847- John P. Jolly, J.P.
source: license- 1751-01/2-42
see also volume 4, page 281

AYRES, JERAMIAH W.
and
GUEST, LUCY

23 Feb 1847- Thomas King, C.C.O.
26 Feb 1847- Richard Wheeler, J.P.
source: license- 1751-01/1-7
see also volume 4, page 253

BOATRIGHT, DREWRY
and
THRASHER, MARY

13 Mar 1847- Thomas King, C.C.O.
13 Mar 1847- John B. Wade, M.G.
source: license- 1751-01/1-13
see also volume 4, page 247

THOMASON, ALEXANDER R.
and
ADDISON, JINCY L.

27 Mar 1847- Thomas King, C.C.O.
28 Mar 1847- John G. York, J.I.C.
source: license- 1751-04/7-148
see also volume 4, page 246

ATTAWAY, JAMES
and
BRUCE (? BRUER?), CATHARINE R.

9 May 1847- Thomas King, C.C.O.
20 June 1847- D. Simmons, M.G.
source: license- 1751-01/1-6
see also volume 4, page 263

SMITH, JAMES
and
MULINAX, ELIZABETH

12 June 1847- Thomas King, C.C.O.
13 June 1847- John H. Patrick, J.I.C.
source: license- 1751-04/7-137
see also volume 4, page 248

RAMSEY, SETH S.
and
MILLER, MARTHA M.

13 June 1847- Thomas King, C.C.O.
13 June 1847- James L. Gillespie, J.P.
source: license- 1751-03/6-122
see also volume 4, page 272

BURNS, JAMES H.
and
NEAL, LOUISA K.

1 July 1847- Thomas King, C.C.O.
1 July 1847- H.C. Carter, V.D.M.
source: license- 1751-01/1-20
see also volume 4, page 261

CHANDLER, DEVEREAX JARRET
and
VARNER, MARTHA HARRIET

29 July 1847- Thomas King, C.C.O.
29 July 1847- Osborn Garner, J.P.
source: license- 1751-01/2-27
see also volume 4, page 265

ROBIRDS(?), SYDNEY C.
and
JACKSON, ARMINDA

1 Aug 1847- Thomas King, C.C.O.
5 Aug 1847- Isaac B. Laurence, J.P.
source: license- 1751-03/6-123
see also volume 4, page 319

AYERS, WILLIS CLAY....
and
HOOPER, NANCY

14 Aug 1847- Thomas King, C.C.O.
19 Sept 1847- John G. York, J.I.C.
source : volume 5, page (2)&(3)

COLLYER, JOHN
and
MORRIS(?), ELIZABETH

24 Aug 1847- Thomas King, C.C.O.
25 Aug 1847- John H. Patrick, J.I.C.
source: license- 1751-01/2-34
see also volume 4, page 268

CAUDEL, GILBERD
and
ALLRED, CARLINE/CAROLINE

29 Aug 1847- Thomas King, C.C.O.
29 Aug 1847- Isaac B. Laurence, J.P.
source: license- 1751-01/2-26
see also volume 4, page 323

SMITH, JOHN W.
and
VICKERY, PATIENCE

31 Aug 1847- Thomas King, C.C.O.
31 Aug 1847- John B. Wade, M.G.
source: license- 1751-04/7-138
see also volume 4, page 271

WHITE, WILLIAM
and
WILLBANKS, LUCINDA A.

1 Sept 1847- Thomas King, C.C.O.
1 Sept 1847- Minyard Sanders, J.P.
source: license- 1751-04/8-162
see also volume 4, page 264

MACKIE, ANDREW H.
and
WESTBROOK, MARTHA M.

7 Sept 1847- Thomas King, C.C.O.
7 Sept 1847- James L. Gillespie, J.P.
source: license- 1751-02/4-92
see also volume 4, page 271

FLEMING, MATTHEW L.
and
HIX, CYNTHIA

9 Sept 1847- Thomas King, C.C.O.
9 Sept 1847- J.H. Aderhold, J.P.
source: license- 1751-02/3-49
see also volume 4, page 26

MEALLER, WILLIAM
and
MILLER, ELIZABETH

13 Sept 1847- Thomas King, C.C.O.
13 Sept 1847- W'm J. King, J.P.
source: license- 1751-03/5-103
see also volume 4, page 312

PAYNE, JAMES W.
and
CRAWFORD, MARGARET

18 Sept 1847- B.F. King, D.C.C.O.
19 Sept 1847- John H. Patrick, J.I.C.
source: license- 1751-03/5-111
see also volume 4, page 265

MIZE, HENRY J.
and
MIZE, MARY ANN ELIZABETH

30 Sept 1847- Thomas King, C.C.O.
30 Sept 1847- W'm Turk, J.I.C.
source: license- 1751-03/5-101
see also volume 4, page 270

GRESHAM, W.S.
and
KNOX, JOSEPHINE M.

4 Oct 1847- Thomas King, C.C.O.
26 Oct 1847- B.F. Mauldin
source: license- 1751-02/3-60
see also volume 4, page 280

RICE, CHARLES
and
CARR, FRANCES

5 Oct 1847- Thomas King, C.C.O.
5 Oct 1847- Job Bowers, J.P.
source: license- 1751-03/6-124
see also volume 4, page 269

GINN, JAMES C.
and
ADDISON, SINTHA

8 Oct 1847- Thomas King, C.C.O.
8 Oct 1847- John G. York, J.I.C.
source: volume 5, page(2)

DOBBS, OLIVER
and
FREEMAN, ELMINA

9 Oct 1847- Thomas King, C.C.O.
10 Oct 1847- Dudley J. Chandeler, J.P.
source: license- 1751-01/2-44
see also volume 4, page 282

ISBELL, JOHN M.
and
BLAIR, NANCY

14 Oct 1847- Thomas King, C.C.O.
14 Oct 1847- Zachariah Thomas, J.P.
source: volume 4, page 307

PHILIPS, NICHOLAS M.
and
OSBORN, CHARITY ANN E.

14 Oct 1847, Thomas King, C.C.O.
14 Oct 1847- John B. Wade, M.G.
source: license- 1751-03/6-114
see also volume 4, page 268

CHEEK, SAMUEL P.
and
BRUCE, MARTHANN

4 Nov 1847- Thomas King, C.C.O.
4 Nov 1847- John B. Wade, M.G.
source: license- 1751-01/2-30
see also volume 4, page 267

SARTIN, LARKIN
and
CAPE, PERMELEY ELIZABETH

4 Nov 1847- Thomas King, C.C.O.
4 Nov 1847- W'm T. Crow, J.P.
source: license- 1751-03/6-128
see also volume 4, page 285

BAU, CROFFORD
and
JUSTICE, ELIZABETH

5 Nov 1847- Thomas King, C.C.O.
6 Nov 1847- Green B. Holbrook, J.P.
source: license- 1751-01/1-9
see also volume 4, page 266

POOL, JACKSON
and
GARRISON, HANNAH E.

23 Nov 1847- Thomas King, C.C.O.
25 Nov 1847- Allen T. Garrison, J.P.
source: license- 1751-03/6-116
see also volume 4, page 318

SLATON, SAM'L H.
and
VERNER, MARTHA

28 Nov 1847- Thomas King, C.C.O.
28 Nov 1847- James L. Gillespie, J.P.
source: license- 1751-04/7-135
see also volume 4, page 293

CRAWFORD, HUSEL(?)
and
CAREY, LUCINDY

29 Nov 1847- Thomas King, C.C.O.
29 Nov 1847- Green B. Holbrook, J.P.
source: license- 1751-01/2-36
see also volume 4, page 273

WARD, EDWARD
and
MEADERS, MALINDA P.

1 Dec 1847- Thomas King, C.C.O.
2 Dec 1847- Allen T. Garrison, J.P.
source: license- 1751-04/8-157
see also volume 4, page 317

WHITE, BENNETT
and
LANGSTON, SARAH K.

1 Dec 1847- Thomas King, C.C.O.
3 Dec 1847- A. Neese, M.G.
source: license- 1751-04/8-162
see also volume 4, page 274

SHACELFORD, FRANCIS M.
and
WATSON, MARY C.

2 Dec 1847- Thomas King, C.C.O.
2 Dec 1847- Green B. Holbrook, J.P.
source: license- 1751-04/7-133
see also volume 4, page 273

MAXFIELD, JEREMIAH
and
ORR, ELIZABETH

2 Dec 1847- Thomas King, C.C.O.
2 Dec 1847- Ja's L. Gillespie, J.P.
source: license- 1751-03/5-97
see also volume 4, page 298

MIZE, WILLIAM J.
and
ORR, MARY

7 Dec 1847- Thomas King, C.C.O.
7 Dec 1847- Tho's Mize, J.P.
source: license- 1751-03/5-101
see also volume 4, page 275

VICKERY, JOSEPH H.
and
CAWTHON, LUCY

8 Dec 1847- Thomas King, C.C.O.
11 Dec 1847- Job Bowers, J.P.
source: license- 1751-04/8-153
see also volume 4, page 279

MARTIN, DR. GABRIEL S.
and
NEAL, MARY F.

13 Dec 1847- Thomas King, C.C.O.
16 Dec 1847- W'm J. Parks, M.G.
source: license- 1751-03/5-95
see also volume 4, page 280

HUNT, ELIJA
and
NEAL, MAHALA H.

15 Dec 1847- Thomas King, C.C.O.
16 Dec 1847- John H. Little, J.P.
source: license- 1751-02/3-74
see also volume 4, page 277

CAREY, THOMAS
and
JENES, NANCY

16 Dec 1847- Thomas King, C.C.O.
16 Dec 1847- John N. Aderhold, J.P.
see also volume 4, page 272

RICE, GEORGE L.
and
MC INTIRE, ELIZABETH A.

22 Dec 1847- Thomas King, C.C.O.
23 Dec 1847- James Polk, J.I.C.-
            Madison Co.
source: license- 1751-03/6-124
see also volume 4, page 277

TURNER, WILLIAM S.
and
STOW, SUSAN

22 Dec 1847- Thomas King, C.C.O.
23 Dec 1847- John G. York, J.I.C.
source: volume 5, page (3)

MARTIN, ROBERT
and
MOULDER, MANDA

23 Dec 1847- Thomas King, C.C.O.
23 Dec 1847- John B. Wade, M.G.
source: license- 1751-03/5-95
see also volume 4, page 284

BLACK, JAMES
and
RICHERSON, JANE E.

23 Dec 1847- Thomas King, C.C.O.
23 Dec 1847- John B. Wade, M.G.
source: license- 1751- 01/1-12
see also volume 4, page 281

AARON, JAMES W.
and
KITCHEN, REBECCA

28 Dec 1847- Thomas King, C.C.O.
28 Dec 1847- James L. Gillespie, J.P.
source: license- 1751-01/1-1
see also volume 4, page 299

BROWN, ASBURY H.
and
CROW, REBECCA J.

3 Jan 1848- Thomas King, C.C.O.
6 Jan 1848- Benjamin Thornton, M.G.
source: license- 1751-01/1-17
see also volume 4, page 278

MASSEY, JOEL
and
BROWN, ANNA P.

5 Jan 1848- Thomas King, C.C.O.
5 Jan 1848- Isaac B. Laurence, J.P.
source: license- 1751-03/5-96
see also volume 4, page 317

STOE, JAMES
and
KITCHENS, ELIZA AN

9 Jan 1848- Thomas King, C.C.O.
9 Jan 1848- James L. Gillespie, J.P.
source: license- 1751-04/7-142
see also volume 4, page 298

CONNALY, BENJAMIN H.
and
GARRISON, CATHARINE

11 Jan 1848- Thomas King, C.C.O.
11 Jan 1848- William J. Wiley, J.P.
source: license- 1751-01/2-34
see also volume 4, page 310

BAKER, ANDERSON
and
HILL, NANCY A.

20 Jan 1848- Thomas King, C.C.O.
20 Jan 1848- James L. Gillespie, J.P.
source: license- 1751-01/1-8
see also volume 4, page 299

HUTCHERSON, JOEL
and
ADAMS, ELIZABETH

20 Jan 1848- Thomas King, C.C.O.
20 Jan 1848- W'm J. Parks, M.G.
source: license- 1751-02/3-74
see also volume 4, page 276

VAUGHAN, WILLIAM
and
CASEY, BARBERY

20 Jan 1848- Thomas King, C.C.O.
20 Jan 1848- W'm T. Crow, J.P.
source: license- 1751-04/8-151
see also volume 4, page 279

WILLBANKS, RICHARD A.
and
WHITE, MARTHA ANN

20 Jan 1848- Thomas King, C.C.O.
20 Jan 1848- Minyard Sanders, J.P.
source: license- 1751-04/8-165
see also volume 4, page 267

MORGAN, JOHN H.
and
POOLE, NANCY

25 Jan 1848- Thomas King, C.C.O.
25 Jan 1848- William Turk, J.I.C.
source: license- 1751-03/5-102
see also volume 4, page 275

MILLER, FLETCHER
and
JAMES, JANE

29 Jan 1848- Thomas King, C.C.O.
30 Jan 1848- J.H. Aderhold, J.P.
source: license- 1751-03/5-99
see also volume 4, page 276

AYRES, FRANCIS M.
and
PAYNE, SARYANNE

29 Jan 1848- Thomas King, C.C.O.
30 Jan 1848- Richard Wheeler, J.P.
source: license- 1751-01/1-7
see also volume 4, page 285

CORTHORN, WILLIAM
and
SMITH, MARGRET

2 Feb 1848- Thomas King, C.C.O.
2 Feb 1848- David Vaughan, J.P.
source: license- 1751-01/2-26
see also volume 4, page 284

CRAFT, WILLIAM C.
and
HALE, MARGARETT E.

3 Feb 1848- Thomas King, C.C.O.
3 Feb 1848- John B. Wade, M.G.
source: license- 1751-01/2-36
see also volume 4, page 294

AYRES, JAMES V.
and
ANDREWS, MARY

8 Feb 1848- Thomas King, C.C.O.
8 Feb 1848- Richard Wheeler, J.P.
source: license- 1751-01/1-7
see also volume 4, page 286

CRIDER, DAVID
and
CHILDS, ELIZABETH

12 Feb 1848- Thomas King, C.C.O.
13 Feb 1848- John A. Davis, M.G.
source: license- 1751-01/2-36
see also volume 4, page 295

SHELNUT, JOSEPH
and
HARRIS, ANN

5 Mar 1848- Thomas King, C.C.O.
5 Mar 1848- Job Bowers, J.P.
source: license- 1751-04/7-133
see also volume 4, page 278

SEWELL, JOHN CHAPPEL
and
BELL, SARAH

7 Mar 1848- Thomas King, C.C.O.
9 Mar 1848- Nelson Osbern, M.G.
source: license- 1751-03/6-132
see also volume 4, page 297

GLOVER, JAMES M.
and
BOWERS, SUSEY A.

16 Mar 1848- Thomas King, C.C.O.
16 Mar 1848- W'm Bowers, J.P.
source: license- 1751-02/3-57
see also volume 4, page 293

BRADY, WILLIAM
and
VAUGHAN, MARGARETT

22 Mar 1848- Thomas King, C.C.O.
22 Mar 1848- I.B. Laurence, J.P.
source: license- 1751-01/1-15
see also volume 4, page 321

WRIGHT, EDWARD W.
and
STOE, SARAH

25 Mar 1848- Dan'l Moseley, J.P. for
               Thomas King, C.C.O.
26 Mar 1848- David Simmons, M.G.
source: license- 1751-04/8-170
see also volume 4, page 294

SILMAN, O.W.
and
CHAMBLEE, NANCY C.

25 Mar 1848- Thomas King, C.C.O.
26 Mar 1848- John E. McCarter, J.P.
source: volume 4, page 309

PRESLAR, HARVY
and
WHITE, ELIZA

2 Apr 1848- Thomas King, C.C.O.
2 Apr 1848- Isaac B. Laurence, J.P.
source: license- 1751-03/117
see also volume 4, page 315

BROWN, BENJAMIN M.
and
MC DOUGAL, MARIAH

20 Apr 1848- Thomas King, C.C.O.
20 Apr 1848- John B. Wade, M.G.
source: license- 1751-01/1-17
see also volume 4, page 296

CROW, JESSE M.
and
RICHARDS, LARRAAN (?)

30 Apr 1848- Thomas King, C.C.O.
30 Apr 1848- Isaac B. Laurence, J.P.
source: license- 1751-01/2-38
see also volume 4, page 316

WHORTON, HENRY D.
and
SARTIN, SOPHRONIA E.

7 May 1848- Thomas King, C.C.O.
7 May 1848- Ja's L. Gillespie, J.P.
source: license- 1751-04/8-164
see also volume 4, page 289

STONE, WILLIAM H.
and
GARNER, MARY C.

11 May 1848- Thomas King, C.C.O.
11 May 1848- Zachariah Thomas, J.P.
source: volume 4, page 306

RANDAL, JAMES
and
MC CALL, FRANCES

13 May 1848- Thomas King, C.C.O.
25 May 1848- D. Simmons, M.G.
source: license- 1751-03/6-122
see also volume 4, page 287

MIZE, HENRY C.
and
ENGLISH, MARY

21 May 1848- Thomas King, C.C.O.
21 May 1848- James L. Gillespie, J.P.
source: license- 1751-03/5-101
see also volume 4, page 290

COX, WILLIAM
and
RESINER(?), EVALINE

22 May 1848- Thomas King, C.C.O.
22 May 1848- Zachariah Thomas, J.P.
source: volume 4, page 304

ROBERTSON, HENRY W.
and
CLARK, CATHERINE B.

23 May 1848- Thomas King, C.C.O.
25 May 1848- Zachariah Thomas, J.P.
source: volume 4, page 304

GARRISON, ENOCH C.
and
MEADERS, OPHA C.

23 May 1848- Thomas King, C.C.O.
23 May 1848- Allen T. Garrison, J.P.
source: license- 1751-02/3-54
see also volume 4, page 318

HARRISON, JAMES A.
and
LITTLE, SARAH JANE

4 June 1848- Thomas King, C.C.O.
4 June 1848- J.H. Aderhold, J.P.
source: license- 1751-02/3-64
see also volume 4, page 292

ANDERSON, DR. HARVEY R.
and
WILLBOURN, MARY E.

9 June 1848- Thomas King, C.C.O.
13 June 1848- A.M. Spalding, M.G.
source: license- 1751-01/1-5
see also volume 4, page 286

TEMPLES, BENJAMIN F.
and
CHEEK, ELIZABETH

3 July 1848- Thomas King, C.C.O.
4 July 1848- W'm Bowers, J.P.
source: license- 1751-04/7-146
see also volume 4, page 288

MOATS, JAMES C.
and
SMITH, SARAH C.

5 July 1848- Thomas King, C.C.O.
6 July 1848- Isaac B. Laurence, J.P.
source: license- 1751-03/5-101
see also volume 4, page 287

WARMACK, THOMAS P.
and
WATERS, JUDHA

5 July 1848- Thomas King, C.C.O.
6 July 1848- John A. Davis, M.G.
source: license- 1751-04/8-157
see also volume 4, page 297

SHERIDAN, THOMAS C.
and
BALLEW, CATHERINE

18 July 1848- Thomas King, C.C.O.
18 July 1848- Thomas Mize, J.P.
source: volume 5, page (1)

SMITH, JAMES M.
and
BRYAN, HARRIETT

24 July 1848- Thomas King, C.C.O.
24 July 1848- Zachariah Thomas, J.P.
source: volume 4, page 304,305

HIDE, GEORGE W.
and
WESTBROOK, LUCY

27 July 1848- Thomas King, C.C.O.
27 July 1848- James L. Gillespie, J.P.
source: license- 1751-02/3-68
see also volume 4, page 289

PHILLIPS, ANSON H.
and
BELL, HARRIET

30 July 1848- Thomas King, C.C.O.
30 July 1848- Job Bowers, J.P.
source: license- 1751-03/6-114
see also volume 4, page 291

KESLER, DAVID
and
CARRY(?), MARTHA

3 Aug 1848- Thomas King, C.C.O.
3 Aug 1848- W'm T. Crow, J.P.
source: license- 1751-02/4-82
see also volume 4, page 300

WHORTON, JOSHUA
and
ENGLISH, LUCY

4 Aug 1848- Thomas King, C.C.O.
4 Aug 1848- James L. Gillespie, J.P.
source: license- 1751-04/8-164
see also volume 4, page 290

MURRAY, WILLIAM F.
and
RICHARDS, ELIZA JANE

5 Aug 1848- Thomas King, C.C.O.
5 Aug 1848- Isaac B. Laurence, J.P.
source: license- 1751-03/5-104
see also volume 4, page 321

DAVIS, L.M.
and
WILLIAMS, NANCY

13 Aug 1848- Thomas King, C.C.O.
13 Aug 1848- Alfred Smith, J.P.
source: license- 1751-01/2-41
see also volume 4, page 311

BROCK, REUBEN C.
and
SMITH, ELIZABETH

14 Aug 1848- Thomas King, C.C.O.
14 Aug 1848- Zachariah Thomas, J.P.
source: volume 4, page 306

MILLER, JAMES H.
and
ASH, MARY L.C.

26 Aug 1848- Thomas King, C.C.O.
27 Aug 1848- John H. Little, J.P.
source: license- 1751-03/5-99
see also volume 4, page 292

GARNER, GEORGE W.
and
COSBY, MARY JANE

26 Aug 1848- Thomas King, C.C.O.
27 Aug 1848- Osbern Garner, J.P.
source: license- 1751-02/3-53
see also volume 4, page 309

HUNT, RICHARD C.
and
ALEXANDER, RACHEL ANN

2 Sept 1848- Thomas King, C.C.O.
4 Sept 1848- John B. Wade, J.P.
source: volume 4, page 303

AYRES, THOMAS
and
BRADLEY, PRISSILLA

3 Sept 1848- Thomas King, C.C.O.
3 Sept 1848- Isaac B. Laurence, J.P.
source: license- 1751-01/1-7
see also volume 4. Indexed page 324,
which is missing.

ACRE, WILLIAM
and
MARTIN/MATIN, MARY

10 Sept 1848- Thomas King, C.C.O.
10 Sept 1848- Isaac B. Laurence, J.P.
source: license- 1751-01/1-1
see also volume 4, page 323

MIZE, JOHN
and
MAXWELL, SARAH

14 Sept 1848- Thomas King, C.C.O.
14 Sept 1848- Ja's L. Gillespie, J.P.
source: license- 1751-03/5-101
see also volume 4, page 288

LEUALLAN, JOHN
and
MARLIN, MANDY(?) A.

14 Sept 1848- Thomas King, C.C.O.
14 Sept 1848- Isaac B. Laurence, J.P.
source: license- 1751-02/4-85 (back of
license shows "Manda A. Martin" and
"Manda Allexandria Martin"
see also volume 4. Indexed page 325,
which is missing.

141

ANDERSON, DAVID
and
ROBERTSON, NANCY

19 Sept 1848- Thomas King, C.C.O.
19 Sept 1848- Isaac B. Laurence, J.P.
              Habersham Co.
source: license- 1751-01/1-5
volume 4 indexed on page 324(missing)

LEAIRD, WILLIAM J.
and
PHILLIPS, ANGELINE R.

23 Sept 1848- Thomas King, C.C.O.
24 Sept 1848- Job Bowers, J.P.
source: license- 1751-02/4-85
see also volume 4, page 291

HILL, WILLIAM R.
and
SHERIDAN, NANCY

5 Oct 1848- Thomas King, C.C.O.
5 Oct 1848- Allen T. Garrison, J.P.
source: license- 1751-02/3-69
see also volume 4, page 322

SANDERS, GEORGE
and
RAMSEY, ELIZABETH

15 Oct 1848- Thomas King, C.C.O.
15 Oct 1848- John B. Wade, M.G.
source: volume 4, page 303,304

GUEST, CURTIS
and
ADDISON, ELIZABETH

31 Oct 1848- Thomas King, C.C.O.
31 Oct 1848- John G. York, J.I.C.
source: volume 5, page(3)

MC CLESKY, JOHN
and
SANDERS, ELIZABETH

2 Nov 1848- Thomas King, C.C.O.
3 Nov 1848- Benj. Thornton, M.G.
source: volume 4, page 302

VICKRY, JAMES V.
and
PEEKE, MARY

10 Nov 1848- Thomas King, C.C.O.
12 Nov 1848- Jedediah Ayers, J.P.
source: license- 1751-04/8-154
see also volume 5, page 8

BANKS, RALPH
and
SHACKELFORD, SARHA

15 Nov 1848- Thomas King, C.C.O.
16 Nov 1848- J.A. Davis, M.G.
source: license- 1751-01/1-9
see also volume 4, page 313

JAMES, JOHN C.
and
WEBB, MARTHA

16 Nov 1848- Thomas King, C.C.O.
16 Nov 1848- J.E. McCarter, J.P.
source: license- 1751-02/4-76
see also volume 4, page 310

HATHCOCK, THOMAS H.
and
HATHCOCK, SARAHAN

23 Nov 1848- Thomas King, C.C.O.
23 Nov 1848- W'm T. Crow, J.P.
source: license- 1751-02/3-65
see also volume 4, page 300

MASSEY, WILLIAM
and
BALLEW, NANCY

23 Nov 1848- Thomas King, C.C.O.
23 Nov 1848- Thomas Mize, J.P.
source: volume 5, page (1)

HILL, DAVID
and
BAUGH, JULIAN

2 Dec 1848- Thomas King, C.C.O.
21 Dec 1848- Allen T. Garrison, J.P.
source: license- 1751-02/3-69
see also volume 4, page 319

MOULDER, JAMES M.
and
ASKEA, SEENE

6 Dec 1848- Thomas King, C.C.O.
14 Dec 1848- Nelson Osbern, M.G.
source: license- 1751-03/5-103
see also volume 4, page 301

WHITEN, JACKSON J.
and
KAZE, MRS. BASHABA

9 Dec 1848- Thomas King, C.C.O.
10 Dec 1848- John A. Davis, M.G.
source: license- 1751-04/8-163
see also volume 4, page 315

HANEY, ROB'T B.
and
HALL, JANE E.

19 Dec 1848- Thomas King, C.C.O.
19 Dec 1848- W'm T. Crow, J.P.
source: license- 1751-02/3-62
see also volume 4, page 301

SMITH, TILMON P.
and
KESLER, MARY ANN

20 Dec 1848- Thomas King, C.C.O.
20 Dec 1848- W'm J. Wiley, J.P.
source: license- 1751-04/7-139
see also volume 4, page 311

CAREY, JAMES L.
and
FOWLER, LUCEY

21 Dec 1848- Thomas King, C.C.O.
21 Dec 1848- W'm T. Crow, J.P.
source: license- 1751-01/2-22
see also volume 4, page 302

SCOTT, JAMES E.
and
SANDERS, ALLIS

25 Dec 1848- Thomas King, C.C.O.
28 Dec 1848- Benj. Thornton, M.G.
source: volume 4, page 303

WATSON, BENJAMIN H.
and
CAUDELL, ELISABETH

28 Dec 1848- R.A.R. Neal, C.C.O.
28 Dec 1848- Isaac B. Laurence, J.P.
source: license- 1751-04/8-158
see also Index to volume 4. Listed on
page 326 which is missing

WATSON, SETH
and
LEUALLEN, MATILDA

4 Jan 1849- R.A.R. Neal, C.C.O.
4 Jan 1849- I.B. Laurence, J.P.
source: license- 1751-04/8-158
see also Index to volume 4. Listed on
page 326 which is missing

JONES, JESSE
and
GARNER, SARAH

7 Jan 1849- R.A.R. Neal, C.C.O.
7 Jan 1849- James H. Chappelier, J.P.
source: volume 5, page (3)

WESTBROOK, WESLEY J.
and
MAYS, MARY MALINDA

10 Jan 1849- R.A.R. Neal, C.C.O.
12 Jan 1849- William Turk, J.I.C.
source: volume 5, page (4)

BANKS, RUSSELL
and
YARBER, MARY

10 Jan 1849- R.A.R. Neal, C.C.O.
12 Jan 1849- Richard Wheeler, J.P.
source: license- 1751-01/1-9
see also volume 4, page 313

WALTERS, CLEMMENT
and
SMITH, REBECAH

15 Jan 1849- R.A.R. Neal, C.C.O.
15 Jan 1849- John A. Davis, M.G.
source: license- 1751-04/8-156
see also volume 4, page 314

WRIGHT, JOHN W.
and
RICHARDSON, MARGARET

18 Jan 1849- R.A.R. Neal, C.C.O.
18 Jan 1849- John B. Wade, M.G.
source: license- 1751-04/8-170
see also volume 5, page 8

SEWELL, RILEY
and
VAUGHN, ADALINE

18 Jan 1849- R.A.R. Neal, C.C.O.
18 Jan 1849- Nelson Osbern, M.G.
source: license- 1751-03/6-132
see also volume 4, page 312,313

ALLRED, ELI T.
and
LEWALLEN, NANCY ANN

22 Jan 1849- R.A.R. Neal, C.C.O.
22 Jan 1849- Allen T. Garrison, J.P.
source: license- 1751-01/1-4
see also volume 4. Indexed page 325,
which is missing

LE CROY PRIESTLEY
and
PEEKE, ELIZABETH

4 Feb 1849- R.A.R. Neal, C.C.O.
4 Feb 1849- John B. Wade, M.G.
source: license- 1751-02/4-85
see also volume 5, page 8

MULLINAX, JOHN M.
and
BELL, CATHERINE

8 Feb 1849- Rob't A.R. Neal, C.C.O.
8 Feb 1849- Nelson Osbern, M.G.
source: license- 1751-03/5-104
see also volume 4, page 312

CANIDA, ANDREW J.
and
THOMASON, NANCY

10 Feb 1849- R.A.R. Neal, C.C.O.
11 Feb 1849- John A. Davis, M.G.
source: license- 1751-01/2-22
see also volume 4, page 313

SHANNON, JAMES D.
and
ADAMS, SARAH

19 Feb 1849- B.F. King, D.C.C.O.
.... - ....
source: license- 1751-04/7-133

WEEMS, ASA
and
SMITH, MRS. ELIZABETH

20 Feb 1849- R.A.R. Neal, C.C.O.
21 Feb 1849- John S. Henley, M.G.
source: license- 1751-04/8-159
see also volume 4, page 314

HIX, C.G.
and
MC FARLIN, SARAH

8 Mar 1849- R.A.R. Neal, C.C.O.
8 Mar 1849- David Simmons, M.G.
source: license- 1751-02/3-70
see also volume 5, page 6

COBB, EDWIN M.
and
HARISON, RHODA E.

8 Mar 1849- R.A.R. Neal, C.C.O.
8 Mar 1849- John H. Aderhold, J.P.
source: license- 1751-01/2-33
see also volume 4, page 322

ECHOLS, WILLIAM E.
and
BEARD, MARGARET W.

8 Mar 1849- R.A.R. Neal, C.C.O.
8 Mar 1849- Richard Wheeler, J.P.
source: license- 1751-02/3-46
see also volume 4. Indexed page 327,
which is missing

144

```
KELLY, OWEN                      24 Mar 1849- John G. York, C.C.O.
    and                         8 Apr 1849- John A. Davis, M.G.
GUEST, HARRIET                  source: volume 5, page(2)


YOUNG, JOHN S.(?)               4 Apr 1849- John G. York, C.C.O.
    and                         4 Apr 1849- Job Bowers, J.P.
JOHNSON, ABIGAIL                source: volume 5, page (2)


PARSON, JOSEPH                  13 Apr 1849- Jno. G. York, C.C.O.
    and                         13 Apr 1849- Thomas Mize, J.P.
RAY, MRS. CLEMENTINE            source: volume 5, page (1)


SHOCKLY, BENJAMIN F.            15 Apr 1849- John G. York, C.C.O.
    and                         15 Apr 1849- James L. Gillespie, J.P.
TONEY, RHODY B.                 source: volume 5, page 6


SMITH, CLEVELAND                28 Apr 1849- John G. York, C.C.O.
    and                         28 Apr 1849- Isaac Lawrence, J.P.
STEPHENS, MARGARETT             source: volume 5, page 161


SANDERS, AARON C.               14 May 1849- John G. York, C.C.O.
    and                         14 May 1849- Minyard Sanders, J.P.
WHITEMORE, LUUCINDA M.          source: license- 1751-03/6-128
                                see also volume 5, page 45


WHORTON, JOSEPH                 15 May 1849- John G. York, C.C.O.
    and                         15 May 1849- Minyard Sanders, J.P.
MURRY, MARY ANN                 source: license- 1751-04/8-164
                                see also volume 5, page 45


BAUGH, ANDERSON                 22 May 1849- John G. York, C.C.O.
    and                         22 May 1849- .....
GREENWAY, SARAH L.              source: volume 5, page 54


AYRES, SAMUEL A.                1 June 1849- John G. York, C.C.O.
    and                         2 June 1849- J.S. Hunley, M.G.
ADAMS, ADALINE A.               source: volume 5, page (4)


WALKER, J.W.                    14 June 1849- John G. York, C.C.O.
    and                         14 June 1849- T. Mize, J.P.
KITCHEN, NANCY JANE             source: license- 1751-04/8-155
                                see also volume 5, page 10


JAMES, WILLIAM                  21 June 1849- John M. Freeman, D.C.C.O.
    and                         21 June 1849- William T. Crow, J.P.
EDWARDS, AMANDA M.              source: volume 5, page 5


BRAY, ALPHONZO                  28 June 1849- John G. York, C.C.O.
    and                         28 June 1849- Nelson Osbern, M.G.
WEST, MINERVA                   source: volume 5, page 5
```

HATHCOCK, JAMES
and
GUEST, MARY ANN

4 July 1849- John G. York, C.C.O.
4 July 1849- John H. Aderhold, J.P.
source: license- 1751-02/3-65
see also volume 5, page 6,7

ALLEN, WILLIAM T.
and
GARRISON, SARAH ANN

15 July 1849- John G. York, C.C.O.
15 July 1849- Isaac B. Lawrence, J.P.
source: volume 4, page 329

BAUGH, JOHN
and
WHITEMORE, NANCY

26 July 1849- John G. York, C.C.O.
.... ¯ ....
source: volume 5, page 67

MURPHEY, JOHN
and
CARDELL(?), ELIZABETH JAEN

3 Aug 1849- John G. York, C.C.O.
3 Aug 1849- Alfred Smith, J.P.
source: license- 1751-03/5-104
see also volume 5, page 9

KING, WILLIAM P.
and
HARRISON, VASTINE B.

18 Aug 1849- John M. Freeman, D.C.C.O.
19 Aug 1849- John M. Freeman, J.P.
source: license- 1751-02/4-83
see also volume 5, page 7

COLLINS, THOMAS
and
EDGE, ELIZABETH

20 Aug 1849- John G. York, C.C.O.
23 Aug 1849- Daniel Mosely, J.P.
source: license- 1751-01/2-34
see also volume 5, page 12

COX, BENJAMAN J.S.
and
HOLBROOK, ELIZABETH A.V.

22 Aug 1849- John G. York, C.C.O.
23 Aug 1849- Nelson Osbern, M.G.
source: license- 1751-01/2-35
see also volume 5, page 7

STUBLEFIELD, LEMUEL
and
DAVIS, ANGELINE

26 Aug 1849- John G. York, C.C.O.
26 Aug 1849- Alfred Smith, J.P.
source: license- 1751-04/7-144
see also volume 5, page 9

SMITH, WILLIAM B.
and
BURGESS, SARRIAH

2 Sept 1849- John G. York, C.C.O.
2 Sept 1849- J.H. Chappelear, J.P.
source: license- 1751-04/7-139
see also volume 5, page 11

HOLLEY, DANIEL W.
and
ALLEN, LOUISIANA T.

5 Sept 1849- John M. Freeman, D.C.C.O.
6 Sept 1849- W'm B. Moss, M.G.
source: license- 1751-02/3-72
see also volume 5, page 9

MITCHELL, THOMAS C.
and
COLLYER, ANNA

5 Sept 1849- John G. York, C.C.O.
9 Sept 1849- Daniel Mosely, J.P.
source: license- 1751-03/5-100
see also volume 5, page 12

MAYBRY, EPHRAIM W.
and
GUEST, NEACY

26 Sept 1849- John G. York, C.C.O.
26 Sept 1849- W'm J. Oliver, J.P.
source: license- 1751-03/5-97
see also volume 5, page 13

LECROY(?), THOMAS C.
and
STOW, SARAH ANN

3 Oct 1849- John G. York, C.C.O.
3 Oct 1849- W'm J. Wiley, J.P.
source: volume 5, page 25

HOWELL, JOSEPH A.
and
GARRISON, MARTHA

11 Oct 1849- John G. York, C.C.O.
11 Oct 1849- Nelson Osbern, M.G.
source: license- 1751-02/3-73
see also volume 5, page 11

WACASTER, DAVID
and
PAYNE, MARY A.

18 Oct 1849- John G. York, C.C.O.
18 Oct 1849- James L. Gillespie, J.P.
source: license- 1751-04/8-155
see also volume 5, page 11

HAYES, WILLIAM
and
SPARKS, LORY F.

21 Oct 1849- John G. York, C.C.O.
21 Oct 1849- Daniel Mosley, J.P.
source: license- 1751-02/3-66
see also volume 5, page 12

SEGARS, ELIJAH L.
and
MASSAY, ELMINA

21 Oct 1849- John G. York, C.C.O.
21 Oct 1849- Isaac B. Lawrence, J.P.
source: volume 4, page 328

ISBELL, ROBERT G.
and
GANT, ELIZABETH J.

24 Oct 1849- John M. Freeman, D.C.C.O.
28 Oct 1849- Osborn Garner, J.P.
source: license- 1751-02/4-75
see also volume 5, page 10

ASKEA, FRANKLIN
and
MULLINAX, SARAH ANN

25 Oct 1849- John G. York, C.C.O.
25 Oct 1849- Jno. M. Freeman, J.P.
source: license- 1751-01/1-6
see also volume 5, page 10

KENNEDAY, JAMES
and
BING, ELIZABETH

29 Oct 1849- John G. York, C.C.O.
29 Oct 1849- Alfred Smith, J.P.
source: volume 5, page 56

BRYAN, JAMES R.
and
DENMAN, SUSAN

1 Nov 1849- John G. York, C.C.O.
1 Nov 1849- J.H. Chappelear, J.P.
source: license- 1751-01/1-18
see also volume 5, page 13

SCOTT, LEWIS
and
WILEY, MARGARET

6 Nov 1849- John G. York, C.C.O.
6 Nov 1849- Daniel Moseley, J.P.
source: license- 1751-03/6-130
see also volume 5, page 44

COX, WILLIAM G.
and
GORTNEY, MARY ANN

15 Nov 1849- John G. York, C.C.O.
15 Nov 1849- Daniel Mosely, J.P.
source: license- 1751-01/2-35
see also volume 5, page 38

CHANDLER, JOSEPH N.
and
BURTON, NANCY

22 Nov 1849- John G. York, C.C.O.
22 Nov 1849- John S. Henly, M.G.
source: volume 5, page 17

KEY, PIERCE C.   28 Nov 1849- John G. York, C.C.O.
   and   29 Nov 1849- T. Newton, V.D.M.
ASH, ELIZABETH H.   source: volume 5, page 17

MOTES, JOHN T.   9 Dec 1849- John G. York, C.C.O.
   and   9 Dec 1849- Isaac B. Laurence, J.P.
SMITH, NANCY C.   source: volume 4, page 328

GARNER, SAMUEL K.   9 Dec 1849- John G. York, C.C.O.
   and   9 Dec 1849- Osbern Garner, J.P.
STOVALL, JANE   source: volume 5, page 56

PHILLIPS, ASA   11 Dec 1849- John G. York, C.C.O.
   and   13 Dec 1849- John S. Henly, M.G.
OSBURN, MARY D. M.   source: volume 5, page 19

GAZAWAY, JOHN   11 Dec 1849- John G. York, C.C.O.
   and   12 Dec 1849- W'm J. Oliver, J.P.
ADDISON, RUTHA   source: license- 1751-02/3-55
                                 see also volume 5, page 14

HOWINGTON, ELDRIDGE W.   13 Dec 1849- John M. Freeman, D.C.C.O.
   and   16 Dec 1849- John P. Jolly, J.P.
FREEMAN, JEMIMA   source: volume 5, page 15

LOONEY, MORGAN H.   17 Dec 1849- John M. Freeman, D.C.C.O.
   and   27 Dec 1849- John S. Henley, M.G.
PARKER, SARAH E.   source: license- 1751-02/4-87
                                 see also volume 5, page 13

PARKER, B.B.   17 Dec 1849- John M. Freeman, D.C.C.O.
   and   26 Dec 1849- Henry Tyler, M.G.
LOONEY, SARAH A.   source: license- 1751-03/5-108
                                 see also volume 5, page 14

MAXWELL, JAMES M.   18 Dec 1849- John G. York, C.C.O.
   and   20 Dec 1849- W'm J. Parks, M.G.
TABOR, MARY F.   source: license- 1751-03/5-97
                                 see also volume 5, page 37

SMITH, WILLIAM S.   23 Dec 1849- John G. York, C.C.O.
   and   23 Dec 1849- Daniel Moseley, J.P.
HANCOCK, SARAH ANN   source: license- 1751-04/7-139
                                 see also volume 5, page 44

WADE, EDWARD J.   24 Dec 1849- John G. York, C.C.O.
   and   25 Dec 1849- David Carson, M.G.
DAVID, JULIAN E.   source: volume 5, page 16

SMALLEY, JOHN   25 Dec 1849- John G. York, C.C.O.
   and   25 Dec 1849- Daniel Moseley, J.P.
EDGE, FLORA   source: license- 1751-04/7-135
                                 see also volume 5, page 37

PRICKETT, JAMES P.
and
THOMAS, EMILY J.

2 Jan 1850- John G. York, C.C.O.
3 Jan 1850- W'm Turk, J.I.C.
source: volume 5, page 18

BOND, RUSSEL P.
and
PHILLIPS, NANCY E.

4 Jan 1850- John G. York, C.C.O.
10 Jan 1850- Nelson Osbern, M.G.
source: volume 5, page 18

GARNER, GEORGE H.
and
WHITWORTH, JULIA W.

4 Jan 1850- John G. York, C.C.O.
4 Jan 1850- Oliver Harrison, J.P.
source: volume 5, page 54

FURR, PAUL
and
DOBBINS, MAHALY

8 Jan 1850- John G. York, C.C.O.
8 Jan 1850- Tho's Mize, J.P.
source: volume 5, page 17

CHEEK, WILLIAM P.
and
BELL, ELIZA

10 Jan 1850- John G. York, C.C.O.
10 Jan 1850- Nelson Osbern, M.G.
source: volume 5, page 18

MULLINAX, BENJAMIN
and
FULBRIGHT, CATHERINE

11 Jan 1850- John M. Freeman, D.C.C.O.
11 Jan 1850- Henry Freeman, J.I.C.
source: license- 1751-03/5-104
see also volume 5, page 14

CHEEKE, ROLIN
and
BALEY, LUSEY

12 Jan 1850- John G. York, C.C.O.
13 Jan 1850- John S. Henley, M.G.
source: license- 1751-01/2-30
see also volume 5, page 77

MC EVAN, ADAM A.
and
SHELL, SARANAN F.

16 Jan 1850- John G. York, C.C.O.
17 Jan 1850- Job Bowers, J.P.
source: volume 5, page 21

MEANS, HUGH
and
GILLESPIE, FRANCES W.

17 Jan 1850- John G. York, C.C.O.
17 Jan 1850- James L. Gillespie, J.P.
source: volume 5, page 16

MABRY, WALTER
and
KELLEY, ELIZABETH

24 Jan 1850- John G. York, C.C.O.
24 Jan 1850- W'm J. Oliver, J.P.
source: volume 5, page 16

HOLCOMB, SHEARWOOD
and
MOSS, MAHALA KATHARINE

4 Feb 1850- John G. York, C.C.O.
15 Feb 1850- John A. Davis, M.G.
source: volume 5, page 19

LORRYMORE, ANDREW
and
HAYNES, LINNEY

7 Feb 1850- John G. York, C.C.O.
7 Feb 1850- John S. Henly, M.G.
source: volume 5, page 20

PARR, THOMAS P.
and
CAUSBEY, ELENDER S.

7 Feb 1850- John G. York, C.C.O.
27 Feb 1850- Green B. Holbrook, J.I.C.
source: volume 5, page 15

CRAIG, JOHN G.
and
SWIFT, SUSAN

11 Feb 1850- John G. York, C.C.O.
21 Feb 1850- Joseph Greyham, M.G.
source: volume 5, page 57

HERRING, BENSON
and
SANDERS, ORPHA

13 Feb 1850- John G. York, C.C.O.
14 Feb 1850- S.B. Sanders, M.G.
source: volume 5, page 22

LANSON(?LAWSON?), JOHN
and
SMITH, NANCY

14 Feb 1850- John G. York, C.C.O.
14 Feb 1850- Green B. Holbrook, J.I.C.
source: volume 5, page 15

MURRAY, ALEXANDER
and
ELLIS, ELIZA N.

17 Feb 1850- John G. York, C.C.O.
17 Feb 1850- Isaac B. Laurence, J.P.
source: volume 4, page 329

DOBBS, ALVIN B.
and
AARON, MARY M.

21 Feb 1850- John G. York, C.C.O.
21 Feb 1850- Green B. Holbrook, J.P.
source: volume 5, page 19

PRUITT, EMPSON
and
MURRAY, LYDIA

2 Mar 1850- John G. York, C.C.O.
3 Mar 1850- Isaac B. Laurence, J.P.
source: volume 4, page 330

MOOD(?), DR. JAMES R.
and
KING, MARTHA

7 Mar 1850- John G. York, C.C.O.
7 Mar 1850- Urban Sinclair Bird, M.G.
source: volume 5, page 20

MC CARTER, JOSEPH M.
and
MC CARTER, REBECCA

8 Mar 1850- John G. York, C.C.O.
10 Mar 1850- W'm J. Wiley, J.P.
source: volume 5, page 22

BOWERS, JEPHTHATH A.
and
ROE, IRMIN

10 Mar 1850- John G. York, C.C.O.
10 Mar 1850- John B. Wade, M.G.
source: volume 5, page 21

JONES, JOHN
and
MULKEY, MARTHA

17 Mar 1850- John G. York, C.C.O.
17 Mar 1850- James H. Chappelear, J.P.
source: volume 5, page 20

SEWELL, JOSHUA
and
VAUGHN, MARY

20 Mar 1850- John G. York, C.C.O.
21 Mar 1850- David Vaughn, J.P.
source: volume 5, page 60

ADISON, SANFORD
and
GAZAWAY, MARY

20 Mar 1850- John G. York, C.C.O.
21 Mar 1850- W'm J. Oliver, J.P.
source: volume 5, page 25

ISBELL, JAMES L.
and
SMITH, MARY ANN

24 Mar 1850- John G. York, C.C.O.
24 Mar 1850- John G. York, C.C.O.
source: volume 5, page 55

PAYNE, WILLIAM
and
LOONY, RHODA

7 Apr 1850- .....
7 Apr 1850- John B. Wade, M.G.
source: volume 5, page 21

VICKERY, ELIAS
and
SKELTON, NELLY

14 Apr 1850- John G. York, C.C.O.
15 Apr 1850- Benjamin Thornton, M.G.
source: volume 5, page 23,24

JORDAN, DREWRY
and
CRIDER, JERUSA

16 Apr 1850- John G. York, C.C.O.
21 Apr 1850- F.H. Attaway, M.G.
source: volume 5, page 23

OSBERN, L.M.
and
MC PHERSON(?), REBECCA

20 Apr 1850- John G. York, C.C.O.
21 Apr 1850- Green B. Holbrook
source: volume 5, page 60

TERREL, JOHNATHON
and
THOMAS, ELIZABETH H.

25 Apr 1850- John G. York, C.C.O.
28 Apr 1850- Green B. Holbrook, J.I.C.
source: license- 1751-04/7-146
see also volume 5, page 46

RAMSEY, DAVID S.
and
TURNER, KATHARINE

12 May 1850- John G. York, C.C.O.
12 May 1850- W'm J. Oliver, J.P.
source: volume 5, page 22,23

LU KROY, GEORGE W.
and
STRANGE, MARY A.

21 May 1850- John G. York, C.C.O.
21 May 1850- Allen T. Garrison, J.P.
source: volume 4, page 330

SOLSBERRY, JOHN
and
PAYNE, MARY

30 May 1850(sic)- John G. York, C.C.O.
5 Apr 1850(sic)- G.B. Holbrooks, J.I.C.
source: volume 5, page 55

WATERS, ANDERSON F.
and
SEWEL, MARY

2 July 1850- John G. York, C.C.O.
2 July 1850- David Vaughn, J.P.
source: volume 5, page 26

CHEEK, HOLLAND B.
and
COKER, MILLEY

6 July 1850(sic)- John G. York, C.C.O.
8 Jan 1851(sic)- James H. Chappelier, J.P.
source: volume 5, page 27

NUN, REUBEN D.
and
DAVID, PILLINA W.

11 July 1850- John M. Freeman, D.C.C.O.
11 July 1850- David W. Patman, M.G.
source: license- 1751-03/5-106
see also volume 5, page 32

POPHAM, BENJAMIN F.
and
PAYNE, EMILIN(?) M.

16 July 1850- John G. York, C.C.O.
21 July 1850- Green B. Holbrook, J.I.C.
source: volume 5, page 24

BRIDGES, JAMES M.
and
COKER, ARMINDA

27 July 1850- John G. York, C.C.O.
27 July 1850- Job Bowers, J.P.
source: license- 1751-01/1-16
see also volume 5, page 33

MYERS, ALEXANDER
and
CHEEK, TRESEY

7 Aug 1850- John G. York, C.C.O.
.... - ....
source: license- 1751-03/5-104
see also volume 5, page 33 which shows
the marriage 7 Aug 1850- Job Bowers, J.P.

HOLLY, WILLIAM
and
HARRISON, FRANCIS A.

9 Aug 1850- John G. York, C.C.O.
11 Aug 1850- John H. Aderhold, J.P.
source: volume 5, page 23

MIZE, JAMES M.
and
ROBERTSON, MANDY J.

10 Aug 1850- John M. Freeman, D.C.C.O.
22 Aug 1850- W'm R. Goss, M.G.
source: license- 1751-03/5-101
see also volume 5, page 27

KING, BENJAMIN F.
and
HARRISON, ELIZABETH C.

19 Aug 1850- John G. York, C.C.O.
19 Aug 1850- John H. Aderhold, J.P.
source: volume 5, page 25

CHEEK, MILTON
and
TEASLEY, HARIET

21 Aug 1850- John G. York, C.C.O.
22 Aug 1850- Samuel B. Sanders, M.G.
source: license- 1751-01/2-30
see also volume 5, page 34

SMITH, ELEAZAR E.
and
OWEN, MARY E.

22 Aug 1850- John G. York, C.C.O.
22 Aug 1850- Job Bowers, J.P.
source: license- 1751-04/7-136
see also volume 5, page 34

HOLLEY, ALEXANDER
and
HOLLEY, MATILDA

26 Aug 1850- John G. York, C.C.O.
27 Aug 1850- Nelson Osbern, M.G.
source: license- 1751-02/3-72
see also volume 5, page 36

FORD, HENRY
and
BARTON, ELENDER

27 Aug 1850- John G. York, C.C.O.
27 Aug 1850- John B. Wade, M.G.
source: license- 1751-02/3-49
see also volume 5, page 46

JONES, JOHN A.
and
MC COLLUM, ELIZABETH E.

28 Aug 1850- John G. York, C.C.O.
30 Aug 1850- F.H. Attaway, M.G.
source: volume , page 26

EDINS, EPHRAIM C.
and
HENDERSON, MARYANN

1 Sept 1850- John G. York, C.C.O.
1 Sept 1850- Alfred Smith, J.P.
source: volume 5, page 24

CARSON, AUGUSTIN L.
and
PAYNE, SARAH E.

14 Sept 1850- John M. Freeman, C.C.O.
19 Sept 1850- ....
source: license- 1751-01/2-24
see also volume 5, page 31

WADE, JAMES
and
ACRE, VINA

15 Sept 1850(sic)- John G. York, C.C.O.
15 Sept 1851(sic)- Isaac B. Lawrence, J.P.
source: volume 5, page 74

SIMMONS, JOSEPH
and
WATERS, MARGARET

16 Sept 1850- John G. York, C.C.O.
16 Sept 1850- Richard Wheeler, J.P.
source: volume 5, page 53

VARNER, GEORGE W.
and
MURRAY, SUSAN ANN

17 Sept 1850- John G. York, C.C.O.
17 Sept 1850- Isaac B. Lawrence, J.P.
source: volume 5, page 57

PULLIAM, THOMAS
and
TABOR, ELIZABETH M.A.

19 Sept 1850- John G. York, C.C.O.
19 Sept 1850- Osborn Garner, J.P.
source: license- 1751-03/6-120
see also volume 5, page 37

TURBYFILL, JAMES H.
and
HOPSON, REBEA

21 Sept 1850- John G. York, C.C.O.
21 Sept 1850- Green B. Holbrook, J.I.C.
source: license- 1751-04/7-150
see also volume 5, page 45

CHEEK, JOHN, JR.
and
ELROD, VINEY

3 Oct 1850- John G. York, C.C.O.
4 Oct 1850- David Vaughan, J.P.
source: volume 5, page 26

WESTBROOKS, FRANCIS M.
and
BEARDIN, MARKEY M.

10 Oct 1850- John G. York, C.C.O.
10 Oct 1850- John P. Jolly, J.P.
source: license- 1751-04/8-160
see also volume 5, page 42

WAID, WILLIAM G.
and
DAVIS, MARY S.P.

11 Oct 1850- John G. York, C.C.O.
13 Oct 1850- David Carson, M.G.
source: volume 5, page 53

WADE, WESLEY G.
and
GRICE, SARAH

17 Oct 1850- John G. York, C.C.O.
17 Oct 1850- John S. Henley, M.G.
source: license- 1751-04/8-155
see also volume 5, page 35

GREENWAY, JOHN H.W.
and
SANDERS, LUCINDA

17 Oct 1850- John G. York, C.C.O.
17 Oct 1850- Minyard Sanders, J.P.
source: license- 1751-02/3-59
see also volume 5, page 43

MEADERS, DANIEL
and
MORGAN, NANCY M.(?)

19 Oct 1850- John G. York, C.C.O.
22 Oct 1850- W'm Turk, J.I.C.
source: volume 5, page 52

PHILLIPS, THOMAS C.
and
JAMES, MARY E.

29 Oct 1850- John G. York, C.C.O.
31 Oct 1850- W'm T. Crow, J.P.
source: volume 5, page 53

VAUGHAN, WILLIAM W.
and
SHATLIN, LOUSINDA

31 Oct 1850- John G. York, C.C.O.
31 Oct 1850- John P. Jolly, J.P.
source: license- 1751-04/8-151
see also volume 5, page 42

VAUGHAN, BENJAMIN
and
SHANNON, DOROTHY K.

11 Nov 1850- Jno. M. Freeman, D.C.C.O.
13 Nov 1850- W'm J. Parks, M.G.
source: license- 1751-04/8-151
see also volume 5, page 28

NEAL, SHALES M.
and
HOLLY, JULIA F.

12 Nov 1850- John G. York, C.C.O.
14 Nov 1850- W'm J. Parks, M.G.
source: license- 1751-03/5-105
see also volume 5, page 28

GRIFFIN, ELIJAH
and
HAMBY, SUSANNAH

19 Nov 1850- John G. York, C.C.O.
19 Nov 1850- Levi Sewell, J.P.
source: license- 1751-02/3-60
see also volume 5, page 44

VICORY/VICKRY, JOHNATHAN H.
and
MC CLUSKY/MC LESKEY, ISABELAH

27 Nov 1850- John G. York, C.C.O.
5 Dec 1850- S.B. Sanders
source: license- 1751-04/8-154
see also volume 5, page 40

YARBOROUGH, JASPER
and
ADAMS, CLARISSA

30 Nov 1850- John G. York, C.C.O.
30 Nov 1850- Dan'l Mosely, J.P.
source: license- 1751-04/8-171
see also volume 5, page 39

CURRY, JOHN
and
PAGE, MARTHA

.. Dec 1850- John G. York, C.C.O.
4 Dec 1850- Minyard Sanders, J.P.
source: volume 5, page 52

BROWN, WILLIAM P.
and
MARTIN, MARY ANN

5 Dec 1850- John G. York, C.C.O.
5 Dec 1850- Isaac B. Lawrence, J.P.
source: volume 5, page 75

KING, MARK W.
and
SUDETH, MARY

7 Dec 1850- John G. York, C.C.O.
8 Dec 1850- Green B. Holbrook, J.I.C.
source: license- 1751-02/4-83
see also volume 5, page 46

ADDISON, TERRIL
and
CARTIN, HARIET

8 Dec 1850- John G. York, C.C.O.
8 Dec 1850- W'm J. Oliver, J.P.
source: license- 1751-01/1-3
see also volume 5, page 38

POPHAM, JOHN L.
   and
CHAPPELEAR, EMILINE

8 Dec 1850- John G. York, C.C.O.
8 Dec 1850- J.H. Chappelear, J.P.
source: license- 1751-03/6-116
see also volume 5, page 43

SHELTON, LEWIS
   and
GOBER, LOUISA C.

12 Dec 1850- John M. Freeman, D.C.C.O.
1 Jan 1851- V.H. Shelton, M.G.
source: license- 1751-04/7-133
see also volume 5, page 36

PRICKETT, WILLIAM P.
   and
WILLBANKS, LOUISA

12 Dec 1850- John G. York, C.C.O.
12 Dec 1850- Minyard Sanders, J.P.
source: volume 5, page 54

OSBERN, HUGH B.
   and
MURRAY, MARY ANN

28 Dec 1850- John G. York, C.C.O.
28 Dec 1850- Isaac B. Lawrence, J.P.
source: volume 5, page 74

SMITH, EZEKIEL C.
   and
STOVALL, LUCY C.

29 Dec 1850- John G. York, C.C.O.
29 Dec 1850- Oliver Harrison, J.P.
source: volume 5, page 55

MITCHELL, JO. H.
   and
JONES, E.

source: volume 5, indexed as page 327.
This page is missing.

END

.......(sirname unknown)
Adarine 13
Elizabeth 18
Tho's 30
..... 27

AARON,ARON
George W. 127
James W. 137
Jesse 21
John F. 126
John R. 99
Mary M. 150
Nancyan 121
Rosa 5
Tho's 28
William 12,54

ABBOT,ABBIT,ABET
Deba 95
Luvinda 102
Mary 47

ACKER(see also Acre)
Mary T. 43
William S. 54

ACOLS see Echols

ACRE(see also Acker)
A. Linton 107
Louvisa 123
Maryan 114
Vina 153
William 141

ADAMS
Absalom 1
Adaline A. 145
Clarissa 154
Elizabeth 81,138
Israel 83
Jesse 81
John J. 113
Julia Ann 105
Mary 124
Mary A. 129
Mehala 91
Nancy 83
Pallaan 127
Sarah 144
Sarah H. 93

ADARINE(see also
ADRINE,ADRIAN)
.... 13

ADCOCK
Louisa 97
Mary Ann 64

ADDISON,ADISON
Brazel 32
Elizabeth 142
Jincy L. 134
Rutha 148
Sanford 151
Sintha 135
Terril 155

ADERHOLD,ADDERHOLD
Anna 38
Catharine 103
Elizabeth 98
Isaac 38
John H. 100
Mary 113
Mary M. 45

ADGE(see also Age,
Edge)
Elizabeth 75

ADRIAN(see also
Adrine, Adarine)
David W. 112

ADRINE(see also
Adrian, Adarine)
Flemen F. 5

AGE(see also Adge)
Sarah 57

AKINS
Carline 90
Elender 76
William 30

ALBRITTON,ALLBRITTON
Eliza 35
Elizabeth 90
Isaac G. 110
James 84
Phillip L. 59

ALEXANDER,ELAXANDER
Cynthia A. 127
Elizabeth 4
Isaac 4
James 116
James S. 53
John M. 119
John P. 46
Mary Elizabeth 124
Rachel Ann 141
Samuel F. 65

ALFRED(see also Allred)
Camely 127

ALLEN
Alfred S. 93
Asa 29
Asenith 60
Benjamin 94
Charles 80
Elizabeth 13,22
Hudson H. 34
James 2
John M. 69
Louisa H. 61
Louisiana T. 146
Mary 95
Mary M. 108
Matilda 34
Matthew 50
Patcy 6
Polly 12
Richard 88
William D. 93
William T. 146

ALLRED(see also Alfred)
Carline/Caroline 134
Eli T. 144
Emily 133
John 22

ALMAN
William 45

ANDERS,ANDRES,ANDREWS
Adam 48
Cleavland 86
Daniel 77
David 124
Elizer 87
Enoch 4
Jane E. 85

BALLEW
  Catherine 140
  Jane 119
  Nancy 142

BANKS
  Levy 4
  Mary 99
  Ralph 142
  Robert T. 57
  Russell 143
  Saryann E. 90

BARBER
  Sampson 33
  William A. 55

BARNES (see also Burns)
  Anne 8

BARNETT
  Jane 31
  Martha 102
  Susan 70

BARRETT
  Eliza H. 71

BARRY (see also Berry)
  Bartley 51

BARTON (see also Burton)
  Cloud 60
  Daniel/David 79
  David O. 131
  Dolly 28
  Elender 152
  Frances 2
  William E. 80

BASKIN
  Mary 62

BATES (see also Baits)
  Adaline 125
  Bryant 125
  James 122

BAUGH, BAU
  Anderson 145
  Crofford 136
  John 146
  Julian 142

BAUZEWELL (see also
  Boswell)
  Miles 19

BAXTER, DACKSTER
  Becca 18
  Dorcas 37
  W'm 3

BEALL, BEAL (see also
  Bell)
  Amelia 31
  Elizabeth 87
  Frederick 62
  Horatio 61
  Josiah 35

Lucy 33
Mat. W. 16
Russel G. 29
Tempe 1
William J. 131

BEARD, BEAIRD (see
  also BAIRD)
  Hennery W. 127
  Margaret W. 144
  Nancy 105
  Polly 33

BEARDIN, BIARDEN
  Charlote M. 133
  John 104
  Markey M. 153

BEASLEY
  Clarasy 21

BEASONS
  Elizabeth 17

BELL, BELLE (see
  also Beall)
  Aaron 80
  Addam 39
  Alison 67
  Catherine 144
  Eliza 149
  Harriet 140
  James 78
  Joseph 109
  Martha 96
  Maryan 107
  Ruth 16
  Sarah 138
  Thomas 14

BELLAMY
  Asa 71
  Elizabeth 62
  Gilbert F. 95
  John 52
  Leavycy 35
  Lovevina 117
  Nicholas 20
  Pleasant 67

BENNET (T)
  Cooper 65
  Ezebeth 64
  Mary 10
  Melissa Irle 86
  Peter 68
  William 102

BERRY (see also Barry)
  John 56

BETENBAU
  Michael 78

BING
  Elizabeth 147
  George A. 111
  James 108
  Martha 58

BIRD (see also Byrd and
  Birtt)
  John Shew 95
  Martha H. 60,77

BIRTT (see also Byrd,
  and Bird and Burt)
  John 33

BLACK
  David M. 105
  Elizabeth 132
  James 137
  James M. 70
  Janet 3
  John 9
  John G.A. 132
  Mary 96
  Mary B. 79
  Sarah 67
  Susannah 89

BLACKWELL
  Ann 17
  Elizabeth 40
  Hensley 90
  Jediah 25
  Jesse 9
  Joel 65
  Lucy 71
  Nancy 101
  Russel 113

BLAIR
  Hugh 94
  John 80
  Levi 49
  Nancy 135
  Sally 32

BLALOCK
  Ella 43

BLANKENSHIP, BLANKINSHIP
  Benjamin 86
  John 109
  Mary 129
  Nancy 39

BOATWRIGHT
  Drewry 133
  Nancy 29

BOBO
  Benjamin H. 66

BOGGS
  Eliza Jane 82

BOHANNON, BOHANAN
  James 2
  James S. 38
  William 14

BOLCH
  Georg A. 52

BOLEN,BOLIN(G) (see
  Bulling, Rollen)
  Amey 6
  Nancy 27
  Prisiley 27

BOLES
  George 8

BOLLS
  Eber M. 21

BOND(S)
  Charity 18
  Eliza 69
  Ephraim M. 94
  Jinney 15
  Leonard 28
  Lindsey 105
  Lucy 79
  Milley 124
  Russell P. 149
  Sarah 98
  Vily 34
  Willis D. 106
  Write 28

BORDERS
  Adaline 62

BORUM
  Mary 56

BOSEL
  William 69

BOSWELL,BOZWELL
  (see also Bauzewell)
  Elizabeth A. 109
  Fatama 114
  James 8,74
  Jasper N. 133
  John 64
  John C. 132
  Sarah 109
  William 23

BOWEN
  Andrew 46
  Andrew W. 85
  Hepsey 15
  Polly 30

BOWERS
  Edy 73
  Jephthath A. 150
  Susey A. 139
  Thomas W. 112

BOX
  Eachel 5

BRADLEY,BRADLY
  Elizabeth 53
  Marry 120
  Prissilla 141
  Sally 128

BRADY
  Enoch 23
  William 139

BRAMLET,BRAMBLETT
  (see also Brumblet)
  John 67
  Mary 31
  Nathaniel 33

BRANAM,BRANNAM,BRANNUM,
  BRANEN,BRONEN(see also
  Brawner)
  Frances 46
  Mary 44, 117
  Nancy 82

BRANTLY
  Joseph A. 23

BRASDLE
  Ann 4
  James 12
  Rebecca 14
  Sarah 11
  Winnefred 15

BRASHER,BRAISHER
  Deanner 12
  Jamimay 17

BRAWNER,BRONNER
  (see also Branam)
  Amelia 2
  Ann 7
  Charlotte 78
  Elizabeth 7
  Jeffers H. 122
  Melissa M. 95
  Sarah 54
  Washington M. 87

BRAY
  Alphomzo 145
  Hillman 124

BREWER,BRUER
  Catharine R. 134
  Henry M. 128
  Jackson M. 130
  Randle 19
  Sarah 65

BREWSTER
  William Pinkney 81

BRIDGES,BRIGES
  Cloe 70
  Delilah 79
  Elizabeth 42
  James M. 152
  Mary 110
  Sarah Ann 128
  Selah 119
  William J. 130
  Wilson 106

BRIGHT
  Charlot(Lottey) 16

BRINDLEY,BRINLEE,
  BRENDLEE
  Asa 30
  Lucinda 22
  Luvice 18

BRITT
  Elizabeth 123

BROCK
  Reuben C. 141
  William 26

BRONEN(see Branam)

BROOKS
  Job 12

BROWN
  Ann 19
  Anna P. 137
  Asbury H. 137
  Benjamin M. 139
  Catharine 9
  Eliza 94
  Hugh 51
  Isaac 9
  James 19,34
  Jensa 12
  Jesse 37
  John 4,6
  Julian 107
  Margarett A. 111
  Mary 88,117
  Polly 121
  Priscilla 5
  Rebekah 4
  Robert 44,122
  Thomas 11
  William 25,35
  William P. 154

BRUCE
  Catharine R. 134
  David L. 130
  Elizabeth 121
  Marthann 135
  Mary 51

BRUMBLET,BRUMLY(see also
  Bramlet)
  Eliza 37
  Stephen 30

BRYAN(T),BRIANT
  Alis 45
  Benjamin K. 106
  Dobia D. 98
  Edith 8
  Elizabeth 34
  Francis C. 132
  Harriett 140
  James R. 147
  Jesse 72
  Jinny 34
  Lovada L. 61
  Lucinda 72
  Martha 52
  Martin 109
  Nancy 84,101

Mary 131
Sary 110
Thomas 5
William R. 73

CARVER
Henry 47

CASEY,CASY,CASEE,
CAZEE,KAZE
Barbarey 138
Bashaba 143
George 115
Jno. 27
Matilda 111
Nancy 64

CASH
Henry C. 38
Howard 97,128
Joseph 108
Lidia H. 33
Peggy 18
Sally 28
Stephen 117

CATLETT
Mary 64
Sary 49
Susannah 62

CAUDEL(L),CAWDELL,
(see also Cadel,
Cardell,Caldwell)
Daniel 128
David 27,42,109
Elisabeth 143
Eliza T. 92
Gilberd 134
Green 107
Hannah 44
Jane 69
Mary 51
Nancy 117
Phebe 48

CAUSBEY(see also Cosby)
Elender S. 150

CAWTHON,CAUTHON,
CORTHORN,CORTHAN
Claburn 29
Elizabeth 128
Fanny 41
Harriett 93
Larkan 118
Lucy 136
Martha 124
Orpha 121
Orville 55
Polly 46
Rhoda,Rody 99,101
Wilkinson T. 47
William 138

CHALMERS(see also
Chambers)
Elizar 62
Jane 96

CHAMBERS(see also
Chalmers)
Elizabeth M. 78
John E. 132
Lene 95
Thomas 94

CHAMBLEE
Nancy C. 139

CHANDLER,CHANLER,
CHANDELAR
Allen 4
Ambrose 42
Anna 118
Asa 53
Clement Q. 129
Daniel 38,49
Devereax Jarret 134
Dudley J. 60
Elizabeth 23,26,116
Elza 65
Frances C. 51
Green 26
Jabes E. 128
Jedediah 20
Joseph N. 147
Lewis 40
Linsey 56
Lucindy 67
Maleda 28
Martha 24,48
Mary 36,99
Matilda 28,42
Nancy M. 116
Peggy 23
Rebecca 43
Rhoda 34
Sarah 130
Stephen 38
Thomas 54
William 53
Wyett 17

CHAPMAN
James M. 128

CHAPPLEAR,CHAPPLIER,
CHAPPELEAR
Benjamin 62
Cassandra 71
Emiline 155
James H. 97
Orpha C. 97
Polley 12

CHATERCIAL
Elizabet 84

CHATHAM,CHITHAM
Almeda 127
Bernicy 49
Chafin,Chafan 14,62
Cyntha 103
Ester 36
Isham 131
James 45
John W. 90
Lemuel 117
Mary 86

Polly 10
Roda 30
Sally 1
Sarah J. 67
Thomas H. 111
William 17,71

CHEEK,CHEAK
Burgess H. 102,131
Charles W. 125
Elizabeth 31,104,140
Holland B. 151
James S. 107
Jane 33
John 72,153
John M.D. 130
Larkin S. 129
Milton 152
Pleasant 81
Priscilla(r) 89,116,122
Rolin 149
Rowland B. 102
Samuel P. 135
Tresey 152
William P. 149

CHILDERS
Thomas 67

CHILDS, CHILES
Elizabeth 138
John 117
Margaret 70
Mirica 96
William 86

CHITWOOD
Dan'l 26

CHRISTIAN
Cinus 39
Einus 39
Elizabeth 11
Fanney 53
George M. 42
Nancy 3
Obed M. 8
Pyride 39
Sarah 37,50

CLARK
Catherine B. 140
David 81
Dicy 28,67
Elizabeth 35
Francis 111
Jacob 57
Jane 53
John 47
John T. 93
Wiley 47
William W. 81
Zacheriah 46

CLARKSON
Elizabeth 42
Jane 113
Joseph 22
Kizia 40

CLEGHORN(E)
Elizabeth 7,14

CLEVELAND,CLEAVLAND
Alpha 91
Anne 27
Arminda B. 75
Elizabeth 97
Jemmima 21
Joseph 7
Thomas G. 133
William E. 118

COBB,COB
Anna 68
Edwin M. 144
Isaac E. 51
Patsy B. 18
Samuel 115

COCKBURN
Jeremiah 46

COCKER see Coker

COCKERHAM(see also
Cockrum)
Elizabeth 71
Mary 65
Matthew B.H. 61
Milley 82

COCKRUM,COCKRAM(see
also Cockerham)
Frd'k 37
Robert 132
Sally 47

COFFEE
Milly 120

COFFIN
Nancy 118

COIL see Coyle

COKER,COCKER
Adaline 87
Alsea T. 97
Arminda 152
Chalton 42
Charlotte 129
Elizabeth 94
Isaiah 114
Izaah 121
Jacob F. 124
Joseph 70
Mary 106
Maryan 66
Milley 151

COLEMAN
Susannah 14

COLLEM
Elizabeth 27

COLLINS,COLLENS
Arinda 86
Benjamin 85

Charles O. 101
Elizabeth 5,11
Mary 6,101
Thomas 146

COLLY
James 98

COLLYER
Anna 146
Christian 81
John 134
Moses 70
Sarah 66
Thomas 6

COMBS
Harriett M. 59

COMPTON
Deneria/Dencria 62

CONE(see also
Cane)
Polly 87

CONNALLY,CONLEY,
CONLY
Benjamin H. 137
Charles M. 37
Christopher 39
Disa 37
Drury 7
Mary 42
Polly 7
Samuel W. 39
Sarah 16
Thursy 32
William 39

CONNER
John 12

COOK
Burrell 5
Cynthia 112
Emily 68
Francis T. 39
Lucy 37
Mary 65
Sarah 23,56

COOPER
Elenor 131
Temple F. 109

CORNELIUS
Absalom 7

CORNELIUSON see
Cuneliuson)

COSBY(see also
Causbey)
Austin W. 55
Mary Jane 141
Nancy 53

COUCH
James 17
Mary 36
Mary M. 70
Reuben 37

COVINGTON,COVINTON
Catherine 9
Eleanor 12
Rebecca 7

COX
Annah 48
Benjamin J.S. 146
Clement W. 114
Elizabeth 15
Leanna 19
Mary J. 88
Matthew 94
Michel 69
Robert R. 6
William 139
William G. 147

COYLE,COIL
Ann 5
Rebekah 3

CRAFT
Elizabeth 21
Polly 130
Sarah Ann 110
William C. 138

CRAIG
John G. 150

CRAWFORD
Elijah 21
Hugh 34
Husel 136
John 30
Margaret 135
Martha Minerva 130
Mary 4
Moses B. 78
Rachael 107
Sarah 63

CRIDER
Alisabeth 121
David 138
Jane 114
Jerusa 151
John 79
Martha S. 107
Sarah 99
Sophia 79
Susan 69

CROMER
Barbary 103
David 115
Hiram 100

CROSS
Elizabeth 21

CROW
  Francess J.A. 112
  Jesse M. 139
  John W. 63
  Levi 59
  Nancy 104
  Perlina A. 132
  Randolph 44
  Rebecca J. 137
  Sarah 109
  Thomas J. 59
  William S. 54
  William T. 40

CRUMP
  Clary Liles 79
  Dinselondy 20
  Hannor 117
  Jane 32
  Maryan 95
  Memery 99
  Missa 4
  Permelia 94
  Rahtha 50
  Richard 13

CUMMINS
  Mary 125
  Melinda 114

CUNELIUSON
  A. 34

CURRY(see also Carey)
  John 72,154

DAILY,DAILEY
  Mary 128
  Susan 66
  William 49

DANIEL
  James 2
  Russel 18

DAVID(see also Davis)
  Julian E. 148
  Nancy H. 89
  Nancy J. 127
  Pillina W. 88,152

DAVIS,DAVES,DAVICE
  (see also David)
  Angeline 146
  Claryann 97
  Coopper B. 120
  Elizabeth 8,10,14,37
  Henry H. 31
  Hezekiah 65
  James 58
  James H. 32
  Jefferson 72
  Jincy 5
  L.M. 141
  Littleton M. 83
  Mary S.P. 153
  Maryann 138
  Matthew 20
  Nancy 23
  Nancy T. 81

Pollyann 46
Robert 92
Thomas D. 129
Van 120
William 13
Winney 29
Young 116

DAVISON,DAVISEN
  Emaline 126
  Nancy B. 44
  Rachael 60

DAWSON
  Elizabeth 125
  Emaline 126

DAY
  Rachel 9

DAYMON
  John 98

DEALE(see also
  Duell)
  William 8

DEAR(see also Deen)
  William 32

DEARING
  Elizabeth 50

DEBENPORT
  Matthew 133

DEEN(see also Dear)
  William 6,29

DEFOOR
  Druciller 41
  Martin 57

DELPORT
  Harriett 70
  James 110

DEMSEY
  Berryman S. 88

DENMAN
  Absalem 11
  Catherine 3
  Christopher 44
  Elizabeth 21
  Felix G. 32
  Hepsebeth 8
  James 29
  John 10
  Morgan 14
  Nancy 122
  Polly 17
  Susan 147
  William 6
  William S. 53

DENT
  Ann 35
  Cloe S. 29

DEVALL
  Imaly E. 93

DEVERALL
  John 45

DICKERSON,DICKASON(see
  also Dixon)
  Joel 69
  John R. 75

DICKERT
  Libby 55

DIXON(see also
  Dickerson)
  Bethana 6
  Daniel 6

DOBBINS
  Mahaly 149

DOBBS,DOBS
  Alvin B. 150
  Delila 45
  Elizabeth 5,13
  Greenberry 60
  James 19
  Lodowick 45
  Martan 52
  Martha 52
  Meeky 26
  Moreman 17
  Oliver 135
  Solomon 56
  William 9

DODD
  9
  David 11
  Jeremiah 105
  Lemuel 48
  Peterson 8
  Sary 1
  Wiley 96

DODSON
  Elizabeth 62

DONAHOO,DUNAHOO
  Cernelius R. 35
  Eleanor 98
  James 25,36
  Mary Ann 90

DOOLEY
  John 29

DORSEY
  Caty 5
  Polly 9
  Priscilla 6

DOWDY
  Armsted 21

DOWNS
Eliza 84
Sarah Ann 61

DUDLEY
John 29

DUELL(see also Deale)
William 68

DUNAGIN
Joseph 33

DUNAHOO see Donahoo

DUNCAN
Aner 72

DUNLOT
Lucy 34

DUNSON
Nancy 115
William 56

DYAR
George W. 96
Joel H. 43

DYE
Stephen 8

EATON
Amanda L. 108
Sarah 129

ECHOLS,ECHOLLS,ACOLS
Abram 34
Ann 25,41
Shapleigh 85
William E. 144

EDGE(see also Adge
and Age)
Elizabeth 146
Flora 148

EDINS,EDDINS
Elizabeth 34
Ephraim C. 153
Martha A. 80

EDWARDS
Amanda M. 145
Edward H. 87
Judah Ann 65
Patsey 33
Sarah 60
Thomas G. 57

ELAXANDER see Alexander
ELLIOTT
Elizabeth 12
Mehelia 22

ELLIS
Eliza N. 150
Martha 56

ELISON
David 13
Moses 21
Nancy 21

ELROD
Viney 153

ELSTON
Allen 15

ENGLISH
Elizar 125
Hiram 80
Lucy 141
Margarett 44
Martha 103
Mary 139
Wesley 99

EPPERSON,EPPERZEN
Charles 75
Hannah 11
James W. 114
Katharine 113
Peter 13

ESKEW(see also
Askew, Askea and
Asca)
John B. 83

EVANS
Adaline 74

EVERETT,EVRETT,EVIT
Elizabeth 18
Rebecca 22
Sary 101

F. GARRELL
Samuel 39

FAGANS(see also
Figgins)
J.Z. 82
Moses 47

FAIN
Mary 66

FANNEN
Jno. 26

FARMER
Lucy 10
William H. 111

FARRAR
Lewis 115

FARROW
Sursey 32

FENOT
Charaty 32

FIELD
Samuel 61
Susanner 29

FIGGENS(see also Fagans)
Peggy 19

FINCH
Catharine 114
Martha 108
Osbern 84
Polly 39
Thomas 114

FINN
Midleton 63

FITZPATRICK
James P. 127

FLEMIN,FLEMING
James L. 19
Jane 9
Malisa 102
Martha 80
Matthew L. 135
Permelia 21

FLOOD
Celesthus E.D. 121
John 93
Patsy 21
Virginia 80
William 67

FORD
Henry 152
James 132
Sarai 95
William 49

FORRESTER,FORESTER
Elender 8
Margaret 2

FORSYTH,FORCYTH
Malinda 113
Nancy 70
William 4

FOWLER
Anna 98
George D. 93
John A. 68
Lucey 143
Lucinda C. 120
Nancy 45
Patcy 33
Polly 33
Susan 115

FREEMAN
Benajah 55
David 113
Elizabeth 75
Elmina 135
Frankey 125
Henry 34,38
Hudson 98
James 48
Jemima 148
Jhonathan 110
Margaret 59
Mary F. 131

Matilda 67
Pliney 117
Polley 49
Sarah G.P. 132
Wesley 117

FRY
Drury 59

FULBRIGHT,FULLBRIGHT
Catherine 149
David 87
Mary 108
May 105
Partheny 52
Susan 118

FULGHAM,FULGUM,FULGIM
Elizabeth 68
Jesse P. 89
Pricilla 82

FULLER
Coper B. 66
Nancy P. 95

FURR
Paul 149

GABLE
Harmon 121

GAINES, GAINS
Elizabeth 117
Susannah 107

GANT
Elizabeth J. 147

GARDINER(see also
Garner)
Samuel 70

GARNER(see also
Gardiner)
Anna 77
Derrel 106
George 75
George H. 149
George W. 130,141
James 116
Lucinda 122
Martha 130
Martin G. 93
Mary 107
Mary C. 139
Nancy 38
Osburn 58
Samuel K. 148
Sarah 89,143
William 115,115

GARRETT
Mahaley 71
Pendleton 79

GARRISON
Barnabas 69
Caleb 5
Candas 47

Cassel 57
Catharine 137
David J. 79
Ellender 24
Enoch C. 140
Hannah E. 136
James 5
James H. 44
Jedidiah 53
Juday E. 28
Martha 147
Martin 94
Nancy 36
Sarah Ann 146
Saulbury 54
Susanna 16
Thomas S. 89
Thomas W. 113
Tryphena 57
William 21

GARTNEY,GORTNEY
Mary Ann 147
Rebecca 29

GARVIN
Micajer 62

GATEWOOD
Roland 12

GAZAWAY,GASAWAY
John 148
Lucindy 94
Mary 151
Thomas 12,18

GIBS
Mima 15

GIBSON
Daniel 36
John 17
Judah 25
Ruhama 17

GIDEON
Francis 19

GILBERT
Elizabeth 18
Prissilla 14
William 14

GILLESPIE,
GILLISPIE
Frances W. 149
James 49
James L. 120
Milton W. 95
Patterson R. 84
Pickens 56

GILLEY(see also
Gulley)
Willis 18

GINN
Charlott S.F. 129
James C. 135

GLASS
Nancy 24

GLAZIER
Charles R. 61

GLENN,GLYNN
Andrew 110
Arminda 94
Catharine 102
Eliza P.W. 86
Elizabeth 67
Franklin 48
William 5

GLOVER
Alpha A. 112
Elizabeth Ann 130
James M. 139
Jane 73
Joseph P. 107
Marhy 78
Maryann 103
Sarah Ann 103
William 13

GOBER
Betsy 37
Daniel 17
Dolly 12
Elizabeth 1,51,93
George 88
Hiram 37
Jiney 33
John 57,92
Louisa C. 155
Margarette 41
Mariah 35
Marian 35
Mary 51
Nancy 22
Orpha 76
Richard 21
Robert H. 90
Sarah 100
William J. 93

GOODE
Daniel 67
George W. 91

GOODSON
Nancy 40
Patsy 60
William 125

GOODWIN
Nancy 13

GOOSBY(see also
Gouldsby)
Judge A.P. 127

GORDON,GORDAN,GORDEN
Alston 80
Elizabeth 115
Henry 92
William 121,129

GORHAM
  Thomas 20

GORTNEY see Gartney

GOULDSBY(see also
  Goosby)
  Charles 109

GOWDY
  Fred'k 13

GRADDY
  Elizabeth 74

GRADY
  William 5

GRAHAM
  Jonathan 46
  W'm R. 70

GRAVES
  Jeremiah 31

GRAY
  Elizabeth 14
  Garret 45
  Jane 55
  Johnson 60

GREEN
  Caleb 101
  John 59
  Nancy 66
  Robert 118
  Tandy H. 37

GREENWAY
  John H.W. 154
  Sarah L. 145

GRESHAM
  W.S. 135

GRICE(see also
  Grose)
  Sarah 153

GRIFFIN
  Asa 28
  Elijah 154
  Hardy 113

GROSE(see also
  Grice)
  Sary 47
  Susy 47

GROOVER,GRUVER
  Milton 91
  John 19

GROVER
  Milley 46

GUEST,GESS,GUESS
  Anny 18
  Curtis 142
  David 77

Harriet 145
Lucy 133
Martha 78
Mary 78
Mary Ann 146
Neacy 146
Russel 129
Sarah 99

GULLEY,GULLY(see
  also Gilley)
  Alpha F.O. 108
  Eliza B. 113
  Richard L. 129

GUNNELLS
  Avis 49
  Sarah Francis 119

GUNTER
  Tempy 97

HACKETT
  Eliza T. 52
  Ellen C. 103

HADDEN(see also
  Headen, Heaton,
  and Hatan)
  Nancy 82

HAGEWOOD(see
  also Hogwood)
  Hesteran 115

HAILING
  Nelly 8

HAINS see Haynes

HALE(see also Hall)
  Margarett E. 138

HALEY (see also
  Holley)
  Dice 25
  James 41
  Lewdeay 10
  Nancy 72
  William 103

HALL(see also Hale)
  Dicia Elvira 128
  Elizabeth 71
  George 36
  Jane E. 143
  Judah 27
  July 35
  Lidy 11
  Robert H. 38
  Seborn 28
  Tabitha 49
  William 10
  William H. 13

HAMBY,HAMBEY(see
  also Hanby)
  J.F.L. 99
  Levy 35
  Susannah 154

HAMILTON,HAMBLETON
  Mordeca Stringer 3
  Parrina 112
  William B. 83

HAMMETT
  James 48

HAMMOND
  Terreas C. 80

HAMPTON
  Henry 40
  William 96

HANBY(see also Hamby)
  Any 39

HANCOCK
  Frances 96
  Isiah 13
  Sarah Ann 148

HAND
  Polly 70

HANES see Haynes

HANEY
  Rob't B. 143

HANLEY(see also Henley)
  Any 39

HANNAN
  Carline W. 58

HARBIN(see also Hardin)
  Sarah 72
  William 82

HARBOUR,HARBER
  Eli J. 123
  Katharine 49
  Martha 79
  Mary 73
  Nancy 53
  Talman 85
  Tho's 2

HARDIN(see also Harbin)
  Evalina 80
  Sandlin 12

HARDY
  Armsted 38
  Freeman 22
  Henry W. 52
  John 75

HARGROVE
  John 4

HARPER
  Andrew K. 74
  John 53

HARRIS(see also
  Harrison)
  Allen 90
  Ann 138
  Charles 8
  Elizabeth 6
  Little 39
  Nathaniel 22
  Patience 16
  Starling 1
  Thomas 7
  Walter/Walton 126
  William 31,61

HARRISON,HARISSON(see
  also Harris)
  Adaline 85
  Adaline B. 117
  Catharine 87
  Clark 122
  Elizabeth 55,85
  Elizabeth C. 152
  Elvira 84
  Frances A. 152
  Francis 42
  Hugh 58
  James A. 140
  John T. 92
  Larkin 42
  Nancy 65,65
  Oliver 77
  Reuben 6
  Rhoda E. 144
  Robert 8,18
  Terrel L. 89
  Vastine B. 146

HATAN(see also Hadden,
  Headen and Heaton)
  Samuel 25

HATHCOCK
  James 146
  Sarahan 142
  Thomas H. 142
  William 50

HAWKINS,HAWKINGS
  Bennet 118
  James M. 104

HAYES,HAYS,HAZE
  Hendricks 119
  Jackson 66
  Jacob 116
  Mary 34
  Nancy 81
  Solathiel 121
  William 147

HAYNES,HAINS,HANES
  Eli T. 79
  Elijah 87
  Hanner 82
  James 114
  James W. 73
  John W. 91
  Linney 149
  Moses 78
  Nancy 58

  Patience 16
  Polly 18
  Sarah 129
  Stephen 59,112

HAZE see Hayes and
  Hazy

HAZY(see also Hayes)
  Scientific 109

HEADEN(see also Hatan,
  Hadden and Heaton)
  Elizabeth 56
  Lousanna 93
  Ollia F. 128

HEATON,HEETON(see
  also Headen,Hatan,
  and Hadden)
  Henry O. 113
  Samuel 25
  William 45

HEDRICK
  Gurdran 10

HEMPHILL
  Caroline 78
  John 105
  Robert 44

HENDERSON
  Elizabeth 10,19
  Joseph 22
  Maryann 153
  Nancy 25
  Sinah 23

HENDRICK(S),HENDRIX
  Elizabeth 121
  Gilford E. 69
  Jeremiah 63
  John C. 86
  John J. 47
  Nancy 16,116
  William 87

HENIG(see also Hening)
  Eliza 38

HENING,HENNINGS(see
  also Henig)
  Harriett S.C. 96
  Margaret 31

HENLEY(see also Hanley)
  Edmond 8
  John S. 112
  Sally 24

HENSLEE
  David S. 27

HENSON,HINSON
  Alsey 50
  Joannah 46
  Nancy 101
  Sarah 64
  William 72

HERIN(G),HERRIN(G),
  HERREN
  Benson 150
  Clarissa 101
  Joel 36
  Mary Elizabeth 110
  Matilda An 126
  William 30

HERVEY
  Eleener 26

HEWEL(see also Howell)
  John 9

HEWSE(see also Hughes,
  and House)
  Polley 2

HEWEY
  Eleener 26

HEYRS(see also Ayers)
  David 20

HICKS see HIX

HIDE see Hyde

HIGGINBOTHAM,HICKUMBOTTAM
  Francis 35
  Rachel 42

HIGGINS,HIGGENS,HEGGINS
  Burwell 16
  Charaty 16
  Elizabeth 16,88
  Enoch 22
  Henry 123
  Polly 22
  Tho's 29

HILBURN
  N.S. 77

HILL
  Adaline 127
  Benjamin C. 131
  Benjamin R. 76
  Caleb 54
  David 142
  Harry M. 118
  Lucinda 86
  Mary 91
  Nancy A. 137
  William 31
  William R. 81,142

HILLHOUSE
  Elijah 42

HINSON see Henson

HIX,HICKS
  C.G. 144
  Cyntha 135
  Elizabeth 128
  Harvey 78
  James 122
  Martha 127

Mary 6
Matilldy 77
Meekey 81

HOBBS
Louisa 32

HOBGOOD see Hopgood

HOBSON,HOPSON
Matilda 108
Rebea 153

HODGE
James 15
John 12

HOGWOOD(see also
Hagewood)
Asa 16

HOLBROOK(S),HOLEBROOK,
HOLDBROOK(S)
Berrian 88
Betsey 33
Christopher 37
Darkes 20
Eleanor 19
Elizabeth A.V. 146
Franklin M. 125
Franky 17
Jinsey 19
John 9
Katharine 86
Mahala 88
Nelly 2
Partheny 86
Pleasant 73
Samuel 12
Thomas P. 78

HOLCOM(B)(E)
Cinthey 88
Elizabeth 18
Jane 105
Katharine 86
Matilda 75
Russell 35
Shearwood 149
Sintha 21
Spencer 60

HOLLAND
Allen W. 18
Benjamin 128
Uvey 5

HOLLEY,HOLLY,HOLEY
(see also Haley)
Alexander 152
Daniel W. 146
Emmily M. 89
James R. 90
John A. 131
Julia F. 154
Louisa H. 69
Martha 84
Mary E. 123
Matilda 152
Pleasant 34

Polley 2
William 34,132,152

HOLLINGSWORTH
Benjamin 3
Hannah 26
James 14
John 22
Mary 3

HOLMES,HOMES
Allen 67
Elizabeth 20
James J. 15
Lucy 20

HOLSANBAKE
Japtha 116

HONEY
William 39

HOOD
Eda S. 39
Elizabeth 126
James H. 68
Mary A. 120
Stephen R. 108

HOODLOW
Mary Ann 112
Sarah A. 120

HOOPER(see also
Hopper)
Clementin C. 89
Elizabeth 79
Emelia 87
Garland 77
Johnson M. 49
Joicy 84
Martha 61
Mary 111
Milly 108
Nancy 134
Patcy 10
Richard 76
Richard L. 126
Susannah 7
Washington H. 96

HOPGOOD,HOBGOOD
Hezekiah 33
Nancy 125
Pamela 66

HOPPER(see also
Hooper)
Winncy 28

HOPSON see Hobson

HORTON
Artimissa 67

HOSEY
Bennet(t) 83,123
Daniel 118
Isaac 120
Levi 70

HOUS(E),HOUZE(see also
Hewse)
Balsory 122
Charlotte 75
Darling B. 34,44
Elizabeth 101
George C. 122
Matilda An 126
Patience 16

HOUSTON
John K. 44

HOWARD
Benjamin 72

HOWEL,HOWELL(see also
Hewel)
Anny 28
Joseph A. 147
Nancy 76
Sarah 68

HOWINGTON
Eldridge W. 148
Polly 26
William R. 60

HUBBARD
Francis 97
Levi 132
Lewis 92
Moriah 94
Partin 104
Toliver W. 107
Zenus 130

HUDGINS(see also
Hutchins)
Nancy 55

HUDSON,HUTSON
Charlette M. 104
Elizabeth 45
Francis A. 119
James P. 119
Milton P. 109
Sary M. 132
William C. 112

HUGHES(see also Hewse)
Elizabeth 59
William 70,101

HULSE(Y)
Anny 20
John 24
Pleasant 17
Sarah 36

HUMPHREYS,HUMPHRIS
Elizabeth 53
George 37
James 38

HUNNICUT
Wilson F. 73

HUNT
  Elija 137
  Elizabeth 24,46
  Esley 66
  Mary 35
  Richard C. 141
  Sinthey 84

HUNTER
  William M. 76

HUTCHENS,HUTCHINS(see
  also Hudgins)
  Francis 79
  Mary E. 77
  Mary M. 77

HUTCHERSON,HUCHERSON
  Abisha 34
  Ann 32
  Joel 138

HYATT
  Elizabeth 73

HYDE,HIDE
  George W. 140
  Nancy 123
  Sally 47
  Sarah 133
  William 85,104

ILEY
  Barbara 58
  Cyntha 60

INGLAND
  David 29
  Rachel 20

INGRAM
  John 100
  Littleton 124
  Martin 24

IRONS
  William 17

ISAAC
  Elizabeth 20

ISBEL(L)
  Allen 71,95
  Clarkey 73
  James L. 151
  John 71
  John M. 135
  Robert G. 147
  Sarah 52

ISOM
  James 18
  John 23

IVIE
  John 24

JACKSON
  Adrew/Adrene J. 107
  Amelia 34
  Arminda 134
  Disey 62
  Loveday 100
  Mahulda 100
  Martha 3
  Mary 54
  Randal L. 100
  Rebeca 72
  Rhoda 52
  Susanah 115
  Thomas 64
  Tillman 125

JAMES(see also Jones,
  and Jeans)
  Jane 138
  John C. 142
  Mary E. 154
  Nicy 70
  William 145

JEANS,JENES(see also
  Jones and James)
  Lucinda 107
  Nancy 28,137

JEFFERS
  John 46

JENKINS,JINKINS
  Jesse 76
  Jincey 45
  Lewis 89
  Liley 60
  Mary E. 103
  Mascy S. 99
  Richard 79
  Thomas 2

JENTRY
  Elizabeth 50

JOHNSON,JOHNSTON
  Abigail 145
  Aggy 64
  Ann 7,36
  Anna 37
  Elizabeth 65
  Henry 98
  James 9
  James R. 94
  Jesse 50
  Jon 51
  Louisa 64
  Martha 109
  Nancey 49
  Rachel 16
  Samuel 38
  Sarah 118

JOLLY
  Annez 77
  John P. 65
  Mary 101
  Nancy 60
  Samuel 87

JONES(see also James
  and Jeans)
  Alfred S. 105
  Ann 29
  Catharine W. 41
  Charles 50
  Charles Wesley 111
  Drewry 28
  E. 155
  Elizabeth 89
  Emily 74
  Frances S. 57
  Harriett 56
  Harriett B. 83
  James D. 97
  Jane 66
  Jesse 143
  John 150
  John A. 82,152
  Joicy 3
  Joseph 15
  Lewis D. 43
  Luiza 40
  Martha 31,35
  Martha A. 111,132
  Martin 28
  Mary 14
  Mary H. 56
  Micajah 30,50
  Nancy 60
  Peyton R. 92
  Rebeccah 52
  Robert 115
  Rody 20
  Rutha 63
  Sarah 24,57,93
  Sarah J. 42
  Sophia 31
  Susan Elizabeth 105
  Syntha H. 98
  Terrell H. 74
  William 28,42

JORDAN,JORDEN,JAOURDEN
  Archabel 61
  Atlanteh O. 106
  Beyna 38
  Drewry 151
  Gray 23
  James 91
  Jane 36
  John 83
  Mary Ann 92
  Tempy 19

JUSTICE
  Elizabeth 136
  Stephen 101

KAZE see Casey

KEELING
  Moses M. 106

KEES(see also Key)
  Delila 3

Izebella 50
James M. 93
John H. 89
Martha 81
Mary 82
Nancy 25,28
Sarah Jane 140

LOGEN
Reuben 7

LOGGINS
Ann 26

LOONEY,LOONY
Joseph C. 54
Leah 124
Mary 123
Morgan H. 148
Rhoda 151
Sarah A. 148

LORD(see also Lard,
and Leaird)
Simeon 116

LORRYMORE
Andrew 149

LOTHEREDG(E)
Benjamin 108
Jacob 114

LOUGHRIDGE see
Laughridge

LOVELADY
Nancy 9

LOVIL
Samuel C. 43

LOVIN(G)
Louiza 38
Sandford 108

LOWERY,LOWRY
Amos 35
Ann 5
Benjamin 18
Charles 5
David 23
Elisha 70
George 15
Isom 62
Jackson 87
James 5,24
John 25
John W. 24
Margaret 17
Nathan 7

LUADING(see also
Leuallen,)
John 34

MABRY,MAYBRY,MABURY
Eli L. 77
Ephraim W. 146
James 66
Joshua 41

Mary 74
Nancy 86
Walter 149

MCALLA(see also
McCalla)
Tho's 6

MCARTEY(see also
McCarter)
Elizabeth 83

MCCALL,MCCAUL
Frances 139
Francis 61
James M. 98
Rebecca 43

MCCALLA(see also
McAlla)
James R. 77

MCCARTER,MCCARTA(see
also McArtey)
Alexander 57
James 12
James H. 42
Joseph M. 150
Malinda 100
Mary 65
Matthew 6
Rebecca 150
Sarah 61
Susan 55
Susannah 124

MCCLAY
Letty 52

MCCLESKY,MCCLUSKEY,
MCLESKEY
Isabelah 154
John 142

MCCOLLAY
Margaret 56

MCCOLLOM,MCCOLLUM
Elizabeth E.   152
Sarah 85

MCCOY
Nancy 29

MCCRACKEN
Cintha 128
Elizabeth 38
Margaret 45
Polly 26

MCCURDY
Archibald J. 105

MCDONALD
Christian E. 126
David A. 80
Hugh 26
James M. 111
Mary 5
Siscilly 108

MCDOUGAL,MCDOOGLE
Aaron 110
Mariah 139
Mary 119

MCDOW
Lucy 57

MCDOWELL
Robert 7

MCEVAN
Adam A. 149

MCEVER
Brice 98

MCFARLAN(D),MCFARLIN
Eleanor 39
Lucinda 58
Martha 102
Polley 71
Rhoda 111
Sallie 32
Sarah 144

MCFARRON
John H. 57
Mary 92

MCINA
Thomas H. 17

MCINTIRE,MCENTIRE,
MCINGTIRE,MACKINTIRE
Daniel 73
Elizabeth 39
Elizabeth A. 137
Jane 39
Joseph 25
Minerva C. 112
Peggy 6
Sarah 15
Susannah 81
Thomas C. 61
Zalenda 26
Zilla 37

MCJENKINS
Jimmy 42

MCJUNKIN
Joseph J. 82

MCKELVY
John 43

MCKIE,MCKEE,MACKIE,
MACKY
Andrew H. 135
Elizabeth 2
Martha 69
Mary 112
Sarah 20

MCKINSEY
Peter 7

MCLANE
Jemima 107

MCLURE
John 32

MCMILLEN
John 28

MCMILLION
John B. 71
Margery 62

MCMULLEN
William 31

MCNEAL
John C. 33
Lucy 3
Nancy 61

MCPHERSON
Rebecca 151

MCQUEEN
Isaac A. 9

MAGEE
John 86

MALDEN see Maulden

MALONE
Emily 91
Laura W. 45
Sarah Jane 119

MANGAM,MANGRAM,MANGUM
Bethena 111
Gilford M. 133
Rhoda 84
Samuel 7

MANLY,MANLEY
Daniel B. 28
Daniel J. 101
Elizabeth 108
Isaac D. 44
Letty 92
Moses 15
Nancy 85
Polly 90
Richard 96
William 63
William G. 108

MARAL
Isham 31

MARBRY
Sallie 35

MAREDITH(see also Merida)
Tignal 31

MARLIN(see also Martin)
Andrew 121
Mandy A. 141

MARSHALL,MARTIAL
Andrew J. 116
James A. 128
Nancy E. 122
Sterling 86

MARTIN(see also
Marlin)
Brison 64
Caroline 121
Cintha 132
Cluff 77
Eliza Emeline 129
Gabriel S. 136
Irena 107
James 52
Manda Allexandria 141
Mary 126,141
Mary Ann 154
Micajah 73
Nancy 16
Robert 137
Sary Armanda 51
Tabitha 52
Westley 33
William 25
William J. 75

MASON
James 97
Squire 55

MASSEY,MASSY,MASEY,
MASSAY
Elmina 147
Ephraim 104
Hester 111
James 114,126
James E. 121
Joel 137
John W. 110
Trephena 111
William 142

MATHEWS
William 109

MATHIS
Millissa 99

MAULDEN,MAULDIN(G),
MALDEN,MAULDLING
Elizabeth 57
Elizer 80
Nancy 42
Sally 76
Virginia 71

MAXFIELD
Jeremiah 136

MAXWELL
James M. 148
Sarah 141

MAYES,MAYS
Charlottie 13
James 22
Jane 20,109
Margarit 123
Mary Malinda 143
Matilda 55
Thomas 18,24
William 14

MAYFIELD
Martha 38

MAYHOE
Nancy 13

MEADOWS,MEADERS,MEADORS
MEDDERS,MEDERS
Christopher 47
Daniel 154
Esther 74
Ginsey W. 98
James L. 121
Jedediah 41
July M. 97
Malinda P. 136
Martha G. 83
Mary E. 120
Melissa 127
Nancy 79
Opha C. 140
Sally 64
William 76

MEALLER(see also Miller)
William 135

MEANS
Hugh 149

MEDLOCK
Elizabeth 21

MEEKS
Elizabeth 80
John 10
Luran 35
Martha 23
Martin 63
Nacey 62
Nacey D. 104
Patcy 7
Susan 35

MELLEN
Michael 24

MERIDA(see also
Maredith)
Lucy 13

MERREL(L)
Elizabeth 2
Mary F. 59

MESSER
Jane 1

MEWBOURN
Mary 58

MICHOLDS
Ann 27

MILLER(see also Mealler)
Adenea   76
Asariel 25
C.... E. 75
Disa 31
Elizabeth 87,135

173

Fletcher 138
James H. 141
James M. 127
John 20
Luse 75
Martha M. 134
Mary 25,66
Robert 24
Sarah/Sary 18,38
Samuel 94

MILLICAN,MILLIGAN,
MULLICAN
...vry 17
Iris 17
Tho's 7
William C. 3

MILNER,MILLNER
Hannah 102
Judith 109
Prudence 37

MILLS
Caroline 74
Chesley 40
Dyal 25
James 64
John 8
Louisa 55
Nancy 65
William 63

MILUM
Elizabeth 62

MINISH
Richard 83

MINYARD,MINIARD
Emaline 109
Fleming 78
James 98
Jeptha 99
Richard 43
Thomas 120
William 81

MITCHEL(L)
Arcada 59
David W. 103
Elizabeth 49,74
James 79
James C. 80
Jo. H. 155
John L. 125
Julian 118
Marian 112
Martha S. 68
Mary 51,81
Nacy 65
Nancy M. 54
Riley 59
Rubin 40
Thomas C. 146
William 48
Winney 79

MIZE,MISE
Clarkson 68
Edea Adline 111
Henry C. 139
Henry J. 135
James M. 152
John 141
Margarit 123
Mary Ann Eliza-
beth 135
Minevy Clementin 126
Sally 9
Sarah 92
Thomas 46
Warren 42
William B. 126
William J. 136

MOLDER,MOULDER
Elizabeth 6,83
Jacob 26
James M. 143
Manda 137
Sallie 30
Vina 112

MONTGOMERY
Sally/Sarah 116

MOOD
James R. 150

MOOR(E),MORE
Ann 11
Mary Ann A. 116
Nancy 7

MORGAN
Cissiah 103
Elizabeth 58
James 68
John 112
John H. 138
Nancy M. 154
Rody 4

MORRIS
Elizabeth 134
Eppe 78
Henry J. 60
Joseph 11
Susan 63
Thomas 83

MORROW
Nancy 56
William 51

MOSLEY
Anderson 107
Sallie 35

MOSS
Alisabeth H. 119
John 29
Mahala Katharine 149
Mary 130
Metilda 119
Nancy 122
Richard K. 110
William W. 119

Richard K. 110
William W. 119

MOTES,MOATS
Drewry V. 46
James C. 140
John T. 148

MOULDER see Molder

MULKEY
John 74
Martha 150

MULLIN
Abba 8
Lathy 11
Melia 8
Sena 8

MULLINAX,MULLENIX
Benjamin 149
Elisabeth 134
Frankey P. 72
John M. 144
Sarah Ann 147

MURDOCK
Cary C. 90
Charles C. 107
Elizabeth S. 44
Polly 69
Prudence 68

MURPHY,MURPHEY
Alexander 14
James 77
John 146

MURRAY,MURREY,MURRY
Alexander 150
Anna 76
Josiah 49
Lydia 150
Mary Ann 145,155
Susan 109
Susan Ann 153
William 123
William F. 141

MYERS
Alexander 152

NAIL(see also Neal)
Ezekiel 8
Sabry 15

NANCE
Eli L. 50
Harriett 31

NEAL,NEEL(see also Nail)
Arminda E. 113
Caroline 55
David J. 89
Elizabeth 41,63,70
Frances 90
John M. 132
Louisa K. 134

174

Malisa 70
Martin 37
Mary 151
Mary A. 147
Midleton 16
Obadiah C. 88
Polly 14
Rhoda,Rody 27,131
Ruth 17
Samuel T. 45
Sarah 89
Sarah E. 153
Saryanne 138
Tho's 8,13,54,63,64
William 87,151

PEARE(see also Pair,
Parr)
Elizabeth 29

PEDAN
James 28

PEAK,PEEK(E)
(see also Pack)
Elizabeth 144
Jackson 128
Lucy 43
Mary 142
Nancy 24
Winney 98

PENDERGRASS
Edwin 122

PENN
William 14

PERKINS
Hiram B. 52

PERRY
Paterick 80
Richard 72
Thomas R. 97
William A. 54

PHILLIPS,PHILIPS
Angeline R. 142
Anson H. 140
Arkada 79
Asa 148
Francis 129
Gatsy 129
H.K. 69
Hanah M.106
James 15,50
Joseph E. 47
Mark 13
Nancy 124
Nancy E. 149
Nicholas M. 135
Paschal C. 84
Thomas A.T. 104
Thomas C. 154

PHIPS
Mary 72

PICKENS
Alexander 73
Elizabeth 73

PICKHAM
George L. 115

PIERCE
James 35
Martin 73
William 33,82

PINSON
Sterling 41

PITCHFORD
William G. 96

POE
Elizabeth 4
John 29
Rebeckah 23

POOL(E)
Frances 107
George W. 104
Jackson 136
James 26
John M. 101
Martha 106
Nancy 138
Rebeca 7
William 40
William R. 74

POPHAM
Benjamin F. 152
John L. 155

PORTER
Aves 63
Elizabeth 125
Epperson 130
John 91
Roady 128

POSEY
Abigail 86

POTTS
Jonathan 97

POWERS
Alexander 76

PRATER
Javers 133
Thomas 133
William 98

PRESLER,PRESLAR(see
also Presley)
Harvy 139
Louvisa 125
Melinda 115

PRESLEY(see also
Presler)
Daniel 95
Eliza J. 105

Sary Caroline 104

PREWETT,PREWIT,PRUIT
Eliza 104
Ely 117
Empson 150
John W. 82
Leah 115
Liviney 117
Mary 113
Philip 83
Polly 40
Robert W. 50
Samuel 124
William H. 117

PRICHETT,PRITCHETT(see
also Prickett and
Pritchard)
Henry 106
Jesse 119
Micagah 127
Sarah 18

PRICKET(T) (see also
Prichett)
James P. 149
Jesse 12
Joel 5
John N. 113
Josiah 27
Julia A. 124
Mary 1
Naoma 34
Sarah M. 133
William P. 155

PRITCHARD,PRICHED(see
also Prichett)
Martha 131
Sion B. 56

PUCKETT
Edmund D. 44
Naoma 34

PULLIAM,PULLAM,PULIAM
Alpha 79
Benjamin R. 121
Benjamin S. 65
Elenor E. 110
Elizabeth 13
Frances 41,116
Homer Virgil 105
Jane 40
Jerusha,Jarusha 13,29
Joseph P. 105
Nancy 44
Sarah 41,57
Thomas 30,153

PURCEL(L),PERCIL
Jacob 78
Jarret 74
Susan 72

PUT
William 23

QUAILS,QUAILES
Hulda 80
Robert 91

QUILLIAN,QUILLEN,
QUILLIAM
Fletcher A. 127
James 18
Osburn P. 98
Sarah Ann 125

RACKLEY
Solomon 16

RAGIN
Dicy 20

RALSTON
.... 20

RAMSEY(see also
Rumsey)
Ann 2
David S. 151
Eli 33
Elizabeth 22,34,87,
133,142
Hampton 64
James 1,53
John 27
Madison 50
Margret 6
Martha 39
Nancy 72
Rachel C. 119
Rhoda 93
Seth S. 134
Wade H. 79

RANDAL
Eliza 117
Elizabeth 122
James 139

RAY,RAE
Alfird 104
Charles M. 103
Charles W.G. 128
Clementine 145
Cloa 7
Elizabeth Susanna 128
George A. 126
Jehu/John 68
Robbert 31
Susan 52
William 75

REBURN
Cornelious 18

REDDIN
.... 20

REDWINE
Elizabeth 10
Jesse 24

REED,READ
Charlotte A. 96
Cintha 48

Elmira P. 102
Elmiry 75
George L. 126
Jacob P. 80
James 117
James A. 70
John L. 102
Joseph 77
Margaret A. 55
Mary 105
Mary M. 50
Nancy 22,58,73
Nathan L. 61
Permela N. 55
Susan W. 48

REEDER
Andrew P. 96

REMP/RENEP/RENESS
Daniel 95

RESE(see also Rose)
Nancy 25

REYNOLDS,RENOLDS
Mary E. 121
Milly 93
Susannah M. 113

RHOADS
William S. 128

RICE
Charles 135
George L. 137
Moses 21
Noah 95
Polly 131
William 17

RICHARDS
Eliza Jane 141
Larraan 139

RICHARDSON,RICHERSON
James G. 131
Jane F. 137
Margaret 144

RICHIE
Martha 80

RICKELS
Josiah 23

RIDLEY
Joab 125

RILEY,RYLEY
Edward 8
Edna 98
Elizabeth 55,110
Lucy 71
Morier 110
Poley 103
William 67

RISENOR,RESINER
Evaline 139
Thomas 91

ROBINS,ROBBINS
Aley 11
William 3

ROBERTS,ROBIRDS
Barnet 48
Jesse 52
Moses 43
Sydney C. 134

ROBERTSON,ROBERSON,
ROBESON,ROBISON,
ROBINSTON
David 28
Eliza 106
Henry W. 140
James 17
Mandy J. 152
Mary 53,73
Nancy 142
Patsey 69
Rebecca 19
Richard 4
Rody 36
Sarah 48
William 55

ROE(see also Ray)
Amanda 111
Anny 106
Elizabeth 132
Irmin 150
Rebeckah 23

ROGERS,RODGERS
Betsy 33
Francis 97
John 92
Johnson 64
Marget 44
Rhody 44
Robert 58

ROPER
Lydia 73

ROSE(see also Rese)
Anny 55
Hardy 49
Jesse 21
Nancy 25
Roda 30
Thomas 7

ROSS
Richard 3

ROUS(E)
Martin 62
Rebecca 108

ROWLAND,ROLLEN(see
also Bollen)
Drury 7
James W. 105
Martha 91
Thomas 119

SHELTON
Absalom H. 56
Lewis 155
Margaret 133
Mary 133
Nancy F. 85
Richmond 36
Wilky 36

SHERIDAN,SHERDAN,
SHERRIDEN,SHURDON
David W. 127
Malinda A. 132
Manda Olivy 120
Nancy 81,142
Thomas C. 140
William 57

SHIPPELLEN
Malinda A. 132

SHIRLEY,SHEARLY
Abraham 84
William 74

SHOCKLEY,SHOCKLY
Aquilla 11
Benjamin F. 145
Elizabeth U.C. 133
Kirney K. 111

SHOEMATE
Berryman D. 32

SHOTWELL
Elizabeth 23
John 24

SILMAN,SILLMAN(see
also Salmons)
Arminda 88
O.W. 139

SIMMONS
Holeman F. 30
Joseph 153
William 59

SIMS,SIMMS
Aggy 39
Elisha 30
Hope 23
Hull 12
John 44
Mahulda 103
Nathaniel 2
Polly 17
Rebecca 27

SISK
Martha R. 52

SISSON,SISSOM
Elizabeth 24
John 1
Thomas S. 117

SKELTON
Ann 46
Joel 124

Nelly 151
Syntha 63

SKIPER
Wilis 102

SLACK
Joseph 56

SLATON,SLAYTON
Benjamin 40
Caryan 118
Elizabeth 69
Kisey 126
Lucinda 85
Martha 88
Sam'l H. 136
William 111

SLOAN
William 52

SMALLWOOD
Mark 123

SMALLY
John 148

SMITH
Ailsey 110
Alford/Alferd 55,71
Ally 33
Ansaline 100
Bailey 133
Cerren 49
Charity 25
Cleveland 145
David 102
Dianah F. 48
Eleazar E. 152
Elizabeth 22,29,113,
141,144
Elizabeth J. 116
Ezekiel 93
Ezekiel C. 155
Fa...ty 85
Franky 10
Henry 31
Hezekiah 12
Isam 114
Jacob 58
James 4,6,32,113,134
James A. 103
James D. 106
James M. 140
Jane 114
Jesse 86,103
Jesse M. 95
John C. 118,121
John R. 117
John T. 23
John W. 134
Johnson T. 44
Joseph N. 84
Marget,Margret,
  Margarett 53,115,138
Mark 33
Martha 89
Mary 88,98,113,127

Mary Ann 151
Mathias 16
Miles 100
Morning 35
Mursy 101
Nancy 28,49,78,150
Nancy C. 148
Penelope 120
Phebe 47
Pheraby 8
Polly 33
Ralph 15
Rebecca(h) 67,144
Russel J. 129
Russel T. 99
Sarah/Sary 34,37,76,81
Sarah C. 140
Sarah E. 132
Susannah 28,85,130
Syntha 89
Thomas 3,16
Thomas A. 126
Tilmon P. 143
Vesta 76
Wiley 68
William 1,3,5,15,85
William B. 57,146
William G. 122
William S. 119,148
William W. 84

SOLSBERRY
John 151

SOSEBEE
Abner 59

SOWELS(see also Sewell)
Ann 1

SPARKS
Elizabeth 8
Jemima 54
L...zaan 128
Lory F. 147
Malinda 57
William J. 34

SPEARS
Elizabeth 9
Roland 32
Sims 112
Sintha 38

SPITTON
Wilky 36

STANDLIN
Young 39

STAPLES
Willim N. 51

STARE
Lewis 130

STARNS
Caty 25

STARRITT
  Benjamin 60
  Malinda 61
  Polley 61
  William 107

STEFLE,STIEFLE
  James 106
  Susan 124

STEGALL
  Lency 42

STEPHENS(see also
  Stephenson)
  Margaret 145
  Rebecca 16
  Stephen B. 107

STEPHENSON(see also
  Stephens)
  Elizabeth 27
  Hannah 119
  Polly 12
  Rebecca 10

STOE,STOW(E)
  James 34,137
  Nancy 42
  Polley 3
  Sarah 139
  Sarah Ann 147
  Susan 137
  Warren 21
  William 62,88

STOKES
  Waddy 61
  William 58

STONE
  Catharine H. 91
  Elizabeth 112
  Hillery 30
  Juley 94
  Susan 77
  William H. 139

STONECYPHER,STONECIPHER
  Anney 66
  Benjamin 11
  Joseph 90
  Susannah 5

STOUT
  Dicy 27

STOVALL,STOVEALL
  David 56
  David C. 76
  Dicy 27
  Ferdinand 48
  George 3
  George W. 86
  Henery F. 90
  James 38,60
  Jane 148
  John 109
  Joseph 88
  Josiah 10

Lucy C. 155
Mary 6,123
Mary Ann 31
Nancy 35
Rebecca W. 101
Sally 38
Susanah 74
Wilkins 71
William 92

STOWE see Stoe

STOWERS
  John 2

STRANGE
  Ann 82
  Elizabeth 33
  Harriett 127
  James H. 105
  Jesse 82
  John 36
  Mary A. 104,151

STRIBLING
  Thomas F. 102

STRICKLAND,STRICTLAND
  Cade D. 11
  Clarissa 126
  Wilson 7

STUBBLEFIELD
  Lemuel 146

STUBS,STUBBS
  Benton 40
  .Catharine H. 100
  James F. 83
  John U. 64
  Matilda C. 116
  Polly P. 48
  Sarah T. 63

SUDETH
  Mary 154

SUMMERS,SOMERS
  Susan 91
  Tena 100

SUMMERVILLE
  Sarah 85

SUTLEY,SUTLY
  David 39
  Mary 43
  Michael 36
  Susan 40

SWAIN
  William 4

SWAN
  Caty 30

SWIFT
  Harriett 96
  Johnithan D. 100
  Mary An 67

Nancy 116
Susan 150
Tyre 34

TABER,TABOR
  Elizabeth M.A. 153
  Francis A. 96
  Isaac 32
  Mary F. 148
  Milly 43
  Susan 57

TALLEY
  Joannah 7

TAPP
  Curtiss 64
  Mary 72
  Willis 36

TATE
  Cooper B. 50
  Eliza C. 39
  Elizabeth 27,46
  Loucinday 61
  Mary 71
  Sarah 48
  Solomon 36

TATOM,TATUM
  Mary J. 56
  William 11

TAYLOR,TAYLER,TAILOR,
  (see also Tyler)
  Elizabeth 16
  Elizabeth B. 21
  George 11
  Hiram 32
  M.D.J. 90
  Spencer 88

TEASLEY
  Hariet 152
  James S. 48
  William 75

TEMPLES
  Benjamin F. 140
  John 111

TERRELL
  Anna 15
  Jonathan 22,151

THOMAS(see also
  Thomason)
  Arminda C. 90
  Elizabeth 14
  Elizabeth H. 151
  Emily J. 149
  Ezekiel,Ezekial 40,47
  James L. 22
  Jesse 52
  John 49
  Madison H. 85
  Mary 83
  Polly 12
  Sallie 28
  Sarah,Sary 92,120
  Susannah 4,120

THOMASON,THOMISON(see
also Thomas, Thompson)
Alexander R. 134
Anny B. 55
John W. 55
Lucy 36
Mary 58
Morning 24
Nancy 144
Rachel 84
Sareptay 95
Solomon D. 43
Willis B.

THOMPSON,TOMPSON(see
also Thomason)
Alfred 82
Elizabeth 8,20
Elvira 72
James A. 27
Jesse 25
Jobe 27
John 27
Jonathan 87
Sarry D. 114
Seborn 21
William 10

THORNTON
Catharine F. 91
Dozier 40
Elijah 9
Eliza 40
Jeremiah J. 75
Martha G. 51
Mary 69
Reuben 47

THRASHER
George 26
Mary 133
Thomas 22
Willi.. 22

THURMOND(see also
Turman)
Parthenia 11

TILLER
Anny 87
Peyton 54

TILLMAN
Berry G. 51

TIMMONS
Williams B. 125

TINSLEY
Desa M. 94

TOLBERT
Matilda 19
Peggy 6

TONEY
Belinda 94
Charles 92
Elizabeth 5
Harris 19

Hedrick 55
John 37
Lewraney 100
Manervey 129
Nancy 24
Rhody B. 145
Sintha 45
William C. 85

TOWNS
Capel 91
Elizabeth 56
Francis H. 126
Francis A. 126
John 9
Nancy 87

TOWNSEND
Joel W. 43

TRENTHAM
Ann 30

TRIMBLE
Arminda 50
Elizabeth 24
Lucy 30
Moses 6

TUCKER
Alfred S. 121
Benjamin 63
Lewis 35
Nancy 63
Nancy Jane 121
Polly 23

TURBYFILL
James H. 153

TURK
Cyntha J. 130
John 82
Margaret M. 132
Milton 78
Theodore 63
William 20
William H. 123

TURMAN(see also
Thurmond)
Alpha 76
Elender 65
Eliza 78
Hulda 102
James 89
Mary 83
Simeon 45

TURNER
As. A. 31
Katharine 151
William S. 137

TYLER(see also Taylor)
Allen 118
Reuben L. 115

UNDERWOOD
Littlebery 68

VANDIVER
Benjamin P. 117

VARNER(see also Verner)
George W. 153
Hannah 23
Martha Harriet 134
Sarah C. 110

VAUGHAN,VAUGHN,VAUN
Adaline 144
Airy 41
Asa 118
Benjamin 154
Calvin 125
David 27
Hendrick 4
James 55
John 67,96
Joshua 112
Margarett 139
Mariah 75
Mary 65,150
Narsisa 42
Otaway W. 62
Perry M. 71
Peter 33
Susannah 54
William 70,138
William H. 115
William W. 154

VAWTER,VAUGHTERS
Hiram 67
Lucinda 50

VERNER(see also Varner)
Elizabeth 90
Ester 105
Jane 123
Martha 136
Sarah Jane 122
Sellender 63

VESSELS
Charlotte 40
Lusinda 77
Olive 13
Polly 30

VICKERY,VICKRY,VICKORY
Delila 92
Elias 94,151
James 128
James V. 142
Johnathan H. 154
Joseph H. 72,136
Mary 91
Milly 67
Patience 134
Rachel 106
Sinthy 130
Thomas 98,110
William 110,124

VILKEY(see also Wilkey)
Syntha 83

VINES
John 40

WACASTER
David 147

WADE,WAID
Anna R. 117
Drisilla 5
Edward J. 148
Henry 19
Henry H. 108
James 55,153
John 43
John H. 103
Lisa 80
Lucy 82
Mary E. 119
Nancy 36
Nancy E.P. 129
Wesley G. 153
William G. 153

WALDEN
Micheal 3

WALKER
J.W. 145
Rebecca 74

WALLACE
William 3

WALLEN
Patsy 18

WALLRAVEN
Elizabeth 24

WALLS
Zacheriah 35

WALTERS,WARTERS,
WATER(S)
Alfred F. 130
Anderson F. 151
Andrew J.M. 91
Clemment 144
Elija 27
Elizabeth 47,52
Green C. 76
Jackson M. 46
Jeremiah 39
Jesse 101
John 31,127
Judha 140
Julian 104
Lear 70
Lewis 92
Luther 102
Margaret 153
Martha Ann 80,126
Mary 75
Maryan,Mary Ann 106,132
Micajah 65
Pheby 31
Polly,Polley 31,105
Rufus K. 99
Thomas 19
William P. 79

WARD (see also Word)
Andrew J. 95
Edward 120,136
Margaret 7
Levy 133

WARE
Asa J. 120

WARMACK
Jesse P. 64
Johnson 98
Thomas P. 140

WARREN
David 2
Nancy 22
Ruben 8

WARWICK
Allen 69

WATKINS,WADKINS
Barnet 11
Griffin 19
Rhody 13
Vincent 19
Wiley 55
William J. 106

WATS
Martha Ann 126

WATSON
Andrew 20
Benjamin H. 143
Elizabeth 112
Harriett S. 44
James V. 126
Lucy 32
Mary C. 136
Samuel 56
Seth 143
Susan 123
Whitfield 109

WAY
William 89

WEATHERLEY
Aaron 53

WEBB
John 131
Martha 142

WEEMS,WEMMS
Asa 144
Elizabeth 96
Freeman 127
Jacob 116
Johnson 66
Pleasant 110

WELBORN,WILLBOURN
Argent 22
Mary E. 140
William R. 35

WELDON
Welbourn 76

WELLS
Tho's 39
William 106

WEST
Lucy A. 116
Malinda 54
Milla 118
Minerva 145
Thomas 26

WESTBROOK(S)
B.A. 126
Bartley A. 131
Francis M. 153
Isabela 110
Joel M. 71
John 28
Joshua 35
Lucy 140
Martha 26
Martha M. 135
Mary M. 105
Milton 84
Polley 8
Reuben W. 49
Sampson L. 129
Sarah T. 131
Stephen B. 46,75
Stephen F. 112
Thomas 22
Thompson 103
Visa 93
Washington 112
Wesley J. 143
Wiley F. 86
William L. 75

WHEELER
Abba 32
Elizabeth 13
Katharine 52
Lucy 12
Richard 74

WHISENANT,WHISONANT
Barbara 47
Henry 86
John Nicholas 130
Peter 101

WHITAKER,WHITYCAR,
WHITTICAR,WHITTAKER
Benjamin 15
John 40
Martha 39
Seaborn 62

WHITE
Alender 26
Benjamin H. 53
Bennett 136
Burrell 41
David 56
Eliza 139
Elizabeth 54
Jerusha 42

Mary 143
Nancy 45
Sarah 99

YEARGAN,YEARGIN
Anny 38
Franklin 114
Nancy 114
William D. 114

YEARLOW
Elizabeth 26

YORK
Debery Cooper 3
John G. 55
Ruth 26
William 52,53

YOUNG
John S. 145
Thomas M. 103

INDEX TO COURT OFFICIALS, MINISTERS, ETC.

The following list includes the most common initials
found following officials' names, designating rank
or position. These definitions represent a consensus
of several opinions as to their possible meanings.

C.C.O.- Clerk, Court of Ordinary
D.C.C.O.- Deputy Clerk, Court of Ordinary
E.M.C.- Elder, Methodist Church
E.M.E.- Elder, Methodist Episcopal
J.I.C.- Justice, Inferior Court
J.P.- Justice of the Peace
M.G., M.O.G.- Minister of the Gospel
O.M. - Ordained Minister
O.M.G.- Ordained Minister of the Gospel
P.G. - Preacher of the Gospel
V.D.M.- (?)

Names may appear more than once on a given page

185

BOWERS, JOB 71,73,78,83,87,88,
89,90,91,92,94,97,99,102,105,
106,107,109,111,112,116,120,
121,122,124,125,129,130,132,
135,136,138,140,142,145,149,152

BOWERS, WILLIA 139,140

BRADY, ENOCK 29

BRAMBLIT, ... 38

BRAMBLET, J. 41

BRAMBLET, JOHN 39,40,41,45,47,
48,49,54,55,62,65,66

BREWSTER, JOHN 31

BROWN, HARDY 30

BROWN, J.R. 8

BROWN, JOHN R. 6,7,13

BROWN, WILLIAM 19

BRYAN, ELI 8

BRYAN, ROYAL 28,38,39,40,41,43,
44,47,52,58,59,61,68,71,72,78

BURGESS, E.M. 94,95,96,97

BURGESS, PLEASANT F. 102,109

BURRIS, JACOB 117

BURROUGHS, WILLIAM 61,65,67,68,
70,71,72,73,77,78,79,81,84,91,
92,96,97,100,101,104,105,106,
108,110,112,116

BURTON, H. 127

BURTON, JOHN 54,76,80

BYERS, JOSEPH 64

CALLAWAY, F. 28,29,31,32,33,34,
37,38,42,44,74

CALLAWAY, FRANCIS 7,8,10,12,14,
15,16,17,18,19,22,23,24,25,28,
29,30,31,32,33,47,51,53

CALLAWAY, FRANCIS C. 10

CALLEN, W'M R. 86,89,95,98

CARROLL, J.W. 131

CARSON, DAVID 49,110,117,132,
148,153

CARTER, H.C. 123,130,134

CATLETT, JOHN 54,56,57,58,60,67,
69,71,75,80,89

CAWTHON/COTHON, CHESLEY 37,45,48,49,
52,57,66,69

CATHON, W'M 37,38

CHAMBERS, ... 116

CHANDLER, ASA 54,67

CHANDLER, DUDLEY J. 135

CHANDLER, H.F. 113,133

CHANDLER, JAMES 8,10,11

CHANDLER, JOSEPH 2,4,6,12,13,23

CHANDLER, Z. 36,37,39,40,59

CHANDLER, ZACHARIAH/ZACHERIAH/ZACH.
38,45,46,49,53

CHAPPEL(L), JOHN B. 52,59,120,121

CHAPPELEAR, J.H. 146,147,155

CHAPPELEAR, JAMES H. 143,150,151

CHATHAM, STEPHEN 34

CHILDERS, JESSE 112

CHILDERS, THOMAS W. 110

CLAYTON, WILLIAM 11

CLEGHORN, WILLIAM 9

CLEVELAND, JOHN 13,15

CLOUD, ADAM 14,15

COLLINS, ELBA 127

COLLINS, JOHN 2,3,5,6,7,8,9,11

CONNER, BOLEY/BOLLY 12,13

COSPER, GEORGE H. 40

COSPER, HNERY 117,119

CRANDAL, S. 75

CROCKER, JOHN 43,45

CROW, WILLIAM T. 110,112,115,120,123,
124,125,136,138,140,142,143,145,154

CRUMP, ROBERT 78,96

DAVID, HENRY 19,23,26,34,35,40,49,51,
54,55,56,58,59,67,75,83,95,109,119

DAVID, ISAAC M. 87,97,98,99,103

DAVIS, J.A. 122,142

DAVIS, JOHN A. 75,76,81,85,86,
88,90,92,96,98,104,105,107,
108,110,114,117,119,120,121,
128,130,133,138,140,143,144,
145,149

DEAN, ALVAN 78,83,85,86,88

DENMAN, WILLIAM 5

DORSEY, ANDREW 29,30,31,32

DUMAS, D. 129

DUNCAN, JOHN 16,20,22,23,24,25,
26

DUNLAP, JOSEPH 34

EDDINS, EPHRAIM C. 118

EVERETT, SAMUEL 1

EVERETT, SAMUEL H. 2,3

FARMER, J.W. 118

FARMER, THOMAS 77,90,94

FREEMAN, JAMES F.W. 111

FREEMAN, JOHN M. 145,146,147,
148,149,152,153,154,155

GRANER, OSBORN 134,141,147,148,
153

GARRETT, WILLIAM 35

GARRISON, ALLEN T. 127,131,136,
140,142,144,151

GARRISON, C. 28

GARRISON, CALEB 25,26,27

GARRISON, D. 44

GARRISON, DAVID 3,4,5,43,54,70,
73,79

GARRISON, LEVI 83

GARRISON, THOMAS 46

GERRALD, SAMUEL S. 35,36

GILLESPIE, JAMES L. 82,87,88,91,
92,93,94,96,127,129,131,133,
134,135,136,137,139,140,141,
145,147,149

GILLESPIE,WILLIAM B. 104,106,
107,110,111,113,114,115

GILMORE, WILLIAM 42,47

GLENN, J.W. 123

GOSS, ISHAM H. 126

GOSS, WILLIAM R. 152

GRAY, JOHN M. 19

GREYHAM, JOSEPH 150

GRIFFITH, CALEB 29

GUEST, MOSES 4,8,18,20,21

GUNNELS, N. 50,59

GUNNELS, NATHAN 44,48,50,51,54,55,
56,57,60,61,63,64,65,66,67,68,70

HALEY, JOEL 100,103

HAMMOND/HAMMONS, J. 31,32,33,34,40,
44

HAMMOND, JOB 48,49,50,53,54,60,62,
63,65,67,68,71,72,89

HARDEN, AUSTIN 14

HARDEN, HENRY 37

HARGROVE, JAMES 34,93,111,122,124,
125

HARRISON, OLIVER 149,155

HENLEY, CLEMOND 28

HENLEY, DARBY 14,23

HENLEY, EDMOND 9,10,11,12,17,20,27,30

HENLEY/HENLY, JOHN S. 144,147,148,
149,153

HERRING, WILLIAM 36,37

HIGHSMITH, THOMAS H. 98

HOLBROOK, G.B. 116,151

HOLBROOK, GREEN B. 103,107,120,127,
135,136,150,151,152,153,154

HOLCOMB, ... 19

HOLCOM(B), ABSALOM 19,21,28,60

HOLLAND, THOMAS 125

HOLLINGSWORTH, BENJAMIN 12

HOLLINGSWORTH, THOMAS 3,4,8,15,26

HOOD, NATHANIEL R. 59

HOOD, S.R. 112,120

HOOD, STEPHEN R. 108,113

HOOPER, J.C. 94,98

HOOPER, OB. 4

187

HUDSON, MILTON P. 91

HUGHES, WILLIAM 39

HUGHING, WILLIAM 39

HULSEY, W. 18

HULSEY, WILLIAM 17,18,19,20,21,
  22,24,25,27

HUMPHRIES, GEORGE W. 63

HUNLY, J.S. 145

HUTCHINS, D. 99

HUTCHINS, DRURY 80,95

HUTTO, JAMES 24,27

HYMER, S. 55,57,58,59,61,62,63,
  65,66,71,73,76,81,86

J., E.V. 25

JACKSON, SAMUEL 42,44,46,47,48,
  51,53,62,63,66

JENKINS, C.D. 53,54,61,66

JENKINS, CHARLES D. 41,42,46,53,
  56

JENKINS, JOHN 3

JOHNSON, A. 124

JOHNSON, WILLIAM 36

JOLLY, JOHN P. 108,110,113,116,
  125,126,130,132,133,148,153,154

JONES, BARTLETT 62,64

JONES, D. 9

JONES, WILLIAM 1,11,13,16,23

KEEL, WILLIAM 41

KENDRICK, AUSTIN 15,16,17

KEY, GEORGE W. 74

KING, B.F. 135,144

KING, BENJAMIN 10,13

KING, THOMAS 36,37,39,41-143

KING, WILLIAM 70,72

KING, WILLIAM J. 135

KNOX, G. 1,2

KNOX/NOX, GEORGE 4,5,6,7

LACY, JOHN 117,124,128

LANE, SAM 22

LANGSTON, ALEXANDER 126

LANGSTON, REUBEN 100

LANGSTON, REUBEN J. 100

LAUGHRIDGE, BENJAMIN 55,56,58,60,64,
  65,67,69,72,73,76,77,79,80,81,82,
  84,85,87,89

LAURENCE, I.B. 127,128,133,139,143

LAURENCE Isaac 145

LAURENCE ISAAC B. 107,108,109,111,
  112,114,116,117,118,119,120,121,122,
  123,125,126,127,128,129,134,137,139,
  140,141,142,143,146,147,148,150,153,
  154,155

LEGG, WILLIAM 27,29

LEWIS, JOHN W. 100

LINKERS, CHARLES L. 38

LITTLE, JAMES 13,16

LITTLE, JAMES H. 6,7,8,9,10,11,12,13,
  15,16,17,18,20,22,25,28,29,30,32,33,
  34,35,36,38

LITTLE, JOHN H. 121,123,132,137,141

LOONEY, A. 31

LOONEY, ADAM 27,29,31

LOONEY, NOAH 56,60,61,64,65,82,86,
  87,89,90,94,95,98,99,102,109,110,
  111,112,117

LOWRY, FRED D. 86

LOWERY, JAMES 7, 14

LOWS, JA'S 10

MC ALPIN, R. 77

MC CARTER, J.E. 131,142

MC CARTER, JOHN E. 139

MC COLLUM, SAM'L 58,68,69

MC DONALD, DONALD 35

MC ENTIRE/MC ENTYRE, JOSEPH 67,68,
  69,71,73,85,88,92

MAGEE, W. 80

MC MILLIAN, JOHN B. 34,36,42,43,44,
  46,107,108,114

MANGUM/MANGRUM, HOWEL(L) 45,47,49,
  52,53,54,55

PITCHFORD, H. 91

PITCHFORD, H.P. 90,92,93,96

POLK, JAMES 137

POSEY, HUMPHREY 84

PULLIAM, ROBERT 55,70

PULLIAM, THOMAS 132

QUILLIAN, C. 30

QUILLIAN, CLEMOND(S) 17,18,19,22,
23,25,26,29,30,32,33

QUILLIAN, JAMES 128

QUILLIAN, R.C. 28

REDWINE, WILLIAM 27

REED, JOS. 17

REED, NATHANIEL R. 60

RIVES, JNO. E. 128

ROGERS, OSBORN 8

ROSS, A.W. 52,103

RUSSELL, HIRAM 56

RYLEE, JAMES 2,7

SANDERS, MINYARD 102,103,104,109,
115,122,124,125,126,128,131,134,
138,145,153,154,155

SANDERS, S.B. 150,154

SANDERS, SAMUEL B. 152

SANDIDGE/SANDRIDGE, G.L. 53,56,
57,59,69

SANDIDGE/SANDRIDGE, John 28,34,
35,45

SANDIVEAR, GEORGE 21

SCARBOROUGH, FREDERICK 123

SEAY, JOHN M. 19

SEWELL, LEVI 125,154

SHACKELFORD, WILLIAM 77

SHELTON, V.H. 155

SHOCKLEY, RICHARD 17,19

SIMMONS, D. 134,139

SIMMONS, DAVID 91,93,96,99,111,
116,130,131,139,144

SMITH, ALFRED 133,14,146,147,153

SMITH, GABRIEL 28

SMITH, JAMES 91,104

SMITH, JAMES R. 51,52,92

SMITH, JOHN M. 32

SMITH, RICHARD 35,50,56,57,61

SPALDING, A.M. 140

STEPHENS, ELIJAH 39,44,48

STONECYPHER, BENJAMIN 66,67,75,83,95

STOVALL, GEORGE 18

STOVALL, JAMES 73,74

STOVALL, JOHN M. 96,97,102

STRICKLAND, JACOB 60,64,65,101

STRIPLING, ROBERT 115,118

STUBBS, FRANCIS 16

TABOR/TABER, JOHN 9,10,12,13

TABOR, WILLIAM 61

TERRELL, WILLIAM 12,20

THARRITON, R. 54

THOMAS Z. 114,116

THOMAS, ZECHARIAH/ZACHARIAH 108,109,
111,114,115,117,118,120,122,126,
130,133,135,139,140,141

THOMASON, S.D. 77,80,87

THOMASON, SOLOMON D. 81,84

THORNTON, BENJAMIN 137,142,143,151

THORNTON, DOZIER 42,46,57,65,66,67

THORTON, M.G. 38

TONEY, HARRIS 40

TOWNSEND, JOEL W. 48,53

TRIBBLE, L.N. 31

TURK, WILLIAM 36,42,101,112,119,126,
135,138,143,149,154

TYLER, HENRY 114,148

UNDERWOOD, L.B. 129

VANDIVER, GEORGE 31,41

VANDIVER, M.W. 57,70,92,115

VANDIVER/VANDIVIER, MATTHEW W.
75,76,79

VANDIVER, SANFORD 120

VAUGHAN, DAVID 89,102,106,116,
118,120,121,124,126,131,132,
138,150,151,153

WADE, J.B. 131

WADE, JOHN B. 79,83,85,87,88,90,
101,105,106,108,110,113,115,116,
118,119,122,123,124,125,127,128,
129,132,133,134,135,137,138,139,
141,142,144,150,151,152

WALTERS, JOSEPH 20

WARMACK, JOHN 18

WEEMS/WIMS, R. 24,28

WELBORN, W.R. 82

WELBORN, WILLIAM R. 72,74,78,80,
82,83,84,85,95,97

WHEELER, RICHARD 131,133,138,143,
144,153

WHITE, CARTER 64

WHITE, EPPY 119

WHITTEN, A.E. 73

WIGGINS, LEM'L R. 129

WILEY, WILLIAM J. 125,126,137,
143,147,150

WILLIAMS, A. 37

WILLIAMS, NATHAN 123

WILLIAMS, R. 37

WILLIAMS, ROBERT 38,40,41,42,44,
46,59,61,64,68,72,75,76,77

WILSON, JOHN 69,72,85,94

WILSON, JOHN S. 65

WOFFORD, BENJAMIN 11

WORD, JOHN B. 80,81

WYNNE, HAMILTON 31

YORK, ASA 77,78,79,81,82,100,101,
102

YORK, JOHN G. 125,126,127,129,131,
134,135,137,142,145-155

COUNTIES OTHER THAN FRANKLIN

ELBERT CO. 98,114,119

HABERSHAM CO. 131,142

MADISON CO. 137

PUTNAM CO. 16,29

.

www.ingramcontent.com/pod-product-compliance
Lightning Source LLC
Chambersburg PA
CBHW031124020426
42333CB00012B/215